RAISE THE ISSUES

An Integrated Approach to Critical Thinking

Carol Numrich

In Cooperation with National Public Radio®

Longman

Raise the Issues
Copyright © 1994 by Longman Publishing Group.
All rights reserved.

Longman, 10 Bank Street, White Plains, NY 10606

Associated companies:
Longman Group Ltd., London
Longman Cheshire Pty., Melbourne
Longman Paul Pty., Auckland
Copp Clark Pitman, Toronto

Distributed in the United Kingdom by Longman Group
Ltd., Longman House, Burnt Mill, Harlow, Essex CM20
2JE, England, and by associated companies, branches,
and representatives throughout the world.

Editorial Director: Joanne Dresner
Senior Development Editor: Debbie Sistino
Development Editor: Penny Laporte
Production-Editorial & Design Director: Helen B. Ambrosio
Text Design: Curt Belshe
Production Technical Assistant: Karen Philippidis
Cover Design: Cavazos Design
Production Supervisors: Richard Bretan, Anne Armeny

Library of Congress Cataloging-in-Publication Data
Numrich, Carol.
 Raise the issues: an integrated approach to critical thinking/
 Carol Numrich. in association with National Public Radio.
 p. cm.
ISBN 0-8013-1014-8
 1. English language—Textbooks for foreign speakers. 2. Critical
thinking. I. National Public Radio (U.S.) II. Title.
PE1128.N85 1994
428.2'4—dc20
                                        93-33842
                                        CIP

8 9 10-VG-9897

Contents

INTRODUCTION   v

1 MEN WHO KNOW WHERE THEIR BULLETS ARE GOING   1
Commentator: Donald McCaig from *All Things Considered*

2 WHEN DOES LIFE BEGIN?   22
Commentator: Andrei Codrescu from *All Things Considered*

3 TO KNOW MORE ABOUT LESS OR LESS ABOUT MORE   44
Commentator: Rod MacLeish from *Weekend Edition*

4 ECONOMIC MIGHT VS. ECOLOGIC RIGHT   70
Commentator: James Trefil from *Morning Edition*

5 "JUST SAY 'NO' TO DRUGS"?   91
Commentator: Linda Chavez from *Morning Edition*

6 BRIDGING AN UNCOMMON PAST WITH A COMMON FUTURE   112
Commentator: Linda Chavez from *Morning Edition*

7 HAVE ALL THE HEROES DIED?   133
Commentator: Frank Deford from *Morning Edition*

8 THE RIGHT TO DIE VS. THE RIGHT TO LIFE   155
Commentator: Philip Gerard from *All Things Considered*

9 REDUCING INEQUALITY IN EDUCATION   177
Commentator: Askia Muhammed from *All Things Considered*

10 ANOTHER FIRST AMENDMENT ISSUE?   202
Commentator: Jerry Stern from *All Things Considered*

TAPESCRIPT   224

ANSWER KEY   231

INTRODUCTION

Raise the Issues: An Integrated Skills Approach to Critical Thinking consists of ten authentic radio commentaries from National Public Radio, and articles or essays excerpted from a variety of magazines, journals, and newspapers.

Designed for very advanced students of English as a Second Language, the text presents an integrated skills approach to developing critical thinking. Each unit presents a controversial issue of international appeal. The students gain an understanding of American values and attitudes as they develop their listening and reading skills. They begin to reevaluate their assumptions and develop their own points of view as they develop their speaking and writing skills. By using material designed for the native speaker, the listening and reading selections provide content that is interesting, relevant, and educational.

SUGGESTIONS FOR USE

The exercises are designed to stimulate an interest in the material by drawing on students' previous knowledge and opinions, and by aiding comprehension through vocabulary and guided listening and reading exercises. In a variety of discussion activities, the students integrate new information and concepts with previously held opinions. In the writing exercises, students are given an opportunity to explore the issues further and use the new language and insights gained.

1 Anticipating the Issue

In this 2–3 minute introductory discussion, students predict what the issue will be and share whatever knowledge of the topic they already have. The title, cartoon, and questions are meant to introduce the content of the unit and motivate the students to read further. The ideas generated by the discussion could be written on the board. After reading the *Background Reading,* students can verify or react to their predictions. The teacher may want to provide additional information to help students understand the cartoon or issue.

2 Background Reading

The *Background Reading* has two purposes: to provide students with facts and cultural information that will help them comprehend the opinion pieces that follow, and to introduce the vocabulary that they will need to understand the listening exercise (Opinion 1). The *Background Reading* takes no position, but rather presents two sides of the issue. Students should read the text silently in class.

Vocabulary: The *Background Reading* in each unit is followed by an exercise to reinforce the difficult or topic-specific vocabulary presented. The exercise types include guessing meaning from context, working with synonyms, defining words, and completing sentences. Students who finish the *Background Reading* quickly can continue to work independently on this exercise while the rest of the class finishes the text.

Summarizing the Issue: This activity will help students check their understanding of the issues presented in the *Background Reading.* In groups, students discuss their interpretation of the main issue. Then they are asked to identify the main arguments made by each side of the issue.

Values Clarification: Before being asked to listen to and read the opinions of others, the students discuss, in groups, their own reactions to or opinions about the issue. This discussion should increase their interest and understanding of the issues and prepare them for the opinion pieces that follow. (After studying the opinions of others, they will be asked to think critically about their original assumptions and decide whether they want to reconsider their opinions in any way.)

3 Opinion 1: Listening

Listening for the Main Idea: The students should listen to the commentary once without stopping the tape. They then choose, from three statements, the best expression of the commentator's main idea. The students may compare their choices in pairs to see whether they have understood the essential point of the commentary. Only one listening is usually required for this exercise, but some classes may want to listen a second time. The teacher may want to ask the class *why* the other two statements given do *not* represent the main idea.

Listening for Details: Students should listen to the commentary a second time. This time they answer multiple-choice questions to help them understand detailed information. The students should first read the questions and possible answers. The teacher can then explain any items the students do not understand. Then the commentary is played. The students choose the correct answers *as they listen,* thus evaluating their listening comprehension. Finally, in pairs, they compare answers. The teacher should encourage the students to defend their answers based on what they think they heard. They should also be encouraged to use the language from the tape to convince the other students of the accuracy of their choices. There will certainly be disagreements over some of the answers; these discussions will help focus attention on the information needed to answer the questions correctly. By listening to the commentary a second time, the students generally comprehend this information. Once again, they should be asked to agree on their answers. If there are still misunderstandings, the tape should be played a third time, with the teacher verifying the answers and pointing out where the information is heard on the tape.

Text Completion and Discrete Listening: In this final listening activity, the students complete a cloze of the listening passage. The cloze is intended to activate the difficult or topic-specific vocabulary they have heard, and to present the commentator's ideas in writing. Students should complete this cloze using their knowledge of vocabulary, text structure, the issue, and their memory of what they have heard. (Note: this is not intended as a dictation.) The teacher should encourage the use of any vocabulary that works in the context. Once the students have filled in the blanks the teacher can play the commentary again to verify their answers. Students' alternative answers can then be examined in a class discussion. The completion of the cloze could also be assigned as homework.

4 Opinion 2: Reading

Reading for the Main Idea: Each unit presents an authentic reading selected from a variety of current periodicals and journals. These selections appear in their original form, or only slightly edited for length and comprehensibility. They present an alternative point of view to that presented in the listening commentary—sometimes in direct opposition to the commentary; at other times just offering another angle on the issue. In some cases glosses have been included to explain cultural or linguistic items.

In this exercise, the students are asked to identify the author's thesis. In selecting the main idea statement, the students will need to separate the essential ideas from the less relevant or extraneous information. They will also need to distinguish the opinions of the author from the opinions of others discussed in the text.

Students can compare their answers in pairs or groups, and the teacher can discuss any areas that caused difficulty in comprehension. The teacher may want to assign the reading and reading exercises as homework.

Reading for Fact vs. Opinion; Reading for Explicit vs. Implicit Meaning; Reading for the Author's Point of View: Once the students have agreed on the author's main idea, the focus moves to the details the author uses to support the main idea. A variety of comprehension exercises encourage the students' understanding of these details. The answers to these exercises are not always "black and white." Students are asked to explore the "gray area" of less literal meaning. For this reason, the answer key presents only "suggested answers." Students should be encouraged to disagree with these answers if they can provide convincing arguments for their own opinions.

In *Reading for Fact vs. Opinion*, students are given statements made by the author in the text, but they must distinguish facts from opinions. Students will discover that authors tend to use a combination of facts and opinions in writing, and through this process will come to realize the benefit of using both in their own writing.

In *Reading for Explicit vs. Implicit Meaning*, students are given statements that could all be supported by the author, but they must refer to the reading to determine whether a particular statement is "explicit" (clearly stated by the author in the same words or in a paraphrased statement), or "implicit" (implied only by what the author has written in the text). This exercise helps build students' awareness of the author's meaning, whether it is stated directly or not. They begin to realize that much of comprehension involves interpretation.

In *Reading for the Author's Point of View*, the students decide whether the statements presented would be supported by the author. Here they are asked to "read between the lines" to comprehend the finer distinctions of the author's point of view. They must distinguish between when an author is discussing the views of others and when he or she is presenting his or her own opinion.

Word Search: This is a vocabulary reinforcement exercise that works well as a homework exercise or as an in-class supplementary exercise for students who finish the comprehension exercises early. The teacher should emphasize that, although a word may have more than one meaning in a dictionary, only the meaning that has been used by the author is given in this exercise. Once the students have read the words in context, they select the best synonym or definition for each. This vocabulary has been grouped according to parts of speech (nouns, verbs, adjectives) to help students focus on *structure*: how the words are used in the text.

5 Synthesizing Two Opinion Pieces

Distinguishing Opinions: In this activity, students are asked to compare and contrast the views of the commentator and the author. The statements presented in this exercise are general value statements about the issue; these may or may not be supported by the opinions of the commentator and/or author. Because this evaluation involves a high level of student interpretation, no answer key is given. In discussing whether the author or commentator might agree with a particular statement, students will find themselves disagreeing as they go back to the two texts to locate information that will support their answers. The teacher may want to guide this activity with a particular answer in mind, but should remain open to the arguments that students give for their own answers.

Students should come to realize, through their group discussion, that the commentator and author may agree on certain points and disagree on others. They will see that the different stances taken on an issue are not always in direct opposition, that issues are more complex than that. They will realize that in disagreement, there is usually an area in which people may agree. This should help students examine a dispute from a variety of viewpoints. They can then begin to take their own position on the issue.

Giving Your Opinion: Once the students have agreed on the viewpoints of the commentator and author, they express their own opinions by agreeing or disagreeing with the same statements. This exercise can also be used as an optional discussion for groups that finish the previous exercise early.

Vocabulary Reinforcement: Combining vocabulary from both the commentary and article/essay, this exercise reinforces the comprehension of words and phrases that were studied in earlier exercises. It asks students to apply or analyze the vocabulary they have studied in a new context. There are a variety of exercise types, including categorization, concept grids, word form identification, and word relations.

6 Speaking

The teacher may want to choose to do one of the speaking activities. These exercises promote communication in the context of decision making. The exercises ask students to draw on all the material presented in the unit and to apply their opinions and those of others to specific cases or specific questions.

Case Study: The case studies in each of the units are true cases from the news. The case study has been written as a summary, incorporating some of the vocabulary and issues presented in the unit. The students are asked to weigh the arguments presented in the case and ultimately to make a decision.

The activities presented in each case vary. Each unit asks the students to first read the case study. Then a role-play, debate, or group discussion follows.

Discussion Questions: These questions can be used to guide a class discussion or for small group discussion. The questions ask the students to come to their own conclusions on the issue. The first question always asks students to reevaluate their original assumptions, that is, the opinions that they had expressed in the Values Clarification exercise. They may find that they have somewhat altered their opinions after examining the views of others, an important stage of critical thinking.

7 Writing

Grammar: Each unit focuses on a grammatical structure used in either the commentary or the article/essay, or in both. These structures have been chosen to respond to the advanced learner's needs in developing more sophisticated forms in writing. Each unit asks the students to review a particular grammar point in the context in which it was presented. The students predict how the particular grammar point is formed and used. They then review various rules and explanations for the grammar. Finally, they practice the grammar point in a structured exercise. (The teacher may want to supplement this exercise with other sources, as the explanations are not intended to be all inclusive.)

Writing Style: This exercise focuses on an interesting and useful style of writing used in either the commentary or the article/essay, or in both. Again, these excerpts have been chosen for their relevance to the advanced learner's needs in developing a more sophisticated style in writing. Each unit asks the students to review a segment of writing. Using guided questions, the students explore the particular style of writing. They then read an explanation for how or why the style is used. Finally, they complete an exercise asking them to analyze further examples of the writing style or to practice using the style in short writing assignments.

Essay Questions: This final exercise represents a culminating activity for the unit. The teacher may want to give the essay as a weekend writing assignment. The questions have been designed to elicit the students' own opinions that have developed throughout the course of the unit. At least one of the questions asked is argumentative in nature. The students are asked to develop their own theses in answering the question. In doing this they should be encouraged to refer to ideas expressed in the readings and commentary and practice using the language techniques (grammar and writing style) presented in the unit.

ACKNOWLEDGMENTS

Many people were instrumental in developing this text. I would like to thank my friends and colleagues at the American Language Program, Columbia University, for their ideas, suggestions, and contributions of material that went into the creation of this book. I wish to give special thanks to:

Patrick Aquilina, Frances Boyd, Robert Cohen, Dick Faust, Tess Ferree, Gail Fingado, Sheri Handel, Liz Henley, Mary Jerome, Maryan Keillor,

Jane Kenefick, Dominique Lap, Michael Maione, Leila May-Landy, Barbara Miller, Judy Miller, David Quinn, Shelley Saltzman, and Linda Schlam.

I would also like to express my appreciation to Paul Rudder, who has provided me with his legal expertise throughout the writing of my books, and to Dan Levine, who gave me important information regarding the Kansas City School District case.

The staff at National Public Radio has provided me with continual support from the idea stage to the production stage. I am particularly indebted to Suzanne Noel, from the Public Information Department, for coordinating this project at NPR. Mary Morgan was also instrumental in the realization of this project, and I thank her for her support. Rosemary McMullen was also very helpful with editorial advice. Several NPR librarians helped me in the various stages of research. I would like to thank Jaclin Gilbert, Beth Howard, Margot McGann, Katherine Plumb, Willette Stinson, and Elisabeth Sullivan for their help. Carol Whitehorn deserves special recognition for providing the legal support for permissions and production. Wendy Blair did a superb job of producing the accompanying audiotape.

I would also like to thank the librarians at Ferguson Library in Stamford, Connecticut, for helping me locate numerous articles and essays.

The editors and staff at Longman continue to believe in my work and have offered me sustained guidance and support throughout yet another project. I would like to thank Joanne Dresner for her continual vision and interest in doing something that has not been done before. I am also indebted to Debbie Sistino for her support and guidance throughout the project and to Polli Heyden for helping with the cartoon research. I am especially grateful to Penny Laporte for her fine work as an editor. Her ability to simplify, improve, and make a manuscript more accessible to students continues to impress me! I would also like to thank Allen Ascher for coming in at the end with helpful insights and Helen Ambrosio for her terrific work as production editor.

Finally, I thank my students for offering their suggestions and helping me understand that I must be open to change. I also thank my husband, Eric, for continuing to support my writing and for sending me upstairs to my computer after dinner each night.

MEN WHO KNOW WHERE THEIR BULLETS ARE GOING

1

"It's tough, but their right to keep and bear arms
must not be infringed."

*Drawing by
Handelsman; © 1991
The New Yorker
Magazine, Inc.*

I. ANTICIPATING THE ISSUE

Discuss your answers to the following questions.

1. Look at the title. Look at the cartoon. What do you think the issue of this unit will be?

2. What is the message or humor of the cartoon?

3. What do you know about the controversy over hunting?

BACKGROUND READING

Read the following text.

Hunting has always been a popular sport in the United States. During the autumn months, wooded areas across the nation are invaded by men driving **pickups** and carrying rifles, in search of anything from large bear to small **grouse**. The most popular hunted animal, though, is the white-tail deer.

The hunting of deer has been largely supported by local governments because the huge deer population in the United States has doubled, even tripled in some states, in just the last decade. The growing deer population has added to an increase in crop damage on farms, the destruction of homeowners' yards, and automobile accidents; thus, state officials encourage deer hunting as a means of keeping these problems under control. Yet, not everyone is in favor of this system as a means to manage the destruction caused by deer, and recently there has been a national debate over whether or not the best solution to controlling the deer population is to kill these graceful creatures.

Hunters favor killing off deer as a means of management. They argue that the deer population is so large that many deer would **starve** anyway, as there is not enough vegetation to accommodate the number of hungry deer roaming around. They also point out that if hunters were restricted from killing deer, even more people would die in automobile accidents. In New York and Pennsylvania, for example, there have been up to 40,000 deer-vehicle accidents reported each year, and many more accidents are unaccounted for because they never get reported to the police. What makes matters worse, they say, is that many of the deer in these collisions may die suffering if they are hit and not killed. A deer's leg could be **severed** in an accident, for instance, and then the animal would limp off into the woods to die a painful death. The automobile driver, in these cases, usually has no means of **putting** the deer **down** to take it out of its misery.

Another argument hunters have in support of their sport is that the increase in deer populations has been an economic burden as well as a health threat to many people. Beautiful gardens have been destroyed; forests have been grazed; farmers' crops have been ruined; and Lyme disease, which is the fastest-growing infectious disease in the U.S. after AIDS, has been spread by deer, as deer are frequently the home to ticks, the insects that carry the disease.

In spite of these arguments favoring hunting as a method to manage deer populations, there are those who see hunters as **villains** and would never support killing animals. Animal advocates believe that hunters have no **soul** because they willingly take the life of another living creature. For them, alternatives such as trapping deer, shipping deer off to other areas, and using birth control techniques are preferable to killing deer for management purposes. These people **dread** the start of deer season because for them the season brings on a series of battles with men who hunt. Anti-hunters and animal welfare groups launch campaigns against hunters annually because they feel that their management argument only justifies the hunter's desire to kill for sport. To oppose the shooting of deer, they encourage people to **post** their property, especially around farmland, to restrict the hunters. Farm animals are often the accidental, and sometimes even intentional, victims of hunting. For example, a farmer in Virginia recently lost several **ewes** that were still feeding their baby lambs, because of a hunter's bullet.

In addition to fighting for the rights of animals, animal-welfare groups, or people who oppose the sport of hunting, focus on the danger hunting poses to suburban areas. As more and more people have tried to **flee** big cities, suburbs have grown. As suburbs have extended deeper into deer territory, deer hunting has posed an increasingly greater threat to suburbanites. Because of the higher number of accidents in these areas, restrictions have been placed on hunting there. Those hunters who dare to shoot their prey within these restricted areas risk being **prosecuted** and may pay heavy fines.

But American law works in various ways. Not long ago, a suburbanite in Westchester County, New York, was granted a special permit to shoot deer near a shopping mall. This was a consequence of a lawsuit against the state in which she had claimed $12,000 damages from deer eating the shrubs in her yard. Residents of the area were outraged by her permit. The fact that she could sue for damages caused by animals and be given, as payment, the right to shoot deer near a populated area simply **unhinged their minds**.

Whether deer will continue to be regarded as cute "Bambis" or be seen as "rats with hoofs" in the U.S. remains an unresolved question.

A   VOCABULARY

The following sentences are taken from the background reading. Try to determine the meaning of the boldfaced words and phrases. Write a synonym or your own definition of the word. Then check the answer key for suggested synonyms or definitions.

1. During the autumn months, wooded areas across the nation are invaded by men driving **pickups** and carrying rifles, in search of anything from large bear to small grouse.

   _____

2. Hunting has always been a popular sport in the United States. Areas across the nation are invaded by men driving pickups and carrying rifles, in search of anything from large bear to small **grouse**.

   _____

3. Hunters favor killing off deer as a means of management. They argue that the deer population is so large that many deer would **starve** anyway, as there is not enough vegetation to accommodate the number of hungry deer roaming around.

   _____

4. A deer's leg could be **severed** in an accident, for instance, and then the animal would limp off into the woods to die a painful death.

_____

5. The automobile driver, in these cases, usually has no means of **putting** the deer **down** to take it out of its misery.

_____

6. In spite of these arguments, there are those who see hunters as **villains** and would never support killing animals.

_____

7. Animal advocates believe that hunters have no **soul** because they willingly take the life of another living creature.

_____

8. These people **dread** the start of deer season because for them the season brings on a series of battles with men who hunt.

_____

9. To oppose the shooting of deer, they encourage people to **post** their property, especially around farmland, to restrict the hunters.

_____

10. For example, a farmer in Virginia recently lost several **ewes** that were still feeding their baby lambs, because of a hunter's bullet.

_____

11. As more and more people have tried to **flee** big cities, suburbs have grown.

_____

12. Those hunters who dare to shoot their prey within these restricted areas risk being **prosecuted** and may pay heavy fines.

_____

13. The fact that she could sue for damages caused by animals and be given, as payment, the right to shoot deer near a populated area simply **unhinged their minds**.

_____

B   **SUMMARIZING THE ISSUE**

Work in small groups. Summarize the issue presented in the background reading. Take notes to complete the following outline.

1. The issue (*state in your own words*):

   _____

   _____

   _____

2. Proponents' (of hunting deer) arguments:

   _____

   _____

   _____

3. Opponents' (of hunting deer) arguments:

   _____

   _____

   _____

 C   **VALUES CLARIFICATION**

Work in small groups. Discuss your answers to the following questions.

1. What is your personal view on hunting? Should people be allowed to hunt for sport? Why or why not?

2. What is your opinion about using hunting as a means of managing the deer population? If hunting were not used to control deer, what other methods could be used?

III.   **OPINION 1: LISTENING**

A ✔ **LISTENING FOR THE MAIN IDEA**

Listen to the commentary. Check the statement that summarizes the commentator's viewpoint.

☐   1. Donald McCaig thinks hunting should be abolished.

(continued on next page)

☐ 2. Donald McCaig supports hunting as a sport.

☐ 3. Donald McCaig feels ambivalent about hunting.

B LISTENING FOR DETAILS

Read the following questions and answers. Listen to the commentary again and circle the best answer. Then compare your answers with those of another student. Listen again if necessary.

1. Where did Donald McCaig recently express positive views on hunters?

    a. In the woods, to the hunters themselves.

    b. On the radio.

    c. At his Virginia sheep farm.

2. What did the boys who shot the ewes do after the killing?

    a. They watched them die from the road.

    b. They left.

    c. They played with the lambs.

3. What reaction did McCaig's wife have toward the incident?

    a. She couldn't sleep.

    b. She nurtured the wounded lambs.

    c. She got sick.

4. What is McCaig's view of hunting?

    a. Young animals should never be killed.

    b. Hunters should know their targets.

    c. Hunting shouldn't cause animals long-lasting pain.

5. How does McCaig generally feel about hunters?

    a. He believes they are not real men.

    b. He thinks they practice their sport with respect for farmers.

    c. He is close friends with them and their families.

6. What will be a difficult task for McCaig now?

        a.   He will have to post his farm.

        b.   He will have to penalize good hunters.

        c.   He will have to nurse the baby lambs.

7. Why does McCaig quote Plato?

        a.   Plato taught us that men are basically evil.

        b.   Plato said that evil men are weakened by their evil acts.

        c.   Plato believed that even the evil man has a good soul.

8. What conclusion does McCaig reach about the boys who killed his ewes?

        a.   They had good reason but made a mistake.

        b.   They don't have the necessary skill to be hunters.

        c.   They will lose any dignity they once had.

C   TEXT COMPLETION AND DISCRETE LISTENING

Read the text of the commentary. Try to fill in the missing words in the text as you remember them. Use your knowledge of text structure, vocabulary, and grammar to help you. Then listen again to the commentary to check your answers, stopping the tape as you fill in the blanks. If you have different answers than the original text, check with your teacher to see if they are acceptable alternatives.

Introduction

Across much of the nation this week, there are _____ parked on the
₁
sides of country roads near the woods, and you can hear the pop of
_____ firing in the distance. Hunters are still out. Recently, commenta-
₂
tor Donald McCaig came on the _____ and said a few kind things about
₃
hunters, but since then there's been some trouble at his Virginia sheep farm,
the kind of incident that farmers _____ .
₄

Commentary

I'd like to speak _____ to the boys in the lime-green Chevrolet who
₅
shot two of our sheep Monday, opening day of deer _____ . . . shot
₆
them from the road and left them to die. Since you boys had to _____ ,
₇

you'd be interested to know what's happened once you'd gone. The _____ you shot had just turned out onto pasture so they could graze; their lambs could frolic and play. When we found them, the lambs were banked up against their dead mothers. I rolled a ewe over, and when we saw the bullet hole, my wife, Anne, cried.

You should understand that we're _____ , and not getting much sleep, and Anne's worked so hard, you see, to _____ those ewes that the thought that someone could just kill them, for the pleasure of it, for a moment that _____ her mind. "How could anyone do this?" she said. "What kind of a person could do this?" And then she threw up.

Hunters—men—don't kill animals with young at their side. Without their mothers, young animals _____ to death. Hunters—men—know where their bullets are going. One of your bullets went through the mother and _____ her lamb's leg, and the vet had to _____ the lamb _____ , she was in such pain. Of course you didn't know that; you had to flee.

You mightn't have noticed our farm is not _____ . Over the years, a good many hunters—men—have hunted deer and turkey, _____ , rabbits, and squirrels here. In the years they've been hunting, none of them has so much as left a gate open. Some of these hunters have taken _____ with us; we've met their families.

I confess my first thought, when we'd found out what you'd done, was to post the farm: "No hunting. No trespassing." But, you see, that would be _____ honest men for what you did. So, today we'll burn two young ewes and one lamb, and we'll try to get the lambs you orphaned on a bottle. That's harder to do than you might think. Of course we've called the sheriff, and if you're caught, we'll _____ . But, I don't expect you'll be caught.

Two thousand years ago, Plato looked around and saw that sometimes evildoers are not caught. Sometimes _____ get away with it. Plato said the evil man has a sick soul, and every cruel, thoughtless act a man commits soils and coarsens his own _____ .

You killed without reason. You are less than you were.

IV.   OPINION 2: READING

A   ✔ READING FOR THE MAIN IDEA

Read the editorial. Check the statement that summarizes the author's viewpoint.

☐   1. Although Bass feels guilty about being a hunter, he must hunt.

☐   2. Bass apologizes for being a hunter because it means that he is a killer.

☐   3. Bass thinks that hunting should not be condemned as a sport.

WHY I HUNT

(A Predator's Meditation)

by Rick Bass

In the fall, it's what I want to do. It would be unnatural and dishonest to sit on my hands; I'm a hunter, a **predator** (in the fall), with eyes in front of my head, like a bear's or a wolf's or even an owl's. **Prey** have their eyes on the sides of their heads, in order to see in all directions, in order to be ready to run. But predators—and that's us, or at least some of us—have our eyes before us, out in front, with which to focus to a single point.

For two months of the year—or until I have killed one deer and one **elk**—that's what I do. I want to be out in the woods, walking quietly, walking slowly, or not walking at all but just sitting in some leaves, completely hidden and motionless—waiting, and waiting. To not **pursue** the thing one wants would be a waste of one's life.

In the fall, I can do things I couldn't do in my normal, civilized life. I can disappear into the woods, and over the next mountain, the next ridge. My **roaming** has meaning—it's no longer just roaming, but hunting. The year's meat supply is in question. My meat, my family's meat—not some rancher's **heifer** from Minnesota. Meat from my valley, where I hope to live and die—where I cut firewood, where I pick huckleberries, where I walk, where I watch the stars—my valley.

For those two months, I am after something: something tangible, something that's moving away from me, and something that I must have for the coming year. It's as simple as that.

Over the next ridge. The new life of stores and towns falls away, and the old life returns. There's a loveliness to looking ahead—looking straight ahead—that only hunting brings out.

The other ten months are okay, too—I can be the artist, can *loll around* eating grapes and reading poetry, but the fall comes like a splash of water to my face on a hot, dusty day; and the dust, and my new ways, new feelings—the ones bound by rules—are washed away, leaving the old ways revealed.

I keep eating those lovely candlelit dinners—grouse and potatoes, and the red, almost purple *heartthrob* steaks from elk; fried trout for breakfast, and homemade huckleberry jam . . . I feel alive. . . . I draw immense strength from those meals—strength to live my life—and it feels good. I eat about a pound and a half of meat a day. The cancer studies for this kind of diet alarm me, but I have to trust that they apply to fatty steroid beef, and cattle that must have been raised in pesticide fields. I was seven miles into the mountains when I shot last year's elk, and I carried him out in three trips over a twenty-four-hour period.

Into those same dark woods I go each year, looking straight ahead, and stopping and listening and turning my head. . . .

Of course, it's possible that there's a greater life force that judges us; and of course, sometimes I feel guilty about being a hunter, a killer—a killer of deer and elk, though not moose, because they're too easy, and not bears, because . . . well, bears themselves are meant to hunt. During part of the year they're predators, not prey. It seems unnatural to hunt predators.

I'm scared, sometimes, that all the animals I've killed—few as they are—add up, and that I'm *liable* for them.

I wouldn't mind paying for them with my life someday—we must all give up our lives—but sometimes I get scared I may have to pay afterward, in the afterlife, for my *gluttony*, my *insatiable* hunger for clean meat, and so much of it.

Nonetheless, I've studied it, and have come up with this: I am who I am, and I've come from the place we all came from—the past—but I still remember, and love, that place. Some of us are glad to be away from that place, but I'm not one of those people—not in the fall.

The worst day I ever had hunting was when I shot an elk in the neck, where I was aiming, but it made me feel strangely ashamed after it was over. I broke the elk's neck, the way I always try to do—

that instant drop—but he *groaned* when I walked up to him. He couldn't have been feeling anything, and I hope it was just air leaving his lungs—but it was still a groan.

For a fact—or rather, for me—hunting's better than killing. It takes a while after it's over—sometimes a long while before you can think of it as meat. You can't go straight from a living animal to 250 pounds of elk steaks. There's too much knife and ax work involved—and you're the one who has to do it—skinning the animal, and pulling the *hide* back to reveal your crime, the meat—and already, sometimes, the call of ravens drifting in black-winged shapes flying through the treetops, past the sun. . . .

Instead of trying to make that instantaneous conversion—which I cannot do—life to meat—what I do is pray, sort of. I give heartfelt, *shaky* thanks to the animal as I clean it—ravens calling to ravens—and I do this with deer and grouse too, and even, If I can remember—which I don't always—with fish. A man or woman who apologizes for hunting is a fool. It's a man's or a woman's choice and he or she must live with it.

I don't do it for profit or gain, and rarely do I tell anyone about it after I've done it.

I watch ravens in the off-season. I think ravens have more of a soul than humans—and I think ravens understand the hunt better than I ever will. Sometimes ravens, in Alaska, lead hunters—wolves, or humans—to prey, and then they eat the pickings from the kill.

Ravens, black as coal, shiny and greasy, flying in the sun, like winged, black devils . . . I feel as if I'm on their side, and it scares me, but it would be a lie in the fall to switch sides: to pretend that I'm not. I'm a killer, sometimes. I wish I weren't, but I am. I've **wrestled with** it but I can't escape it, any more than—until death—one can escape one's skin.

_____

Rick Bass lives in Montana.

B   READING FOR EXPLICIT AND IMPLICIT MEANING

Read the following statements. All of the statements would be supported by the author. Do you think the author states the ideas explicitly (E) or implicitly (I)? Write E or I next to each statement. Compare your answers with those of another student. If your answers differ, go back to the text to find out why. The first two have been done for you. (Statement 1 is "E" because Bass states explicitly that he is a predator: "I'm a hunter, a predator ..." Statement 2 is "I" because Bass does not state this explicitly. He suggests that predators are more aggressive than prey by saying that predators look ahead of them, implying that they are always hunting for prey.)

_E_   1. Bass is a predator.

_I_   2. Predators are more aggressive than prey.

_____   3. Bass's roaming has more meaning in the fall.

_____   4. Bass doesn't like to eat rancher's meat from Minnesota.

_____   5. For ten months out of the year, Bass lives by rules.

_____   6. Wild game is healthier than cattle raised for meat.

_____   7. A hunter is a killer.

_____   8. Bass doesn't hunt bear.

_____   9. Bass is afraid he might have to pay for killing animals.

_____   10. People were originally meant to kill animals.

(continued on next page)

_____ 11. Hunting is better than killing.

_____ 12. Bass thanks the deer and grouse that he kills.

_____ 13. Bass never apologizes for his sport.

_____ 14. Ravens have more of a soul than humans.

_____ 15. Bass's desire to hunt animals is stronger than his guilt.

C   WORD SEARCH

Find boldfaced words in the essay that have similar meaning to the following and write them below.

Nouns

skin of an animal: _____

animal to be taken as food: _____

young cow: _____

wandering: _____

largest living deer: _____

excessive eating: _____

animal that hunts after other animals: _____

Verbs

struggled with: _____

follow (in order to capture or kill): _____

move in a lazy manner: _____

made a sound of pain: _____

Adjectives

responsible: _____

incapable of being satisfied: _____

blood red: _____

questionable: _____

V. **SYNTHESIZING TWO OPINION PIECES**

A. ✔ **DISTINGUISHING OPINIONS**

Authors can have different viewpoints, but their opinions can sometimes be similar. Review opinion 1 on pages 7–8 and opinion 2 on pages 9–11.

Work in groups. Read the statements below. Discuss whether McCaig and/or Bass would agree with them. Put a check (✔) in the box if you think they would agree. Leave the box empty if they would disagree or if there is no evidence to support the statement in their opinion.

Discuss how and why the two opinions are the same or different. (In the first statement, for example, McCaig would probably not agree, especially since there are some people, like the boys who killed his ewes, who kill without reason. Bass, however, would agree. He says that he, like the rest of us, comes from a past that he loves, implying that it was a time when hunting was used by all as a means of survival.)

	McCaig: Commentator (Opinion 1)	Bass: Author (Opinion 2)
Hunting is the birthright of all humans.		✔
Hunters are killers.		
Some people who hunt are insensitive to their killing.		
Hunting should be more restricted than it is.		
We have to accept the fact that hunting may cause some animals to suffer.		
Hunters are generally responsible.		
A reason to hunt is to provide a family with food.		

B GIVING YOUR OPINION

After you have distinguished the opinions of the commentator and the author, express your own opinions on the previous statements. Discuss them with the other students in your group.

C VOCABULARY REINFORCEMENT: CATEGORIZATION

Work in small groups. The following list of nouns and verbs comes from vocabulary (or related forms of vocabulary) in the commentary and essay. Discuss the meaning of each and write them under the most appropriate word category below.

deer	groan	predator	roam
dread	grouse	prey	sever
elk	loll around	prosecute	starve
flee	post	put (something) down	unhinge

Categorize verbs from the list above that describe:

Movement:

_____ _____

_____ _____

A legal action:

_____ _____

A separation of some kind:

_____ _____

An eventual death:

_____ _____

Dealing with something unpleasant:

_____ _____

_____ _____

Categorize nouns from the list above that describe:

Those in the hunt:

_____ _____

_____ _____

Animals that can be hunted:

_____ _____

_____ _____

VI.   SPEAKING

A   ✔ CASE STUDY: THE *MAINE V. ROGERSON* CASE

The following reading presents a true case that raises the issue of whether hunting is an acceptable sport.

Study the case.

On a November afternoon, Mrs. Karen Wood walked into her backyard on the outskirts of Bangor, Maine, and was fatally shot by a local hunter. The hunter, 47-year-old Donald Rogerson, later said that he had mistaken her white mittens for the tail of a deer. He walked ahead, looking for a deer, and found Karen Ann Wood with a single gunshot wound in the chest. She died at the scene. Mr. Rogerson was arrested that evening and charged with manslaughter, an act that involves the reckless or criminally negligent killing of another human being.

Mrs. Wood, a mother of one-year-old twin baby girls, had moved from Iowa to Maine with her husband and family only a few months before her death. Their new house was built at the end of a dead-end street, on land that had once been open to hunters. The house is located five miles from Bangor International Airport, so jet airliners often fly directly overhead. On the day she stepped out into her yard and was shot, she was wearing a blue coat and white mittens. It is not clear why she went outside. Perhaps she had wanted to warn the hunters that they were too close to her property. But how did she know they were there? The first shot that was fired was the bullet that killed her.

Rogerson was 319 feet from the Woods' house when he shot Mrs. Wood. Under Maine law, a hunter can shoot no closer than 300 feet from a residence. There was no evidence that a deer had been near the Woods' house that day: No other deer, no blood, no droppings, and no deer tracks could be found.

Mr. Rogerson is the produce manager of a supermarket in Bangor. He is well respected in the community. As soon as the news of the accidental killing came out, people rushed to his defense and made statements on his character on television and in local newspapers. He was a solid citizen, according to his neighbors; he had been named "employee of the year" at the supermarket where he worked; as a Boy Scout leader, he had led boys from the community on hikes up mountains. Moreover, he expressed remorse for what he had done. *The Bangor Daily News* called it a "double tragedy."

The case has stirred up a debate between people who have always lived in Maine and those who have arrived more recently; these two groups tend to represent hunters and anti-hunters. In fact, it has fueled an "us versus them" quarrel in the community. People defending Rogerson claim that the accident might not have occurred if Mrs. Wood had been wearing orange clothing, a common practice in the northern woods during hunting season. These people are also reluctant to restrict hunting. The sport generates $150 million a year for the economy of Maine, a relatively poor state. On the other side, though, residents question Mr. Rogerson's mistaking Mrs. Wood's mittens for the tail of a deer and claim that Mr. Rogerson should be prosecuted for manslaughter.

Prepare for a role play. Read the situation and the roles, and follow the procedure.

The Situation

Mr. Rogerson has been charged with manslaughter. Before his trial, however, Mr. Rogerson's defense attorneys will attempt to "plea bargain" with the prosecuting attorneys, who represent the state. (Plea bargaining is a pre-trial hearing in which defense attorneys will try to negotiate a less serious penalty by pleading guilty to a lesser crime. This saves time and money and ensures a conviction.) The defense attorneys will try to convince the prosecuting attorneys to lessen Rogerson's charge from "manslaughter," the unlawful killing of a human being without purposeful harm, to a "misdemeanor," a charge much less serious.

The Roles

1. **The Defense Attorneys:** You represent Mr. Rogerson. You think his charge is too strong. Before an official indictment is made, you will attempt to lessen Rogerson's charge to a misdemeanor. You will focus on Rogerson's character and the fact that Mrs. Wood's death was an accident.

2. **The Prosecuting Attorneys:** You represent the state. You will attempt to formally charge Rogerson with manslaughter. You will refer to three other hunting deaths in Maine, in which human beings were mistaken for animals; two of them resulted in convictions and jail terms. You will focus on Rogerson's responsibility for Mrs. Wood's death. However, you do have "an interest" in plea bargaining because it would guarantee Rogerson's conviction (in a formal court hearing, he might be found innocent and never be convicted). In addition, less time and money would be spent in court if you plea bargain for a lesser charge.

The Procedure

1. The class divides into two groups (you may prefer to divide into several small groups of two roles). Each group of attorneys prepares a list of arguments supporting its position.

2. The two groups come together for plea bargaining.

3. The prosecuting attorneys present and explain the manslaughter charge as it stands.

4. The defense attorneys present and explain their reasons for wanting the charge reduced to a misdemeanor.

5. The two groups negotiate to reach a decision.

B   DISCUSSION QUESTIONS

Work in groups. Discuss your answers to the following questions.

1. Go back to the questions in the values clarification exercise (p. 5). Do you have the same opinions now, or have you changed your opinions in any way after examining the views of others?

2. What message does Donald McCaig convey about hunters when he prefaces several comments with, "Hunters—men . . ."? What message does he convey about the hunters who shot his ewes? Do you agree with his assessment of hunters?

3. Describe the guilt Rick Bass feels about being a hunter. What is it about his sport that makes him feel uneasy? Why does he continue to hunt? Can you think of other sports, habits, or rituals that people have or practice in spite of the guilt they might feel about them?

VII.   WRITING

A   ✓ GRAMMAR: MODAL PERFECTS

Notice

Notice the verb forms in the following sentences taken from the commentary and the essay:

> You **mightn't have noticed** [that] our farm is not posted.

> The cancer studies for this kind of diet alarm me, but I have to trust that they apply to fatty steroid beef, and cattle that **must have been raised** in pesticide fields.

In which of the statements is the writer more certain? Explain the differences of certainty in each sentence.

Explanation

Modal perfects are used to make statements about actions in the past.

Notice the difference in meaning in the following modal perfect sentences (each example is illustrated in both the active and passive verb forms):

Might have

> *The hunters **might have shot** the deer.*

> *The deer **might have been shot** by the hunters.*

In the above sentences, the writer is not sure whether the hunters did, in fact, shoot the deer. (The writer is making a logical deduction but is only 50 percent sure of the statement.)

Could have

> *The hunters **could have shot** the deer.*

> *The deer **could have been shot** by the hunters.*

In these sentences . . .

1. the writer refers to a possible action in the past that was not taken. Shooting the deer was a possibility, but the hunters chose not to do it.

or

2. as with "might have," the writer is not sure whether the hunters did, in fact, shoot the deer, but he or she is making a logical deduction.

Must have

> *The hunters **must have shot** the deer.*

> *The deer **must have been shot** by the hunters.*

With the "must" modal in this form, the writer is quite certain (90 percent or so) that the action did happen in the past. The writer was not at the scene, but judging from observation or other information, he or she can deduce that the hunters did shoot the deer.

Should have

> *The hunters **should have shot** the deer.*

> *The deer **should have been shot** by the hunters.*

In these sentences, the deer was not shot. The person making the statement is providing advice or a strong opinion contrary to what actually happened.

Exercise

Complete the following statements with the verb in parentheses and the correct modal perfect. Use Donald McCaig's commentary as the context for the sentence meaning. Pay attention to the active and passive forms of the verbs.

1. The boys who shot McCaig's ewes (not) _____ (flee) after killing them.

2. Those boys (not) _____ (bring up) in a family in which morals were taught!

3. The boys (not) _____ (realize) that their bullets had hit a lamb.

4. McCaig _____ (give up), leaving the orphaned lambs to die, but he and his wife decided to try to get them on a bottle.

5. Anne was clearly sickened by the event, but she also _____ (be) very sad.

6. The lamb with the bullet wound (not) _____ (keep) alive without more suffering.

7. McCaig and his wife _____ (like) the hunters who hunted on their land, since they had dinner with them.

8. McCaig _____ (post) his farm, because farmers have the right to forbid trespassers to enter their property, but he decided against it because of his positive feelings toward hunters.

9. Honest hunters _____ (penalize) by "No Trespassing" signs if McCaig had posted the farm.

10. The boys (not) _____ (kill) without reason because now they are less than they were.

B   WRITING STYLE: DESCRIPTION

Notice

Notice Rick Bass's style of writing. Bass uses effective description in his essay. What kind of language does he use to do this?

Explanation

Bass uses several techniques in his writing that illustrate good description:

1. *An appeal to the senses.* Effective description includes details that relate to the senses: sight, sound, smell, taste, or touch.

2. *Careful word choice.* The right words can make a description come alive. Effective choice of nouns, verbs, and adjectives can convey exact images.

3. *Choice of details to create an overall dominant impression.* From the writer's choice of details, readers should be able to feel a dominant impression: a mood, an atmosphere, a scene.

4. *Figurative language.* Figurative language forces the reader to create images in his or her mind. A writer can artistically suggest comparisons, and thus develop more complex ideas, through various types of figurative language:

   a. *Simile*: A simile is a direct comparison and usually contains the words "as" or "like." In this type of figurative language, the writer compares two things explicitly: *she smells like a rose; he's as skinny as a rail.* In this way, there is never any doubt about what is being compared.

   b. *Metaphor*: Unlike the simile, the metaphor states a comparison implicitly and does not use words such as "as" or "like" in the comparison. This is a more subtle way of suggesting how one thing is like another: *her teeth were a set of pearls; he's really just a lamb.*

   c. *Symbol*: Symbols can also suggest comparisons, but in an even more abstract and indirect way. A symbol is used by a writer to represent a significant idea or value that can be recognized both in the writer's essay and in the outside world. It can be an object, a person, an animal, a name, etc.

Exercise

Using the above criteria for effective descriptions, analyze Bass's essay by answering the following questions.

1. Which of the *senses* does Bass appeal to in his writing?

   _____

   _____

2. Take notes on Bass's *word choice* for the following descriptions. List specific words he uses to convey exact meaning about . . .

   a. His lovely candlelit dinners: _____

   b. The elk he shot:_____

   c. Ravens:_____

3. What *overall dominant impression* is created by Bass's choice of details in his description?

   _____

   _____

4. Find an example of the following types of figurative language in Bass's essay:

a. simile: _____

b. metaphor: _____

c. symbol: _____

C   ESSAY QUESTIONS

Choose one of the following topics. Try to integrate ideas, vocabulary, and writing techniques that you have studied in this unit. If you choose to write the essay (question 1), try to incorporate the following:

- an introductory paragraph that presents both sides of the argument and clearly states your thesis (whether you support hunting or not);

- paragraphs (at least three) that develop your argument with supporting evidence;

- a conclusion that reinforces the position you have taken. It should also end with a new idea (a warning, prediction, value judgment) that has not been mentioned before.

1. Hunting, in many parts of the United States, is described by many outdoor enthusiasts as "a tradition older than voting." Income from the sale of permits generates large revenues for many states, and hunting has been an effective management system for animal populations gone out of control. Yet, as suburbs have developed and expanded into wooded land, more and more hunting accidents have been reported each year. Moreover, many people have become increasingly sensitized to animals' rights and have begun to reject hunting as sport.

   Write an essay in which you argue for or against the continuation of hunting as a sport.

2. Write a letter to the editor of the *The Bangor Daily News* stating your opinion of the Karen Wood Case.

Cartoon by Don Wright,
The Palm Beach Post.

I. ANTICIPATING THE ISSUE

Discuss your answers to the following questions.

1. Look at the title. Look at the cartoon. What do you think the issue of this unit will be?

2. What is the message or humor of the cartoon?

3. What do you know about new advances in medical technology?

BACKGROUND READING

Read the following text.

With advances in medical technology has come a **convergence** of new medical and legal issues. It seems that laws cannot be written fast enough to keep up with the new problems posed by technology. The **propositions** for creating new laws are numerous, but decisions are only just beginning to be made.

When a couple in Tennessee, Mary Sue Davis and Junior Davis, decided to get a divorce, a new ethical question was introduced into the courts of law: When does a human life begin? Mary Sue Davis, who is **infertile**, had had a series of complications with pregnancy and decided to get help from an infertility clinic. As the couple wanted very much to have children, they had decided to attempt in vitro fertilization, a process by which a husband's sperm and his wife's egg are fertilized in a **petri dish**, outside the woman's body. The embryo, the fertilized egg, is then implanted into the woman's body. Because the Davises had experienced six previous unsuccessful attempts at in vitro fertilization, their doctors recommended freezing some of Mrs. Davis's successfully fertilized eggs. With this procedure, the eggs could later be **thawed** to be implanted in Mrs. Davis's **uterine cavity** during any of her ovulation cycles.

But, on February 23, 1989, Mr. Davis filed for a divorce, marking the first legal battle over frozen embryos produced through in vitro fertilization. Just as children are fought over in legal **custody** cases, the court had to decide who had the right to the fertilized eggs. Mrs. Davis had tried to become pregnant for years and did not want the eggs **disposed of**. She had spent too much time and energy on trying to get pregnant and was not willing to abandon her last chance of having children. Mr. Davis, on the other hand, was not interested in seeing the eggs "**hatch**," as he did not want to see his wife bear his children after their divorce.

The Davises' case has **spawned** a series of new cases involving the rights to embryos, as well as a national debate over how we view life. Some argue that the frozen embryos, consisting of only **undifferentiated cells**, cannot be viewed as human beings as they have not yet formed into a unique individual. Others argue that life starts at **conception**, so that the moment the egg is fertilized in a petri dish, what is produced must be viewed as a human being. As the couple began to argue over the fertilized eggs, the judge in the divorce trial was being asked to do medical, legal, and ethical **somersaults** in deciding whether the Davises' embryos were just frozen **lumps**, marital property waiting to be divided up, or persons with some rights to legal protection. His decision would have even further **implications** for abortion and right-to-life advocates.

After listening to both the husband and wife **contending** for the right to their embryos, the Tennessee Circuit Court judge ruled that the embryos were people, not property, and they were turned over to the mother. Mr. Davis later announced that he would appeal the court's decision.

A   VOCABULARY

The following sentences are taken from the background reading. Try to determine the meaning of the boldfaced words and phrases. Write a synonym or your own definition of the word. Then check the answer key for suggested synonyms or definitions.

1. With advances in medical technology has come a **convergence** of new medical and legal issues.

   _____

2. The **propositions** for creating new laws are numerous, but decisions are only just beginning to be made.

   _____

3. Mary Sue Davis, who is **infertile**, had had a series of complications with pregnancy and decided to get help from an infertility clinic.

   _____

4. As the couple wanted very much to have children, they had decided to attempt in vitro fertilization, a process by which a husband's sperm and his wife's egg are fertilized in a **petri dish**, outside the woman's body.

   _____

5. With this procedure, the eggs could later be **thawed** to be implanted in Mrs. Davis's uterine cavity during any of her ovulation cycles.

   _____

6. With this procedure, the eggs could later be thawed to be implanted in Mrs. Davis's **uterine cavity** during any of her ovulation cycles.

   _____

7. Just as children are fought over in legal **custody** cases, the court had to decide who had the right to the fertilized eggs.

   _____

8. Mrs. Davis had tried to become pregnant for years and did not want the eggs **disposed of**.

   _____

9. Mr. Davis, on the other hand, was not interested in seeing the eggs "**hatch**," as he did not want to see his wife bear his children after their divorce.

   _____

10. The Davises' case has *spawned* a series of new cases involving the rights to embryos, as well as a national debate over how we view life.

_____

11. Some argue that the frozen embryos, consisting of only ***undifferentiated cells***, cannot be viewed as human beings as they have not yet formed into a unique individual.

_____

12. Others argue that life starts at ***conception***, so that the moment the egg is fertilized in a petri dish, what is produced must be viewed as a human being.

_____

13. As the couple began to argue over the fertilized eggs, the judge in the divorce trial was being asked to do medical, legal, and ethical ***somersaults*** in deciding whether the Davises' embryos were just frozen lumps, marital property waiting to be divided up, or persons with some rights to legal protection.

_____

14. As the couple began to argue over the fertilized eggs, the judge in the divorce trial was being asked to do medical, legal, and ethical somersaults in deciding whether the Davises' embryos were just frozen ***lumps***, marital property waiting to be divided up, or persons with some rights to legal protection.

_____

15. His decision would have even further ***implications*** for abortion and right-to-life advocates.

_____

16. After listening to both the husband and wife ***contending*** for the right to their embryos, the Tennessee Circuit Court judge ruled that the embryos were people, not property, and they were turned over to the mother.

_____

B   SUMMARIZING THE ISSUE

Work in small groups. Summarize the issue presented in the background reading. Take notes to complete the following outline.

1. The issue (*state in your own words*) :

_____

_____

_____

(continued on next page)

2. The wife's view:

_____

_____

_____

3. The husband's view:

_____

_____

_____

4. The judge's view:

_____

_____

_____

C   VALUES CLARIFICATION

Work in small groups. Discuss your answers to the following questions.

1. If you were the judge in the Tennessee case, how would you have ruled?

2. What, in your opinion, are the implications of the Tennessee judge's ruling? How could this ruling affect other areas of life?

III.   OPINION 1: LISTENING

A   LISTENING FOR THE MAIN IDEA

Listen to the commentary. Check the statement that summarizes the commentator's viewpoint.

☐ 1. We need to define when life begins.

☐ 2. Mr. and Mrs. Davis should not make their custody battle a public one.

☐ 3. Our laws are not prepared to deal with new ethical questions.

B   LISTENING FOR DETAILS

Read the following questions and answers. Listen to the commentary and circle the best answer. Then compare your answers with those of another student. Listen again if necessary.

1. What concern does the commentator have about the Tennessee case?

    a. The medical and legal issues should be separated.

    b. The case is too complex for Tennessee's state court.

    c. The case is not limited to the Tennessee couple's case.

2. How do the couple's attorneys view the frozen embryos?

    a. One sees them as matter, the other as life.

    b. One sees them as belonging to the wife, the other as belonging to the husband.

    c. One sees them as eggs that should be thrown away, the other as eggs that should hatch.

3. What is interesting about Louisiana's state law?

    a. Lawmakers haven't yet defined when a human being becomes a human being.

    b. The legal definition of conception is unclear.

    c. Fertilization in a petri dish is not permitted.

4. Which opinion is <u>not</u> mentioned as a human's beginning?

    a. Life begins when a fetus moves.

    b. Life begins when a baby is born.

    c. Life begins when a citizen proves he is worthy.

5. What ironic comment does the commentator make?

    a. Lawyers can't agree on the definition of life.

    b. Each embryo represents a different personality with its own rights.

    c. We need to test our laws through the different ways we define these embryos.

6. What conclusion does the commentator reach?

    a. Mr. and Mrs. Davis should not have gotten a divorce.

    b. Life must begin at conception.

    c. The Davises' custody battle raises larger issues than the future of their embryos.

C TEXT COMPLETION AND DISCRETE LISTENING

Read the text of the commentary. Try to fill in the missing words in the text as you remember them. Use your knowledge of text structure, vocabulary, and grammar to help you. Then listen again to the commentary to check your answers, stopping the tape as you fill in the blanks. If you have different answers than the original text, check with your teacher to see if they are acceptable alternatives.

Introduction

In this country, the _____ of medical and legal issues is being spotlight-
1
ed this summer in the case of the Tennessee couple and their frozen embryos.
As with many other things he reads about these days, commentator Andrei
Codrescu finds the case complicated by _____ .
2

Commentary

The husband, Junior Lewis Davis, wants the fertilized eggs _____ of.
3
The wife, Mary Sue Davis, is infertile and wants the eggs to _____ . The
4
husband's lawyer calls the eggs "a group of undifferentiated _____ ,"
5
while the wife's attorney has labeled them "preborn children." Between these
two definitions lies the entire range of current _____ as to when exactly
6
does a human being become one.

Here in Louisiana, life begins at _____ . But, the law's unclear whether
7
what goes on in a _____ dish can possibly be called "conception." Other
8
laws envision a human as beginning either from the minute it loses its flippers or
from the time it does its first uterine _____ . Other opinions maintain that
9
there are no human beings until they complete a scouting program or even pass
an SAT test. I've heard an advocate for the _____ that human beings
10
aren't human beings until they prove it themselves, in a court of law.

Clearly, there are seven _____ for seven embryos, in every case.
11
The seven frozen embryos in the Tennessee case could be used as tests for the
various laws. One embryo could be a group of undifferentiated cells; that one
would be _____ . Another could testify to the validity of petri dish con-
12
ception; that one could stay. Another could be raised into a fine Boy Scout and

sent out to fight drugs for the President; that one can prove it's a human being in a White House _____ .
                                                13

One shouldn't look at these embryos as merely frozen _____ , con-
                                                                  14
tending for definition. They are seeds of the very laws they might _____ .
                                                                            15
Mr. and Mrs. Davis should not fight for these eggs as if they were a private matter between themselves and their petri dish. They are sitting on the very basis of our future definition of human beings. Their divorce _____ the
                                                                        16
divorce of the diverse philosophies at work here. They should work out a _____ arrangement for these eggs that requires a constitutional lawyer
          17
to babysit.

IV.   OPINION 2: READING

A ✔ READING FOR THE MAIN IDEA

Read the article. Check the statement that summarizes the author's viewpoint.

- ☐ 1. We must recognize the fact that life begins at conception.
- ☐ 2. We should consider the negative consequences of medical technology.
- ☐ 3. Couples must think more seriously about their custody agreements before divorce.

The Eggs

by Betty McCollister

Frozen fertilized eggs provide as telling an example as one could find of how our ingenious technology, far from solving problems, keeps creating them—problems we humans cannot even begin to *unsnarl*.

Mary Sue and Junior Lewis Davis, in the course of their nine-year marriage, found themselves unable to have the babies they had hoped for. Desperate,

(continued on next page)

they resorted to the complicated, painful, costly procedures involved in *in vitro* fertilization. Nine embryos and two failed implantations later, the marriage fell apart.

The seven remaining eggs continued in frozen *limbo* while lawyers and judges *grappled with* questions which have no clear or easy answers. One, of course, is when life begins. But one can no more determine the precise instant life begins than the precise instant an infant becomes a *toddler*, a toddler a child, a child an adolescent, an adolescent an adult, and so on. There is no precise instant of transition from one stage of life to the next. Life is a *continuum*—an ever-changing, ever-developing process of growth and development until eventual old age and death. One might as well try to determine the precise instant a *surge* of sea water becomes a wave.

However, on September 21, 1989, Tennessee Circuit Judge W. Dale Young ruled that life begins at conception and therefore the seven remaining eggs deserve consideration as potential children. He then awarded temporary custody of the eggs to Mary Sue Davis, ruling that she would better serve the interests of those children. This case is believed to be the first of its type in the United States.

During the trial, Mary Sue Davis argued that she has gone through a great deal to have the baby she longs for and claimed that the eggs represented her only chance. Junior Davis argued that he is a product of a *broken home* and cannot bear to *inflict* what he *endured* on a child of his. He does not feel that the eggs are human beings. He says that Young's decision *infringes upon* his rights by forcing him to become a father against his wishes and that he will seek a "stay[1] of implantation." pending appeal[2] in higher state courts.

Both parties invite sympathy. Both deserve credit for recognizing that bringing a child into the world is a serious, long-term responsibility. A baby becomes human through *prolonged*, intensive social interaction. This is why Judge Young and the anti-abortionists who assert that life begins at conception are talking *arrant* nonsense. Life was in the egg and sperm before fertilization; life exists in every genetically coded egg and sperm, most of which are never fertilized at all. Whatever these seven *infinitesimal blobs* may be potentially, they are not now fully human. They cannot become so without successful implantation into a woman's womb—an *iffy* undertaking—and then years of loving *nurture*.

Nor is the question of when life begins the only thorny one this case raises. Now that the law has concluded that each egg is a human being, what happens if implantation fails again? Is the doctor who implanted it guilty of murder? Is Mary Sue Davis guilty because she allowed it?

These are all unanswerable questions, suggesting yet another: As our galloping technology *outstrips* our capacity to handle it wisely, shouldn't we assess its limitations rather than encourage its *unbridled* expansion?

Technology cannot care for the babies we already have—millions of whom die every year of starvation before the age of five. It cannot *purify* the water and air it has polluted. It cannot prevent disastrous oil spills caused by human stupidity and greed or deal with the consequences. For that matter, it cannot control human stupidity and greed.

The highest human qualities are and always have been the capacity to love, cooperate, imagine, *envision*, transmit values, and provide a secure environment for the young. These qualities worked for our hunter-gatherer *forebears* and *bestowed* on our species its humanity. Technology cannot create or substitute for these qualities. On the contrary, it often works against them.

Medical technology has made it possible for these eggs to be fertilized. But it cannot *mend* a broken marriage or guarantee a fulfilling family life for the children who would develop from them.

[1]A hold put on a process until a further decision is made.

[2]The taking of a case to a higher court for a rehearing and new decision.

Source: "The Eggs," by Betty McCollister, first appeared in the Nov./Dec. 1989 issue of *The Humanist* and is reprinted with permission.

B | READING FOR FACT VS. OPINION

In developing critical thinking skills, it is necessary to distinguish facts from opinions. In McCollister's article, both facts and opinions are used to support the author's main idea. Read the following statements. Next to each statement write F if it is a fact or O if it is an opinion. Compare your answers with those of another student.

The answer to statement 1 is "O" because the belief that technology creates problems more than it solves them is the author's thesis, her own conclusion or opinion. This statement is not a fact. In statement 2, however, the answer is "F" because it is a fact that the couple was infertile, unable to have children.

__O__ 1. Frozen fertilized eggs provide as telling an example as one could find of how our ingenious technology, far from solving problems, keeps creating them.

__F__ 2. Mary Sue and Junior Lewis Davis, in the course of their nine-year marriage, found themselves unable to have the babies they had hoped for.

_____ 3. But one can no more determine the precise instant life begins than the precise instant an infant becomes a toddler, a toddler a child, a child an adolescent, an adolescent an adult, and so on.

_____ 4. However, on September 21, 1989, Tennessee Circuit Judge W. Dale Young ruled that life begins at conception and therefore the seven remaining eggs deserve consideration as potential children.

_____ 5. Both parties invite sympathy.

_____ 6. Life was in the egg and sperm before fertilization.

_____ 7. Mr. Davis does not want his children that would come from these embryos to live the life he lived.

_____ 8. Both Mr. and Mrs. Davis seem concerned about the welfare of the embryos.

_____ 9. Life begins before conception.

_____ 10. Whatever these seven infinitesimal blobs may be potentially, they are not now fully human.

_____ 11. Technology cannot care for the babies we already have—millions of whom die every year of starvation before the age of five.

_____ 12. The highest human qualities are and always have been the capacity to love, cooperate, imagine, envision, transmit values, and provide a secure environment for the young.

_____ 13. Medical technology has made it possible for these eggs to be fertilized.

C WORD SEARCH

Find the boldfaced words in the essay that have similar meaning to the following and write them below.

Nouns

small round masses: _____

family after divorce or separation: _____

condition of being forgotten: _____

swelling forward movement:_____

ancestors:_____

baby who can just walk: _____

a process:_____

care: _____

Adjectives

extremely small:_____

questionable: _____

extreme:_____

not controlled: _____

extended: _____

Verbs

repair:_____

tried to deal with: _____

suffered:_____

violates: _____

figure out: _____

cleanse: _____

gave as an offering: _____

impose:_____

picture:_____

goes faster or farther than: _____

V. SYNTHESIZING TWO OPINION PIECES

A ✓ DISTINGUISHING OPINIONS

Authors can have different viewpoints, but their opinions can sometimes be similar. Review opinion 1 on pages 28–29 and opinion 2 on pages 29–31.

Work in groups. Read the statements below. Discuss whether Codrescu and/or McCollister would agree with them. Put a check (✓) in the box if you think they would agree. Leave the box empty if they would disagree or if there is no evidence to support the statement in their opinion.

Discuss how and why the two opinions are the same or different. (In the first statement, for example, Codrescu does not take a stand about when life begins. He only examines the views of those involved in the case. Consequently, this box should be left blank. McCollister, however, would agree. She states that those who assert that life begins at conception are talking arrant nonsense.)

	Codrescu: Commentator (Opinion 1)	McCollister: Author (Opinion 2)
Life may not begin at conception.		✓
Mrs. Davis had the right to keep her embryos.		
Embryos should be viewed more as people than as property.		
Mr. Davis should not be expected to be a parent to any of the seven embryos.		
Our current laws are insufficient in solving ethical issues.		
We need to define what constitutes a human being.		
Technology has gone too far.		

B GIVING YOUR OPINION

After you have distinguished the opinions of the commentator and the author, express your own opinions or statements. Discuss them with the other students in your group.

C VOCABULARY REINFORCEMENT: VERBS

The following verbs come from the commentary and the article. Look at the verbs, then read the sentences. Complete the sentences with the verbs. Be sure to use the correct verb form.

dispose of	bestow	spawn	conceive	endure
envision	grapple with	imply	mend	unbridle

1. The Davis case was the first custody battle over frozen embryos, but their case _____ many more court cases of the same kind.

2. Embryos _____ never _____ outside of a woman's body before in vitro fertilization.

3. The judge in the Davis case must _____ the question of when life begins.

4. The question of whether human life can possibly _____ in a petri dish is a difficult one.

5. Anti-abortion advocates applauded the judge's decision because it _____ that the destruction of an embryo was equal to murder.

6. By the twenty-first century, scientific discoveries in medicine _____ more ethical issues than we can even imagine today.

7. Mr. Davis was determined to make his wife _____ the frozen embryos.

8. If Mrs. Davis (not) _____ so much turmoil and disappointment in trying to get pregnant, she might not have fought so hard for her embryos.

9. By the time they went to court over the embryos, Mr. and Mrs. Davis probably couldn't imagine _____ their broken marriage.

10. _____ its gift of creating new life, technology now poses new ethical dilemmas for society.

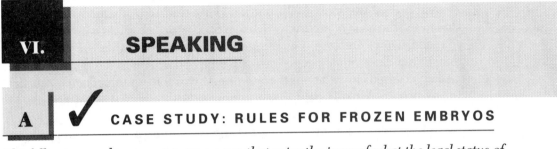

VI.   SPEAKING

A   ✔   CASE STUDY: RULES FOR FROZEN EMBRYOS

The following reading presents true cases that raise the issue of what the legal status of frozen embryos should be. Study the cases.

Work in small groups. Put yourself in the role of an ethics committee member who has been asked to establish rules for the handling and disposition of frozen embryos. Consider the issues that have been raised by doctors, the public, and the church. Draft your rules. Present them to the rest of the class.

Now that the field of medicine offers new possibilities for conception, more and more infertile couples are trying techniques in advanced technology in order to have children. Success with techniques such as in vitro fertilization have brought much happiness to many families, but at the same time, this new technology has caused a great deal of suffering to many other families. The laws are incapable of dealing with many of the new dilemmas posed by this new technology, and rules for the handling of frozen embryos, in particular, must be established.

Along with the Davises' case, there have been many other cases in which the definition of, and future for, frozen embryos has been unclear. For example, a couple who had entered an in vitro fertilization program in Norfolk, Virginia, moved from their home in New Jersey to a new home in California. The wife, Mrs. York, had had three unsuccessful implants with her frozen embryos in Virginia. When the couple arrived in California, they requested that their remaining frozen embryos be shipped to Los Angeles' Good Samaritan Hospital, where Mrs. York's new doctor would supervise her fourth attempt at implantation. To the couple's surprise, the institute in Virginia denied the couple's request and refused to send them their embryos. Apparently, the couple had signed a consent agreement that gave them no rights to the embryos outside the institute. The institute claimed that the Yorks had only four choices: they could return to Virginia for another attempt at implantation; they could donate their embryos to another couple; they could give up their embryos for scientific experimentation; or they could have the embryos destroyed.

The Yorks tried to get a written order from a court of law to demand that the embryos be sent to them. But the judge refused their request and ordered that the case be tried by a jury the following fall. Time, however, was a critical element for the Yorks, as Mrs. York is 39, and in vitro implants become significantly more difficult for women over the age of 40. In addition, the Yorks' embryo had been frozen for 24 months and the longest recorded freezing of an embryo that was successfully implanted in a woman is 28 months. This case has raised the issue of embryo ownership once again, as well as whether or not the donation of embryos is an appropriate alternative when a couple can no longer use them. Some people view this type of donation as the same thing as selling children. In addition, the use of embryos for experimentation shocks many people, but it is clear that experiments with embryos could provide a better understanding of hereditary diseases.

In another case, the issue of the *rights* of embryos has been raised. A wealthy California couple who wanted to have a child sought the services of a fertility clinic in Melbourne, Australia. Elsa Rios, 37, had been treated with fertility drugs and had successfully produced three frozen embryos with the sperm from an anonymous donor, as her husband, Mario Rios, was infertile. One embryo was implanted in Mrs. Rios's uterus while the other two were frozen for later use. Unfortunately, she spontaneously aborted the embryo that had been implanted. Feeling upset by the whole experience, Mrs. Rios decided to wait a while before trying to become pregnant again.

Then, a year or so later, the Rioses were killed in a plane crash. They died without wills but with an estate worth $8 million. The only family "survivors" were the two frozen embryos. Not surprisingly, many women from Australia, as well as from abroad, volunteered to be impregnated.

Many people got involved in the case. The state assembled a committee, headed by a law professor, which concluded that the embryos should be destroyed. At the same time, the Australian right-to-life movement and the Catholic church recommended that the case of "orphan embryos" be presented to the legislature. The legislature then passed a law that guaranteed the preservation of frozen embryos, in case another infertile couple wanted them. It is still not clear whether or not the Rioses' embryos will survive if they are thawed. In the meantime, the California courts have refused any inheritance to the embryos, based on the California state law that requires beneficiaries to an estate to be born or *in utero* at the time of the parents' death.

This case has raised the issue of when and how we decide what should be done with an embryo in the event of death. Another issue raised by this case is the question of an embryo's viability. Should frozen embryos be destroyed after a certain amount of time? Today, frozen embryos cannot last that long. But what will happen in the future if, for example, the period of viability of frozen embryos becomes indefinite? It may become difficult to determine where people are from and what their relations are. What if a man and woman from donated embryos married without realizing that they were, in fact, brother and sister? These are only some of the implications of our new technology.

B DISCUSSION QUESTIONS

In groups, discuss your answers to the following questions.

1. Go back to the questions in the values clarification exercise (p. 26). Do you have the same opinions now, or have you changed your opinions in any way after examining the views of others?

2. Andrei Codrescu makes the comment that Mr. and Mrs. Davis "should work out a custody arrangement for these eggs that requires a constitutional lawyer to babysit." What do you think he is suggesting? What do you think the government can do in future cases such as this one?

3. Betty McCollister writes that life exists before conception. Do you agree with her? What is your definition of life?

VII. WRITING

A ✔ GRAMMAR: NEGATIVE INVERSION

Notice

Notice the structure of the following sentence from the editorial:

> **Nor** *is the question of when life begins the only thorny one this case raises.*

The subject of this sentence (*the question of when life begins*) comes after the verb (*is*). Why does the verb come before the subject in this sentence?

How would the **meaning** change if the above sentence were written in a more standard way (subject + verb)?

> *The question of when life begins is not the only thorny one this case raises, either.*

Explanation

Structure

Negative inversion (or question word order) is used when a sentence begins with adverbs and phrases containing a negative idea. Instead of the normal sequence of *subject + verb* in the sentence, we use *verb + subject*.

Notice that if there is a complex verb, we invert the first auxiliary and the subject:

*Rarely **has** a judge **been** asked to define when life begins in a court case.*

Meaning

If we rewrite the sentence from the reading selection to begin with the subject followed by the verb, it has less emphasis. Negative inversion is used to make statements more emphatic. It is used in both spoken and written English, though it is more frequently used in writing.

The following phrases are commonly used with this form.

Explicit negation:

At no other time . . .
By no means . . .
In no case . . .
In no way . . .
Never . . .
No longer . . .
Nowhere . . .
* Not + until + (time phrase) . . .
* Not + since + (time phrase) . . .
On no account . . .
Under no circumstances . . .

Implied negation:

Hardly ever . . .
In few cases . . .
Only + (time phrase/clause) . . .
Rarely . . .
Seldom . . .

Negative conjunctions:

Neither . . .
Nor . . .
Not only . . . but also . . .

*With these expressions, the inversion always follows the time phrase.
*Not until their divorce **did the Davises** need to decide the future of their embryos.*

Exercise

Practice using the negative inversion form. Rewrite the following sentences to make more emphatic statements about the case you studied in Opinion 1. Use the negative phrase in parentheses to begin your statement. Make any other necessary changes. (The first one has been done for you.)

1. The Davis case was the first. There hadn't ever been a divorce case in which the custody battle was over frozen embryos. (never . . .)

   Never had there been a divorce case in which the custody battle was over frozen embryos.

2. Now that Mr. Davis was divorced he didn't want children. (on no account . . .)

3. The subject of where life begins has not been an issue in many divorce cases. (in few cases . . .)

_____

4. Mr. Davis did not realize that he would have to fight over embryos in court when he asked his wife for a divorce. Mrs. Davis didn't either. (neither . . .)

_____

5. Mrs. Davis was not willing to give up her chance of becoming pregnant with the frozen embryos. (under no circumstances . . .)

_____

6. Mrs. Davis could not consider having children until she sought the help of in vitro fertilization. (not until . . .)

_____

7. Mrs. Davis's attorney viewed the embryos as human life. The judge also saw them as "preborn children." (not only . . . but also)

_____

8. This is the first time in history that technology has outstripped our ability to resolve legal issues. (at no other time . . .)

_____

9. Developed countries are the only places where people fight over frozen embryos. (only . . .)

_____

10. Lawmakers won't ignore the Davis case when deciding how to define when life begins. (by no means . . .)

_____

B   WRITING STYLE: INTRODUCTIONS AND CONCLUSIONS

Notice

Notice the way Betty McCollister, the author of "The Eggs," introduces and concludes her essay:

What does McCollister do to introduce her essay?

How is her conclusion the same as or different from her introduction?

Explanation

An effective introduction will introduce the writer's thesis and give the reader an idea of the direction that the essay will take.

McCollister captures her reader's attention by doing two things: She introduces the thesis of her essay (we cannot yet solve problems created by advancing technology), and she presents an example which illustrates her thesis (she will develop her idea through the example of frozen fertilized eggs).

McCollister concludes her essay by returning to the idea she expressed in her introduction. She does more than just repeat what she said in the introduction. She repeats the idea that technology cannot solve the problem of frozen fertilized eggs, but she uses new words to say this. She also takes a new view of the same idea.

An effective conclusion will often repeat the writer's thesis in a different way and take a new view of the same idea in order to leave the reader thinking.

There are many different ways to introduce an essay. Here are just a few:

a. *Facts and statistics:* Introducing your essay with some surprising facts or statistics can capture your reader's interest.

b. *Short generalization:* A simple sentence that catches the reader's attention and introduces the topic can sometimes be the most effective.

c. *Historical reference:* A useful way to introduce a topic is to provide some historical information about it. Historical reference can often provide relevant background information to show the importance of the topic being discussed.

d. *Example or anecdote:* An example or short description of an event or story can be an effective introduction to an essay, when it illustrates the thesis that will be developed by the writer.

e. *Questions:* Questions can also pique the reader's interest. By posing one or more questions in the introduction, the writer can involve the reader and set up a structure for the development of the essay.

f. *Quotation:* Sometimes the words of others can best introduce a topic. If a quotation introduces your thesis in a unique way, this could be an effective beginning.

There are also many different ways to conclude an essay. Here are just a few:

a. *Summary:* One of the most typical (though not always the most interesting) ways to conclude an essay is to summarize the main points that have been discussed in the essay. (If this type of conclusion is used, try to avoid simplistic expressions such as "In conclusion," "In summary," "Finally.")

b. *Example/anecdote:* Ending with a particular example or story that illustrates the thesis can be a powerful way to conclude an essay.

c. *Quotations:* A quotation can sometimes best sum up a writer's thesis. Someone else's words are sometimes the strongest way to conclude an essay.

d. *Call for action:* Giving advice or ending with a plea for action is sometimes the most appropriate ending. With this type of conclusion, the reader is left thinking about his or her responsibility for acting on what has been discussed in the essay.

e. *Question:* Leaving your reader with a question that remains to be answered can be a strong ending. If your essay has explored a problem but has not offered a particular solution, this might be an effective ending.

f. *Prediction or own conclusion:* Writers may choose to conclude their essays by making a prediction about the future; or after analyzing a problem, the writer may draw his or her own conclusion about it.

Exercises

1. Go back to Codrescu's commentary (pp. 28–29). Decide which style of introduction and which style of conclusion he uses in his commentary. Write the type of introduction and conclusion that best describes his style. (Refer to the previous lists.)

Introduction: _____

Conclusion: _____

Compare your answers with those of another student to see if you agree.

2. Look at the following introductions and conclusions written by a variety of authors. Using the list above, try to identify the style(s) that the writer has used to introduce or conclude his or her topic. Write the type under each example.

Introductions

"As a firefighter, I have seen many people die in hotel fires. Most could have saved themselves had they been prepared. There are *over 10,000 hotel fires per year in the United States. In 1979, the latest year for which figures are available, there were 11,500 such fires, resulting in 140 deaths and 1,225 injuries." (R. H. Kauffman)*

From: "How to Survive a Hotel Fire," copyright © 1981 by Jazerant Corporation, NY, as quoted in Models for Writers: Short Essays for Composition, 3d Ed., edited by Alfred Rosa and Paul Eschholz, St. Martin's Press, 1989.

"In the house where I grew up, it was our custom to leave the front door on the latch at night. I don't know if that was a local term or if it is universal; 'on the latch' meant the door was closed but not locked. None of us carried keys; the last one in for the evening would close up, and that was it." (Bob Greene)

From Tribune Company Syndicated, Inc., as quoted in Critical Reading & Writing for Advanced ESL Students, by Sharon Scull, Prentice-Hall, 1987.

"What was the critical, underlying, formative condition of the Truman Administration? What, ten years after his death, was important about Harry S. Truman? What did his administration contribute to the future course of the United States? What made it possible for him to achieve the major initiatives that he under-took—initiatives that still affect our role in the world today?" (Robert J. Donovan)

From The Tumultuous Years: The Presidency of Harry S. Truman 1949–1953, as quoted in Critical Reading & Writing for Advanced ESL Students, by Sharon Scull, Prentice-Hall, 1987.

Conclusions

"This town does not actually exist, but it might easily have a thousand counterparts in America or elsewhere in the world. I know of no community that has experienced all the misfortunes I describe. Yet every one of these disasters has actually happened somewhere, and many real communities have already suffered a substantial number of them. A grim specter has crept upon us almost unnoticed, and this imagined tragedy may easily become a stark reality we all shall know." (Rachel Carson)

From "Fable for Tomorrow" in Silent Spring, by Rachel Carson, Houghton Mifflin Company, 1962, as quoted in Models for Writers: Short Essays for Composition, 3d Ed., edited by Alfred Rosa and Paul Eschholz, St. Martin's Press, 1989.

"Some years ago Yale University law professor Charles L. Black, Jr., wrote: '. . . forced feeding on trivial fare is not itself a trivial matter.' I think this society is being force-fed with trivial fare, and I

*fear that the effects on our habits of mind, our language, our toler-
ance for effort, and our appetite for complexity are only dimly perceived. If I am wrong, we will have done no harm to look at the
issue skeptically and critically, to consider how we should be resist-
ing it. I hope you will join me in doing so." (Robert MacNeil)*

From "The Trouble with Television," by Robert MacNeil, Reader's Digest, March 1985, *as quoted in* Models
for Writers: Short Essays for Composition, 3d Ed., *edited by Alfred Rosa and Paul Eschholz, St. Martin's
Press, 1989.*

---

*"In the game of golf there is an old saying for those times when a
bad shot takes a miraculous bounce off a tree or a rock and winds
up in or near the hole. The saying is: 'It's not how—it's how many.'
That's my feeling about the death sentence: 'It's not how—it's
when.'" (Mike Royko)*

From The Chicago Sun Times, 1983, *as quoted in* Critical Reading & Writing for Advanced ESL Students, *by
Sharon Scull, Prentice-Hall, 1987.*

C   ESSAY QUESTIONS

*Choose one of the following topics and write an essay. Try to integrate ideas, vocabu-
lary, and writing techniques that you have studied in this unit. In question 1, try to
incorporate the following:*

- an introductory paragraph that presents both sides of the argument and clearly states your thesis;

- paragraphs (at least three) that develop your argument with supporting evidence;

- a conclusion that reinforces the position you have taken. It should also end with a new idea (a warning, prediction, value judgment) that has not been mentioned before.

1. Isaac Asimov, a scientist and famous science fiction writer, claimed that the only solution to new problems is by further advancing technology.

   Do you agree with Isaac Asimov? Write an essay in which you use the case of frozen embryos to support your opinion.

2. Write an essay in which you discuss the future of "spare embryos," those embryos that couples reject because of death, divorce, disabilities, or change of mind. Who do you think should decide the fate of these embryos? What should that fate be?

TO KNOW MORE ABOUT LESS OR LESS ABOUT MORE

ACADEMIC ADVISOR

VS Hixson

Cartoon by Vivian Scott Hixson, from the *Chronicle of Higher Education.*

"I started out in English, and then I went into sociology, and then for two semesters I was into biology, but what I really want is a physics major. Is there any way I can do that and graduate next semester?"

I. ANTICIPATING THE ISSUE

Discuss your answers to the following questions.

1. Look at the title. Look at the cartoon. What do you think the issue of this unit will be?

2. What is the message or humor of the cartoon?

3. What do you know about the problems of school curricula?

II. BACKGROUND READING

Read the following text.

With the emergence of the technological age, it has become increasingly difficult to be a knowledgeable person: There is just too much information to know
something about everything. So what should an educated person be in the
twenty-first century? It isn't always clear whether one should try to become a
specialist or a generalist in today's world. Some people have focused their education, developing skills in one area; specialists now flourish in every field of
life. ***Inversely***, others continue to believe that a well-rounded education offers
the most in life; generalists typically follow a liberal arts education but may
never become experts in any field.

The Greek poet, Archilochus, had already described this difference
between generalists and specialists with the ***metaphor***, "The fox knows many
things, but the ***hedgehog*** knows one big thing." It's not clear whether there
were more foxes or hedgehogs in ancient Greece, but today there appear to be
an ***inordinate*** number of hedgehogs, people who know very little about the
world, ***save*** their field of expertise. This, in fact, has been a criticism of today's
American colleges and universities, that they are producing too many hedgehogs.

In the 1960s, most American colleges and universities offered a generalist
approach to education. In response to student protests, universities began
offering many innovative courses. For example, they added Asian Studies and
African Studies to their curricula in an effort to extend education beyond the
mores of Western society. Students began "doing their own thing," taking
courses in just about every subject imaginable, from Transcendental
Meditation to Swahili storytelling. Students believed these courses ***enriched***
their minds. But as university students began to focus on more and more of
these less common subject areas, critics began to abound. They believed that
much of education had become useless. Employers began to make ***derisive***
comments about the quality of college graduates. As ***"jacks-of-all-trades,"***
they could "function" in most areas of life but might never "excel" in any. The
college degree of the 1960s was viewed by many as ***rot***. Too many subjects, too
general an approach to education, may have resulted in too little because of too
much.

In the 1970s and 1980s, with new technologies creating new job opportunities, an emphasis on specialization appeared in American education. More
vocational courses were offered in colleges and universities, especially as computer programming jobs became available. Business schools flourished as more

and more graduate students could enter fields that offered specialized jobs with high salaries, such as investment banking and stock trading. But with the media coverage of junk bond[1] trading and the crimes committed by insider-information[2] **scoundrels** on Wall Street, even the reputation of the MBA (Master's in Business Administration) degree was **sullied**. The more narrowly focused approach to professional education also seemed to fail.

One of the **dilemmas** of this decade has been whether to approach modern education in terms of the generalist or the specialist. Some universities require all students to take a common core of courses from a broad range of disciplines, appealing to the generalist approach to education. Yet, choosing the core courses in light of today's explosion in information and diverse multicultural student populations has not been an easy task. How does one select what it is that everyone should know? Other universities continue to tailor their courses to the more immediate professional needs of their students, appealing to the specialist approach to education. But without a core curriculum, students often lack the shared knowledge necessary to participate effectively in an integrated society.

A coherent vision of an educated person in the twenty-first century has yet to be defined.

[1] Junk bond: a high-risk bond.

[2] Insider information: taking advantage of corporate knowledge for personal profit.

A   VOCABULARY

Look at the boldfaced words and phrases in the following sentences. From the context of the background reading, determine the better meaning. Circle your answer.

1. **Inversely,** others continue to believe that a well-rounded education offers the most in life.

   a. similarly

   b. on the other hand

2. The Greek poet, Archilochus, had already described this difference between generalists and specialists with the **metaphor,** "The fox knows many things, but the hedgehog knows one big thing."

   a. the use of words to mean something other than the literal meaning

   b. the use of music to create a message

3. "The fox knows many things, but the **hedgehog** knows one big thing."

   a. large domestic animal

   b. small wild animal

4. Today there appear to be an **inordinate** number of hedgehogs.

   a. excessive

   b. disorderly

5. Today there appear to be an inordinate number of hedgehogs, people who know very little about the world, **save** their field of expertise.

   a. except for

   b. especially

6. They added Asian Studies and African Studies to their curricula in an effort to extend education beyond the **mores** of western society.

   a. literary works   b. customs

7. Students believed these courses **enriched** their minds.

   a. improved in quality   b. improved in quantity

8. Employers began to make **derisive** comments about the quality of college graduates.

   a. scornful   b. complimentary

9. As **"jacks-of-all-trades,"** they could "function" in most areas of life but might never "excel" in any.

   a. experts in industry   b. people who do a little of everything

10. The college degree of the 1960s was viewed by many as **rot.**

    a. nonsense   b. the answer

11. The media exposed the crimes committed by insider-information **scoundrels** on Wall Street.

    a. wealthy money makers   b. people with no moral principles

12. But with the media coverage of junk bond trading and the crimes committed by insider-information scoundrels on Wall Street, even the reputation of the MBA degree was **sullied.**

    a. discredited   b. glorified

13. One of the **dilemmas** of this decade has been whether to approach modern education in terms of the generalist or the specialist.

    a. problems with no possible answer b. situations with both favorable and unfavorable choices

B   SUMMARIZING THE ISSUE

Work in small groups. Summarize the issue presented in the background reading. Take notes to complete the following outline.

1. The issue (*state in your own words*) :

   _____

   _____

   _____

(*continued on next page*)

2. The Specialists' Approach:

    a. Advantages _____

    _____

    b. Disadvantages _____

    _____

3. The Generalists' Approach:

    a. Advantages _____

    _____

    b. Disadvantages _____

    _____

C   VALUES CLARIFICATION

Work in small groups. Discuss your answers to the following questions.

1. Would you describe your own education as being more specialist or generalist? How would you evaluate this approach from where you are today?

2. Do you agree with the concept of a core curriculum in higher education? If so, what should be included in this core?

III.   OPINION 1: LISTENING

A LISTENING FOR THE MAIN IDEA

Listen to the commentary. Check the statement that summarizes the commentator's viewpoint.

☐   1. A generalist approach to education is necessary for today's world.

☐   2. A specialist approach to education is necessary for today's world.

☐   3. Both a generalist approach and a specialist approach to education are necessary for today's world.

B   LISTENING FOR DETAILS

Read the following questions and answers. Listen to the commentary again and circle the best answer. Then compare your answers with those of another student. Listen again if necessary.

1. What is the subject of Rod MacLeish's essay?

   a. Experts are the same as specialists.

   b. We should believe someone who knows more about less.

   c. We need to ask which is better: knowing more about less or less about more.

2. From Archilochus's Fragment 103 we learn that

   a. the fox was wiser.

   b. the hedgehog was wiser.

   c. it's not clear whether the fox or hedgehog was wiser.

3. Why is Fragment 103 a metaphor for modern life?

   a. We need more specialists.

   b. Specialists know too much.

   c. Generalists have less influence today.

4. Why are hedgehogs dangerous, according to the commentator?

   a. They invent new chemicals.

   b. They may have forgotten history.

   c. They make too much money on Wall Street.

5. In the commentator's opinion, hedgehogs

   a. may have become more powerful with the emergence of an industrial society.

   b. are bad for society.

   c. cannot really influence our lives.

6. How does Western society view the generalist today?

   a. As a failure.

   b. As a necessity.

   c. As a master.

(continued on next page)

7. What was the message of the Oxford classicist?

    a. You have to work hard on your own to succeed.

    b. You need to study many subjects to think critically.

    c. It's important to be able to think about one big thing.

8. What conclusion does MacLeish reach in his essay?

    a. Those in power may not be generalist enough.

    b. There are too many people talking rot.

    c. There aren't enough people who can think anymore.

C   TEXT COMPLETION AND DISCRETE LISTENING

Read the text of the commentary. Try to fill in the missing words in the text as you remember them. Use your knowledge of text structure, vocabulary, and grammar to help you. Then listen again to the commentary to check your answers, stopping the tape as you fill in the blanks. If you have different answers than the original text, check with your teacher to see if they are acceptable alternatives.

Introduction

Common wisdom has it that an expert is someone who knows more and more about less and less. Substitute the word " _____ " for "expert," and ask whether it's better to believe someone who knows _____ about less or less about more and you have the subject of writer Rod MacLeish's essay this morning.

Commentary

Archilochus, the Greek poet, left us only bits and pieces of his writings; the most famous is Fragment 103: The fox knows many things, but the _____ knows one big thing. No one is certain about Fragment 103's original meaning. But it has become a metaphor for a modern _____ : the increasing dominance of Western society by specialists, hedgehogs, if you will. This means, inversely, the decline in influence of _____ foxes.

    The supremacy of hedgehogs is dangerous because it creates a climate of rarefied ignorance. The man who invents an exotic new form of chemical weaponry has probably forgotten—if he ever knew—the generalist's view of history, with its lessons about the origins of war. The junk bond and insider-information _____ , who sullied the reputation of Wall Street, were obsessed with the one big thing they knew. The prudence and moral balance, which comes from a _____ general vision of society, were lost on them.

Perhaps the dominant power of the specialist hedgehogs was _____ , as science and technology became increasingly complex after the mid-nineteenth century. The argument here is not *against* specialists, but rather their _____ influence over our lives. In the _____ of Western society, the generalist fox, who knows (but is not expert in) many things, is dismissed with such _____ clichés as "jack-of-all- _____ , master of none."

At the turn of this century, there was an acerbic classicist at Oxford who used to tell newly arriving students, "Nothing you will learn here in the course of your studies will be of any use to you in later life _____ only this: If you pay attention and work hard, you may eventually come to know when a man is talking rot." In other words, Oxford taught you how to think by teaching you many subjects that _____ and broadened the mind. The hedgehogs know how to think, but only about one big thing. The time may be approaching when the people who dominate our lives won't know when a man is talking _____ .

IV.   OPINION 2: READING

A ✔ READING FOR THE MAIN IDEA

Read the article. Check the statement that summarizes the author's viewpoint.

☐   1.   We need a specialist approach to education for today's specialized world.

☐   2.   A generalist's approach to education must focus more on the classics and less on technology.

☐   3.   Today's generalist approach to education is no longer relevant for today's world.

Liberal Arts for the Twenty-First Century

by M. Garrett Bauman

Tortured by *vocationalism*, charges of irrelevance, erosion of standards, declining enrollments, *calcified* faculty, and lack of coordination, the current liberal arts *paradigm* seems to be disintegrating. And truly, our students, who will be asked to manage the most complex century in history, are not well served by what we now offer.

Our current degree was *predicated* on a specialized social state, an expanding industrial base, and the belief that plentiful resources existed to create a materialist state. Technologists and scientists would create the material means, social scientists would manage society, and humanists would handle the community's spiritual matters. We still organize liberal arts programs as though this specialized world existed or could exist. It does not and cannot.

Tomorrow's graduates enter the post-industrial age; they face global energy and resource depletion, a cancer *scourge* induced by various types of pollution, and a world in which one billion people live in absolute poverty. The technological dream *recedes* each year.

Ecologists predict almost unanimously that by the end of the century humans will exterminate 20 percent of all *fellow* species alive on the planet in 1975. Computers and robotics will replace more human labor than have all of history's tools combined. One-fourth of all nations on the planet are currently at war and have been for a decade. Are our specialized social managers *faring* any better than the technologists?

Individuals *clamor* ever louder for human rights, empowerment, and creative expression while the arts and humanities are largely viewed as irrelevant. Are we becoming either more human or humane? These are the *salient* facts, the problems and parameters of the world our graduates must manage.

The present liberal arts degree does not provide the thinking skills and necessary knowledge to make wise decisions for this emerging world because it suffers from three *flaws*.

1. As this century races to its end, we must realize liberal arts is the stuff of time, not *stasis*. Liberal arts is changing faster than ever, but not fast enough to accommodate the increasing pace of history. We cannot make ideas *run the gauntlet* of centuries before admitting them to academia. This is not a call to teach *trendy*, contemporary writers instead of Shakespeare, or Fritjof Capra[1] instead of Plato. It is a call to account for major changes in the human condition—our relationship to nature, technology, and ourselves—that have occurred during the last twenty years, changes *backlogged* in the liberal arts' waiting room. This law results in the "unemployability" of many graduates: Their education *is* largely irrelevant to the

[1] A philosopher and physicist.

(continued on next page)

concerns of contemporary society. The other practical justification of the liberal arts—that it creates well-informed citizens—is also *suspect*.

The second and third flaws relate directly to what has been the proudest, most long-standing claim of the liberal arts: that it provides a broad education that prepares one to focus on a variety of specific problems. We claim—more loudly as enrollments decline—that we train students to be educationally self-sufficient by providing the ability to grasp the overall nature of problems and a variety of tools to solve them and that liberal arts provides the essential knowledge an educated person must have of his or her age. Yet in practice we *edge* grudgingly toward this integrative vision and *lag* in offering the necessary knowledge for wise decision making.

2. Liberal arts has neither accepted technology as an extension of the human brain nor has it done its traditional job of *synthesizing* the expanding world of knowledge. Many humanists still treat technology as though it were an alien invader and proceed by fits and starts. For instance, we encourage computer literacy and train technologists before we have figured out how to train them to be ethically literate.

3. Liberal arts today resembles a farm of scattered fields. After students nibble dozens of disconnected courses, we tell them: "Now use your critical abilities to synthesize all that." We don't directly teach the integrative skills we say are a graduate's prime attribute.

The liberal arts are neither *bankrupt* nor lazy. It was easy to debate, clarify, standardize, and integrate learning when universities spend two hundred years debating the angel-on-a-pin issue or fifty years debating evolution. In the last twenty years, by contrast, we have explored space, created life artificially, *whisked* from heavy industry to the silicon chip, and seen more lives appear on earth than during the entire medieval age. More writers, artists, and theorists with more variety of ideas walk the planet than ever before (the United States alone publishes enough new books to fill the great Library of Alexandria[2] every seventeen years). In short, we're creating the past faster than ever and the sum of what humankind has learned—both technologically and in the realm of ideas—is becoming ever more *lopsided* in favor of the recent past. Liberal arts education needs to catch up.

[2]Alexandria: a city in Egypt famous for its library.

Source: from "Liberal Arts for the Twenty-First Century," M. Garrett Bauman, *Journal of Higher Education*, Vol. 58, No. 1 (Jan./Feb. 1987), reprinted by permission. Copyright 1987 by the Ohio State University Press. All rights reserved.

B   READING FOR FACT VS. OPINION

In developing critical thinking skills, it is necessary to distinguish facts from opinions. When expressing opinions, authors use either facts or opinions (or both) to support their ideas.

(continued on next page)

In Bauman's article, both facts and opinions are used to support the author's main idea. Read the following statements. Next to each statement write F if it is a fact or O if it is an opinion. Compare your reactions with those of another student.

_____ 1. Tortured by vocationalism, charges of irrelevance, erosion of standards, declining enrollments, calcified faculty, and lack of coordination, the current liberal arts paradigm seems to be disintegrating.

_____ 2. Tomorrow's graduates enter the postindustrial age; they face global energy and resource depletion, a cancer scourge induced by various types of pollution, and a world in which one billion people live in absolute poverty.

_____ 3. Ecologists predict almost unanimously that by the end of the century humans will exterminate 20 percent of all fellow species alive on the planet in 1975.

_____ 4. One-fourth of all nations on the planet are currently at war and have been for a decade.

_____ 5. The present liberal arts degree does not provide the thinking skills and necessary knowledge to make wise decisions for this emerging world because it suffers from three flaws.

_____ 6. Liberal arts is changing faster than ever, but not fast enough to accommodate the increasing pace of history.

_____ 7. The other practical justification of the liberal arts—that it creates well-informed citizens—is also suspect.

_____ 8. We claim—more loudly as enrollments decline—that we train students to be educationally self-sufficient by providing the ability to grasp the overall nature of problems and a variety of tools to solve them and that liberal arts provides the essential knowledge an educated person must have of his or her age.

_____ 9. Many humanists still treat technology as though it were an alien invader and proceed by fits and starts.

_____ 10. The liberal arts are neither bankrupt nor lazy.

_____ 11. In the last twenty years, by contrast, we have explored space, created life artificially, whisked from heavy industry to the silicon chip, and seen more lives appear on earth than during the entire medieval age.

_____ 12. More writers, artists, and theorists with more variety of ideas walk the planet than ever before (the United States alone publishes enough new books to fill the great Library of Alexandria every seventeen years).

_____ 13. Liberal arts education needs to catch up.

C   WORD SEARCH

Find boldfaced words in the article that have similar meaning to the following and write them below.

Nouns

mistakes: _____

combining: _____

model; example: _____

cause of great suffering: _____

stagnation; motionlessness: _____

educational emphasis on trade or industry: _____

Adjectives

fashionable: _____

outstanding; easily noticed: _____

possibly false; questionable: _____

of the same class or kind: _____

inflexible; hardened: _____

leaning to one side: _____

based: _____

accumulated and not processed: _____

depleted; completely without use: _____

Verbs

fall behind: _____

are exposed to continuous severe criticism: _____

(continued on next page)

move forward slowly: _____

demand loudly and continually: _____

getting along; doing: _____

becomes more distant: _____

moved quickly and suddenly: _____

V. SYNTHESIZING TWO OPINION PIECES

A ✓ DISTINGUISHING OPINIONS

Authors can have different viewpoints, but their opinions can sometimes be similar. Review opinion 1 on pages 50–51 and opinion 2 on pages 52–53.

Work in groups. Read the statements below. Discuss whether MacLeish and/or Bauman would agree with them. Put a check (✓) in the box if you think they would agree. Leave the box empty if they would disagree or if there is no evidence to support the statement in their opinion.

Discuss how and why the two opinions are the same or different. (In the first statement, for example, MacLeish would disagree. He states that the supremacy of hedgehogs is dangerous, and as specialists, they know more about less. Bauman, however, would probably agree with the statement because he says the liberal arts are largely irrelevant to today's world.)

	MacLeish: Commentator (Opinion 1)	Bauman: Author (Opinion 2)
It's better to know more about less than less about more.		✓
Specialists are more dangerous to society than generalists.		
Technology is not a friend to general education.		
The generalist fox, or liberal arts major, is a "jack-of-all-trades, master of none."		

Studying many subjects, such as in a liberal arts curriculum, broadens one's view of the world and creates better citizens.		
Educating society for tomorrow is more difficult than it was in the past.		
A generalist's education should include an in-depth view of history.		

B   GIVING YOUR OPINION

After you have distinguished the opinions of the commentator and the author, express your own opinions on the above statements. Discuss them with the other students in your group.

C   VOCABULARY REINFORCEMENT: WORD FORMS

Work in small groups. In the following chart you will find vocabulary from the commentary and the article. Fill in the chart with the appropriate word forms for each vocabulary item. (An X has been placed in the box if there is no related word form.) Use a dictionary to help you if you are not sure.

NOUNS	VERBS	ADJECTIVES	ADVERBS
		bankrupt	X
		calcified	X
	clamor		X
		derisive	X
	edge		X
		enriched	X
	X	fellow	X
flaw	X		X
X	X	inordinate	
			inversely
	lag		X
metaphor	X		
	recede		
		suspect	X
	synthesize		X
	X	trendy	X

Read the following sentences. Fill in the blank spaces with the most appropriate vocabulary item from the above chart. In some cases there may be more than one possibility. Be sure to use the correct form of the word you choose.

1. In the 1960s, many new _____ courses replaced the common, classic courses in the college curriculum.

2. The school tuition was so _____ high that the student had to take on a part-time job while studying at the university.

3. One of the main arguments for a liberal arts curriculum is that it is an _____ for the mind.

4. People who worked on Wall Street quickly became _____ when it was clear that they were making huge sums of easy money.

5. In times of _____ , when there is little money available to experiment with new courses, school curricula usually take on a more generalist focus.

6. If colleges do not catch up with the times by offering the courses that students need to function in today's society, students may look for other means of educating themselves and colleges may close due to _____ .

7. As professors fight to maintain their discipline's status within a university, _____ comments may sometimes be heard about the value of a colleague's course.

8. With a generalist approach to learning, students are asked to _____ the various subjects they study into a unified whole.

9. While one student might benefit most from a generalist approach to education, a _____ classmate might accomplish more with a specialized approach.

10. Fragment 103 explains _____ the difference between generalists and specialists.

VI. SPEAKING

A ✓ CASE STUDY: HARVARD UNIVERSITY'S CORE CURRICULUM

The following reading presents a true case that raises the issue of whether a core curriculum is an appropriate solution to educating university students today. Study the case.

Work in small groups. Discuss what Harvard University should do about its core curriculum (continue the core, drop the core, modify the core). Present your conclusions to the rest of the class.

While many colleges and universities have moved to offer a more specialized curricula to accommodate students' needs for new job markets, other institutes of higher education have held on to their generalist approach to education and continue to offer a liberal arts curriculum. In an effort to provide a broad education that prepares students to deal with a variety of problems, many of these colleges and universities offer a core curriculum, a series of required courses for all students. The idea behind a core curriculum is that it provides the essential knowledge that all educated people should have to participate in the larger society.

The core curriculum offered at Harvard University has long been a model for a successful program of general education. Yet, today many professors and students are dissatisfied with Harvard's core.

Harvard has had a long tradition of requiring broad-based learning. The university first instituted a general-education program in 1949–1950. In those years, course requirements tended to reflect an emphasis on broadening students' knowledge in Western thought and literature. The aim then was for students to develop a broad interdisciplinary overview of fundamental topics so that, when they studied their major, they had a context in which to fit it.

By the 1960s, however, Harvard's curriculum, like those of most American colleges and universities, had changed dramatically. More and more courses qualified as basic requirement courses. By 1969, Harvard offered more than a hundred courses that satisfied the general-education requirement, many of them no longer resembling traditional required courses, many of them esoteric in nature. For example, courses such as "The Scandinavian Cinema" could replace the traditional "Epic and Novel." "Drug Use and Adolescent Development" could be chosen in place of "The Growth of Modern Western Society." These courses seemed to represent contemporary needs, but to many critics, it appeared that Harvard's original general-education program had become merely a list of distribution requirements.

In the 1970s, educational trends changed once again. Harvard's curriculum, like the curricula in many universities, had been severely criticized for having gone "too far." Realizing that reform was necessary, but not wanting to dictate any specific curricula, the Harvard administration created a core curriculum that would emphasize "critical faculties," or thinking skills, rather than "specific knowledge." When a task force for the core curriculum was appointed to propose the new requirements, they stated, "There are simply too many facts, too many theories, too many subjects, too many specializations to permit arranging all knowledge into an acceptable hierarchy." So, instead of emphasizing content in their core, the task force would emphasize educational theory or method. In this way, professors were less threatened by a core curriculum that might not emphasize their particular discipline. In fact, the core was overwhelmingly supported by the faculty and adopted in 1978, and by 1981, the Harvard approach was the most frequently mentioned and recommended as an example of a quality core curriculum.

Harvard's core curriculum still exists today. The philosophy behind the core is that "every Harvard graduate should be broadly educated, as well as trained in a particular academic specialty." It assumes that "students need some guidance in achieving this goal." The Harvard core is divided into six categories of ten courses:

1. Social Analysis
2. Moral Reasoning
3. Historical Study A & B
4. Science A & B
5. Foreign Cultures
6. Literature and Arts A, B, & C

All undergraduates must take at least eight of these courses in addition to their major.

This core, though widely acclaimed by many, has not been without criticism. Some professors claim that it is no different than the smattering of courses that was offered in the 1960s. What makes matters worse, they say, is that there is no mathematics requirement, a subject generally agreed upon as ideal for teaching thinking skills. No introductory foreign-language courses are included in the core, either. Another criticism is that, ironically, students can meet their core requirements without taking a single course that focuses on Western culture; this intentional omission has been explained by some as the university's fear of appearing ethnocentric or even racist by focusing on Western views. Yet, most students *are* required to study a foreign culture. While this requirement is meant to expose students to a new culture so that they might reexamine the values of their own culture, students claim that many of the foreign cultures courses do not, in fact, "develop students' critical facilities." Some faculty say that they feel a loss of ownership with the core curriculum, as they are less free to pursue their specialized research and develop courses that interest them.

The Harvard administration, along with faculty who support the core curriculum, claim that the core "seeks to introduce students to the major approaches to knowledge in areas that the faculty considers indispensable to undergraduate education." The philosophy underlying the core is that educated people are those who can analyze facts, rather than those who know many facts. They support the core because, they say, the core courses emphasize a particular way of thinking, even though the subject matter may be different.

While they pave the way for some of the country's most promising students, the faculty at Harvard continue to debate the relevance of the university's core curriculum.

B   DISCUSSION QUESTIONS

Work in groups. Discuss your answers to the following questions.

1. Go back to the questions in the values clarification exercise (p. 48). Do you have the same opinions now, or have you changed your opinions in any way after examining the views of others?

2. Bauman, in his essay, claims that the liberal arts need to catch up with what humankind has learned, especially in the recent past. Do you agree with him? What needs to be included in a liberal arts, or generalist, curriculum? What balance, if any, should be struck between traditional studies and newer knowledge stemming from technological discoveries?

3. George Reedy, a retired professor of journalism from Marquette University, writes in his farewell speech:

   > *The doom of the specialist draws closer every time someone punches the keys on a word processor. Of course, we will still need doctors, lawyers, plumbers, and electricians. But will there still be a brisk market for all the specialties we have fostered in the economic and social fields? I doubt it. The future will belong to those who know how to handle the combinations of information that come out of the computer, what we used to call the "generalist." The day of the generalist is just over the horizon and we had better be ready for it.*

   Do you agree with Reedy's prediction? If so, what are those specialties that will no longer be needed and how will a generalist approach solve the problem of dying specialties?

A ✔ GRAMMAR: ELEMENTS IN PUNCTUATION

Notice

Notice the punctuation in Bauman's article. Examine the following sentences (a–h), focusing on the highlighted punctuation marks. With another student, try to determine the different rules for using each of these punctuation marks.

The Semicolon (;)

a. This flaw results in the "unemployability" of many graduates; their education is largely irrelevant to the concerns of contemporary society.

The Colon (:)

b. The second and third flaws relate directly to what has been the proudest, most long-standing claim of the liberal arts: that it provides a broad education that prepares one to focus on a variety of specific problems.

c. After students nibble dozens of disconnected courses, we tell them: "Now use your critical abilities to synthesize all that."

Quotation Marks (" ")

d. Conversation heard in a hallway: "What are you majoring in?" "Oh, just liberal arts."

e. This flaw results in the "unemployability" of many graduates.

The Dash (—)

f. It is a call to account for major changes in the human condition—our relationship to nature, technology, and ourselves—that have occurred during the last twenty years, changes backlogged in the liberal arts' waiting room.

g. In short, we're creating the past faster than ever and the sum of what humankind has learned—both technologically and in the realm of ideas—is becoming ever more lopsided in favor of the recent past.

Parentheses ( )

h. More writers, artists, and theorists with more variety of ideas walk the planet than ever before (the United States alone publishes enough new books to fill the great Library of Alexandria every seventeen years).

Explanation

The Semicolon

The semicolon is similar to the period in that it ends an independent clause before a new one begins. The difference is that an independent clause that follows a semicolon is closely connected to the preceding independent clause. It usually gives further information about the first clause. In sentence "a" above, Bauman further explains why many graduates are unemployable by explaining the irrelevancy of their education. The two clauses are closely connected.

The Colon

The colon indicates to the reader that what follows is closely tied to the preceding clause. It *explains, restates in new words,* or *gives details about* what has been written in the first clause. The following explains Bauman's two uses of the colon from sentences b and c above.

   b. <u>Explanation or interpretation:</u> The phrase "that it provides a broad education that prepares one to focus on a variety of specific problems" explains or interprets what Bauman perceives to be the most long-standing claim of the liberal arts. Consequently, this clause is followed by a colon.
   c. <u>Introduction to quotations:</u> If a quotation effectively supports or contributes to the preceding clause, it is introduced by a colon. Here Bauman quotes what we tell students.

Other Uses of the Colon

<u>Listing:</u>
The Harvard core is divided into six categories:
   1. Social Analysis
   2. Moral Reasoning
   3. Historical Study A & B
   4. Science A & B
   5. Foreign Cultures
   6. Literature and Arts A, B, & C

<u>Function of form:</u>
Time: *arrives at 11:45*
Bible reference: *Nehemiah 11:7*
Salutation in formal letters: *Dear Ms. Brown:*

Titles with subtitles: *Recasting America: Culture and Politics in the Age of Cold War*

Quotation Marks

Quotation marks are used for many different purposes. In Bauman's article two uses are illustrated. Refer to sentences "d" and "e" above.

d. <u>Exact words of a speaker:</u> Notice that both the student's question and the other student's answer are enclosed with quotation marks. The second quotation mark appears **after** the end punctuation marks (question mark or period).

e. <u>Technical terms:</u> Bauman has enclosed the word *unemployability* in quotation marks, as it is frequently used among college graduates and professors to describe the dismal state of graduates trying to find jobs. Special expressions, slang, and words used to express special meaning can also be written with quotation marks.

Other Uses of Quotation Marks

<u>Titles:</u> Titles of essays, short stories, articles, poems, and songs are presented within quotation marks.

"Mending Wall" *is a poem written by Robert Frost.*

<u>Quotations within quotations:</u> If you quote a writer who has quoted someone else, the original quotation is written in single quotes.

Bauman writes, "After students nibble dozens of disconnected courses, we tell them: 'Now use your critical thinking abilities to synthesize all that.'"

The Dash

When writers use the dash, they are indicating a break in thought or that an example will follow. It is a stronger separation than the comma and less formal than the colon. The dash is not frequently used in writing. Use it only when more formal marks of punctuation seem inappropriate. Refer to the sentences on p. 62.)

f. <u>Replacement of particular words:</u> When we indicate that an example will follow, we generally use expressions such as *namely, that is, in other words, specifically, such as.* The dash can replace these words. Notice that Bauman provides us with three examples of what he considers to be "major changes in the human condition" after the dash.

g. <u>An interruption in thought:</u> A writer may add a thought in the middle of a sentence, something that gives more detailed information about what has been stated. In this case, the dash is used to separate the interruption from the main sentence. Bauman interjects, almost as an afterthought, the fact that humankind's learning is from both technology and ideas.

Parentheses

Extra information or examples are presented within parentheses. However, when this punctuation mark is used, it lessens the importance of the information included within the parentheses. Notice in sentence "h" that the fact that "the United States alone publishes enough new books to fill the great Library of Alexandria every seventeen years" is really incidental to the main idea.

In some cases, either parentheses, a dash, or commas can be used to separate a group of words, without changing the meaning.

Exercise

Punctuation is used in written language to convey a specific meaning. When we speak, however, we use stress, pause, and intonation to convey that same meaning.

You listened to Rod MacLeish's essay, which was broadcast over the radio as a commentary. To understand his commentary, you had to perceive stress, pause, and intonation.

Look at his commentary again in the written form. The punctuation marks have been removed. Consider the elements of punctuation already discussed. Add the appropriate marks in each of the blanks.

Introduction

Common wisdom has it that an expert is someone who knows more and more about less and less. Substitute the word __ specialist __ for __ expert, __ and ask whether it's better to believe someone who knows more about less or less about more and you have the subject of writer Rod MacLeish's essay this morning.

Commentary

Archilochus, the Greek poet, left us only bits and pieces of his writings__ the most famous is Fragment 103__ The fox knows many things, but the hedgehog knows one big thing. No one is certain about Fragment 103's original meaning. But it has become a metaphor for a modern dilemma__ the increasing dominance of Western society by specialists__ hedgehogs, if you will. This means, inversely, the decline in influence of generalist foxes.

The supremacy of hedgehogs is dangerous because it creates a climate of rarefied ignorance. The man who invents an exotic new form of chemical weaponry has probably forgotten __ if he ever knew __ the generalist's view of history, with its lessons about the origins of war. The junk bond and insider-information scoundrels, who sullied the reputation of Wall Street, were obsessed with the one big thing they knew. The prudence and moral balance which comes from a broad general vision of society were lost on them.

Perhaps the dominant power of the specialist hedgehogs was inevitable, as science and technology became increasingly complex after the mid-nineteenth century. The argument here is not *against* specialists, but rather their inordinate influence over our lives. In the mores of Western society, the generalist fox, who knows __ but is not expert in __ many things, is dismissed with such derisive clichés as __ jack-of-all-trades, master of none.__

At the turn of this century, there was an acerbic classicist at Oxford who used to tell newly arriving students __ __ Nothing you will learn here in the course of your studies will be of any use to you in later life save only this__ If you pay attention and work hard, you may eventually come to know when a man is talking rot.__ In other words, Oxford taught you how to think by teaching you many subjects that enriched and broadened the mind. The hedgehogs know how to think, but only about one big thing. The time may be approaching when the people who dominate our lives won't know when a man is talking rot.

B   WRITING STYLE: FIGURATIVE LANGUAGE

Notice

Notice the two examples of figurative language used by MacLeish in his commentary. He refers to a metaphor and also mentions a commonly used cliché. What is the difference between a metaphor and a cliché?

a. metaphor: The fox knows many things, but the hedgehog knows one big thing.

b. cliché: Jack-of-all-trades, master of none.

Can you identify which of the following two examples from the author's essay is a metaphor and which is a cliché? What do you think the boldfaced expressions mean?

c. Many humanists still treat technology as though it were an alien invader and proceed ***by fits and starts.***

     d. After students **nibble** dozens of disconnected courses, we tell them: "now use your critical abilities to synthesize all that."

Explanation

In example "a," MacLeish explains that the expression is a metaphor: Words that apply literally to one kind of object or idea are applied to another to show a comparison.

In this metaphor, animal characteristics are referred to in order to elicit the difference between a generalist and specialist. In example "d," Bauman uses the word "nibble" to describe students taking many different courses. As the word "nibble" is usually used to describe eating small bits, it is used figuratively here to describe an approach to learning.

Metaphor is used, especially in writing, to add **forcefulness, expression,** or **detail.** Ordinary language may seem too bland to express strong feelings or ideas. A metaphor adds freshness or creativity to our writing. In addition, a metaphor can sometimes be used to make an abstract concept more concrete.

In example "b," MacLeish refers to a cliché. A cliché may have once functioned as a metaphor, but because of its frequent use in everyday language it has lost the force and expression of a metaphor. People will use the expression "jack-of-all-trades, master of none" without really thinking of its intended meaning. In example "c," Bauman also uses a cliché to describe the way many humanists approach learning technology. To proceed "by fits and starts" means to proceed intermittently, with a burst of activity after periods of relative inactivity. Because this expression has been used so often in everyday language, it too has lost some of its original metaphoric value.

Exercise

Work with a partner. Read the following sentences illustrating figurative language. Try to decide whether the sentence illustrates a metaphor or cliché, and write an "M" or "C" in front of each one. Then write what you think the meaning of the boldfaced phrase is.

_____ 1. With the explosion of new knowledge and professions, getting a degree in higher education is **a whole new ballgame**.

_____

_____ 2. Many employers complain that a general education doesn't prepare employees for the specific tasks required on the job; when employees fill new positions, they **can't cut the mustard**.

_____

_____ 3. During the 1960s, many American universities offered courses that were not typically offered by academic departments and somewhat **off the beaten path**.

_____

_____ 4. Education is **hanging on** until you've **caught on!**

_____

(continued on next page)

_____ 5. Education makes a people easy to lead but difficult to **drive**; easy to govern but impossible to **enslave**.

_____

_____ 6. Because universities now offer many new courses in new technological fields, some of the classics have **gone by the wayside.**

_____

_____ 7. Getting a college degree is **only half the battle.** Finding a good job is the real task.

_____

_____ 8. Students will **avoid** some required courses **like the plague** and do anything they can to get out of taking them.

_____

_____ 9. A common criticism of specialists is that they become so knowledgeable and focused on their area of specialization that **they can't see the forest for the trees.**

_____

_____ 10. The **tributaries of knowledge** become more diverse every day, but if we only let ourselves **flow** in one direction we may never reach **the larger sea.**

_____

_____ 11. A common criticism of generalists is that they have **so many irons in the fire** that they never really learn any one thing well.

_____

_____ 12. When an open curriculum began to fail, administrators had to **go back to the drawing board** to determine which courses they should require of students.

_____

_____ 13. Generalists approach learning with an interest in everything, **leaving no stone unturned**.

_____

_____ 14. The great universities may teach **all the branches but not necessarily all the roots.**

_____

_____ 15. Tests, unfortunately, are often the **drivers** of education that put students on a limited **road** to knowledge.

_____

C   ESSAY QUESTIONS

Choose one of the following topics and write an essay. Try to integrate ideas, vocabulary, and writing techniques that you have studied in this unit. In this essay, try to incorporate the following:

- an introductory paragraph that (1) presents arguments in favor of the specialist/generalist approaches to education, and (2) clearly states your thesis;

- paragraphs (at least three) that develop your argument with supporting evidence;

- a conclusion that reinforces the position you have taken. It should also end with a new idea (a warning, prediction, value judgment) that has not been mentioned before.

1. At some universities in the United States, undergraduate students are allowed to design individualized majors, self-designed courses of study for students who may not find their calling in a traditional college department. Majors such as "Documentary Film and Native American Studies" and "Comparative Communism: China and Russia" have been created by students to fit their individual interests. Faculty claim that, although these majors may seem narrow, they allow for a broad-based education and that students tend to be quite motivated and do well in them. Students explain that a university education is now too expensive for them to waste time studying subjects that do not interest them or help them in their career goals.

   What is your reaction to this new program of study, given the arguments for specialized and generalized approaches to higher education? Write an essay in which you express your opinion.

2. Some people argue that the professionalization of professors and the proliferation of academic specialists have created institutions of higher learning that resemble industrial life. Others say that universities have done a good job of maintaining their academic priorities and continue to hold their traditional role in helping to shape a human community.

   Take a stand. Write an essay in which you support one of these views of university education. Include examples to support your views.

ECONOMIC MIGHT VS. ECOLOGIC RIGHT

Cartoon by John Deering, the Arkansas Democrat-Gazette.

I.   ANTICIPATING THE ISSUE

Discuss your answers to the following questions.

1. Look at the title. Look at the cartoon. What do you think the issue of this unit will be?

2. What is the message or humor of the cartoon?

3. What do you know about endangered species?

BACKGROUND READING

Read the following text.

Somewhere between 10,000 and 15,000 years ago, man's first clash with nature may have begun. Historians and philosophers agree that since the development of agriculture, human beings have had an effect on the natural **habitat** of many plant and animal **species**. As human populations have increased, so has the **demise** of other living things: As many as 6,000 species are disappearing each year from deforestation, a number 10,000 times greater than before man appeared on the planet. In one day alone, say scientists, some 45 kinds of plants and animals will die. In one year alone, some 17,500 species will be **wiped out.**

In 1977, the United States Congress took an important step to help the ever-increasing number of **endangered** species; it passed a law known as the Endangered Species Act. Through this law, the government officially recognizes the right of all species to share life on the planet. The law mandates protection for "endangered species," those that may become **extinct**, and "threatened species," those likely to become endangered in the near future. The act has already helped to save the gray wolf, the bald eagle, and the alligator from extinction. At the same time, the act has been powerful in altering or stopping many plans for land construction and development. For example, a highway-widening project in Illinois was rerouted in order to protect a rare plant, the prairie bush clover. The construction of a **dam** was stopped in Tennessee to protect a tiny endangered snail.

With the enforcement of the Endangered Species Act, some species have gained more public recognition than others. Pressure groups have pushed to protect those endangered animals that people love and adore. Elephants, **whooping cranes**, whales, and the spotted owl, for example, have received far more media attention than have the smaller, less known, and less attractive species that are also endangered. Of the 676 native American species that are threatened, only 24 or so have received attention; yet, it is the tiny species, such as bugs and bacteria, that keep the planet in balance. Scientists are becoming ever more concerned with the fact that without equal concern for these species, the planet's biological **diversity** will be destroyed, leaving us with a loss of potential new foods and drugs. Their forecast for the future of this planet is a **somber** one.

On the other hand, some scientists argue that the extinction issue is being exaggerated, and that people are "crying wolf" by describing the loss of species as more alarming than it really is. History proves that every species will eventually become extinct. They argue that conservationist-scientists may be **overselling** their case by creating fears of **doom.** Evolution of species, they say, naturally involves the extinction of species; man has no control.

In addition, many people point to the fact that the world is already lacking in resources, food, and adequate health care. Concerned more with economic survival, they ask whether it is, in fact, realistic to **make a fuss** over saving the elephant or other species that may become extinct many years from now, when people have families to feed tomorrow. They see saving endangered species as somewhat **schizophrenic** as it interferes with or contradicts human goals. These people question a law that puts the continuance of lower forms of life above man's own survival.

While the debate continues over how much effort should be made to save species from extinction, the addition of 3,800 species on the endangered species list is **impending**, and many loggers, real estate developers, ranchers, and shrimpers find decreasing opportunities to make a living.

A VOCABULARY

Look at the boldfaced words and phrases in the background reading. Try to determine their meaning from the context. Then, complete the following sentences to show you understand their meaning. Compare your sentences with those of another student. Check a dictionary if you disagree about the meanings.

1. The natural **habitat** of the whale is

   _____

2. One **species** that once lived on the earth but lives here no longer is

   _____

3. If someone has reached his or her **demise**, he or she is

   _____

4. If the fish in a lake were **wiped out**, they would be

   _____

5. An **endangered** species that is starting to come back today is

   _____

6. A mammal that has been **extinct** for millions of years is the

   _____

7. If a **dam** were built on the body of water nearest you, there would probably be

   _____

8. To see **whooping cranes**, you might have to go to

   _____

9. If a nation has cultural **diversity**, it probably has

   _____

10. A **somber** prediction for the future is

   _____

11. People who are ***overselling*** their ideas are usually

_____

12. Fortune-tellers who predict ***doom*** are predicting

_____

13. When people ***make a fuss*** about politics, they usually

_____

14. If you have a ***schizophrenic*** attitude toward a problem, it means that

_____

15. If there is an ***impending*** storm, the sky is

_____

B   SUMMARIZING THE ISSUE

Work in small groups. Summarize the issue presented in the background reading. Take notes to complete the following outline.

1. The issue (*state in your own words*):

_____

_____

_____

2. Proponents' (of saving endangered species) arguments:

_____

_____

3. Opponents' (of saving endangered species) arguments:

_____

_____

_____

C   VALUES CLARIFICATION

Work in small groups. Discuss your answers to the following questions.

1. What is your reaction to the Endangered Species Act? Where do you stand in the debate between saving species from extinction and allowing man to develop?

(continued on next page)

2. Is there an issue of endangered species in your country? What opinion do you have toward your government's policies, if there are any, on endangered species?

III. OPINION 1: LISTENING

A ✔ LISTENING FOR THE MAIN IDEA

Listen to the commentary. Check the statement that summarizes the commentator's viewpoint.

☐ 1. Because of man, many living things have become extinct.

☐ 2. The dangers of extinction may not be as serious as they are made out to be.

☐ 3. The extinction rate today is much more serious than it was in the past.

B LISTENING FOR DETAILS

Read the following questions and answers. Listen to the commentary again and circle the best answer. Then compare your answers with those of another student. Listen again if necessary.

1. What will be the consequence of a new dam in the Amazon?

    a. The Amazon will start to dry up.

    b. Trees will die.

    c. Endangered species will be saved.

2. Which of the following issues are Jim Trefil's colleagues concerned about?

    a. Animals are being destroyed faster than plants.

    b. Tropical rain forests cannot be reproduced.

    c. Mankind contributes to the death of animals and plants.

3. How does Jim Trefil react to his colleagues' arguments?

    a. With concern because of his family.

    b. In two different ways.

    c. He has started to cut more trees.

4. What conclusion does he reach about the dangers of extinction?

    a.   He is disturbed by the exaggeration.

    b.   He worries that people are not concerned about them.

    c.   He is afraid that the situation is worse than it seems.

5. How does Trefil explain the death of species?

    a.   The death of species is no different than that of humans.

    b.   The death of species was rare 600 million years ago.

    c.   Governments haven't done enough to prevent the death of species.

6. How does Trefil view the current rate of extinction?

    a.   It is impossible to compare it with the past.

    b.   He says no one thinks it is severe.

    c.   He is skeptical of the warnings about it.

7. What problem does Trefil have with the word "species"?

    a.   No spectacular species are considered endangered.

    b.   Most people are only interested in saving well-known species.

    c.   All beetles are counted as one species.

8. Why might people stop listening to scientists?

    a.   They haven't been honest about the real extinction issue.

    b.   They are more concerned about the extinction of bugs than the extinction of large animals.

    c.   They cannot make objective decisions about extinction.

C   TEXT COMPLETION AND DISCRETE LISTENING

Read the text of the commentary. Try to fill in the missing words in the text as you remember it. Use your knowledge of text structure, vocabulary, and grammar to help you. Then listen again to the commentary to check your answers, stopping the tape as you fill in the blanks. If you have different answers than the original text, check with your teacher to see if they are acceptable alternatives.

Introduction

Seven weeks from now, a new _____ in the Amazon will flood millions
₁
of trees and animals out of the rain forest. Environmentalists have criticized

the plan because they say many _____ animal species will be destroyed.
Physicist Jim Trefil has been thinking about the situation in the Amazon, and
he has these observations.

Commentary

Some of my _____ are starting to publicize their worries about the rate
at which plants and animals are disappearing from the earth. Things like the
destruction of the tropical rain forest are described in _____ tones. The
destruction of a _____ , we are told, is equivalent to the destruction of
all the species that live in that habitat. We are told that mankind must not contribute to the _____ of other living things.

I have to admit that my reaction to this line of reasoning is a bit
_____ . On the one hand, I have a strong emotional commitment to the
notion that any argument that keeps people from cutting down a tree is a good
argument. For years, I've managed a twenty-acre wood lot in Virginia, taking
out _____ to keep my family warm in the winter.

And yet, I've been trained as a scientist. And one of the first
_____ of that training was to learn to put feelings aside and examine
arguments _____ on their merits.

When I do that with the arguments about the dangers of extinctions
and loss of biological _____ , some very disturbing questions arise in my
mind. I worry that the people involved may be _____ their case, that
the situation may be neither as serious nor as dangerous as they say.

Species, like individuals, do not live _____ . Over the past 600
million years, almost every form of life that existed on the earth has become
_____ . Paleontologists estimate that, even in normal times, species
become extinct at the rate of several hundred per year. Governments can no
more pass laws to stop the death of species than they can pass laws to stop the
deaths of individuals. _____ is just another part of life.

So the real question is how the extinction _____ today compares to what it's been in the past. I don't know the answer to this question, but I don't think anyone else does _____ . I do know that until it's answered, I'm going to be very skeptical of headlines about impending _____ .

     Another problem I have is with this word "species." When we hear that a species is endangered, we usually think of whales or _____ cranes or ivory-billed woodpeckers—something spectacular. In fact, most of the tropical species that are being _____ _____ today are insects that live in very restricted locations. The beetles in one mountain valley may look just like their _____ in the next valley. But they're counted as separate species because of very fine technical differences between them.

     My experience has been that when people learn that all this _____ is being made over bugs and not large animals, they feel cheated and lose interest in the whole _____ question. People listen to what scientists have to say because they believe we are capable of making objective _____ , regardless of our own beliefs and feelings. If the public comes to regard us as just another pressure group crying wolf, they may just stop listening. If that happens, we will have lost the most important _____ of all.

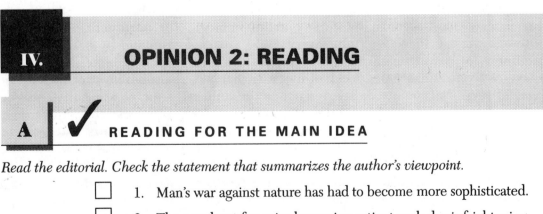

IV.   OPINION 2: READING

A ✔ READING FOR THE MAIN IDEA

Read the editorial. Check the statement that summarizes the author's viewpoint.

    ☐ 1. Man's war against nature has had to become more sophisticated.

    ☐ 2. The number of species becoming extinct each day is frightening.

    ☐ 3. We must accept the fact that extinction is part of evolution.

All Creatures Great And Dying

by Jon Bowermaster

Ever since man came busting out of the last Ice Age 11,000 years ago, armed with sharpened sticks, traps, and snares, he has had a nasty habit of *wreaking havoc* on plants and animals.

Occasionally the *annihilation* was unintentional, as when predators were introduced by early explorers to remote locales—such as the dodo on the island of Mauritius. More often, man was merely making room for one thing: himself. The first time he swept across North America, man wiped out saber-tooth cats, mastodons, mammoths, huge ground sloths, short-faced bears, and dire wolves. Centuries later, when the British colonists came ashore in South Carolina, they found, according to one account, "endless Numbers of Panthers, Tygers, Wolves, and other Beasts of Prey." Needless to say, the newcomers wasted little time in wasting them, too. The winning of the West that followed included the *butchering* of the buffalo, along with varieties of grizzly bears, wolves, foxes, and cougars.

By the late nineteenth century, with the advent of industrial technology and modern farming, man's weapons of choice in his continuing war against nature had become more sophisticated. Today parking lots, pesticides, waste dumps, and industrial pollutants of all stripes are the new spears, though the victims remain the same—plants, animals, and their homes. Grasslands and wetlands are increasingly replaced by subdivisions and *malls*. Trees and lakes are poisoned by acid rain. Tropical forests are *slashed* and burned at the rate of 100 acres a minute. As population density soars from South America to Southeast Asia, economic *might* continues to overrule ecologic right. Since 1900, Africa's wildlife population has declined by more than seventy percent as the human population has grown sixfold.

The number of wildlife extinctions and endangered species is *mind-boggling*. In the early twentieth century, the earth was losing one species a year; today, it's one species a day—400 times the natural rate. By comparison, it's estimated that dinosaur species *died off* at a rate of one every 1,000 years. By the middle of the next century, according to the Nature Conservancy, one-half of all the earth's present species may be lost, largely as a result of man's greed, cruelty, and vanity.

In the United States alone, there are 565 animals on the U.S. Fish and Wildlife Service's list of endangered species; outside the U.S., the projected figure is 508. Calculating the number of endangered plants and invertebrates is difficult: On one *hectare* of any rain forest live *countless* species of plants and insects that exist nowhere else; if that hectare of hardwood is *razed*— whether to make cardboard packing boxes for VCRs or disposable chopsticks—the species are gone forever. Some estimates of endangered plants and invertebrates run as high as 40,000.

One school of biological theorists contends that extinction is evolutionary, arguing that we all have to go sometime. But there's a big difference between natural and unnatural death. Already the Tasmanian wolf, the laughing owls of New Zealand, the Caribbean monk seals, and many more are *history*. And while there are some efforts underway to rescue a handful of species—in the U.S., for example, a number of zoos have had success breeding and bringing back such species as condors, ferrets, and Siberian tigers—they represent a *drop in the bucket*, particularly at a time when only thirty Spanish lynxes and thirty Western swamp tortoises remain, and when entire species of insects are *vacated* every day. While much of the public *handwringing* over (and Hollywood fund-raisers on behalf of) endangered species is done in the name of the "glamour" animals—like blue whales and bald eagles (which are actually staging a comeback of sorts, after a twenty-year, $25 million campaign)—the unparalleled horror of today's carnage lies more in the sheer number of plants that are disappearing.

When the dinosaurs were killed off 65 million years ago, flowering plants survived. Today dozens are being *eradicated* weekly, many before they can even be named or studied. The tragedy in their extinction is that many hold potential cures for everything from cancer to AIDS. Twenty-five percent of the *pharmaceuticals* in use in America today contain ingredients originally derived from wild plants. The Madagascar periwinkle, for example, is a key ingredient in curing lymphatic *leukemia*; the South American ipecac is used to treat amoebic dysentery; hormone medicines like cortisone and diosgenin (the active ingredient in birth control pills) were developed from wild yams; the heart medicine strophanthin comes from a wild West African vine.

But aren't there plenty of *shrubs* and vines to go around? Who's going to miss an odd thousand or so of the 30 million different kinds of insects that crawl the face of the earth? Certainly evolution will continue even as we pave and pollute the planet. Unfortunately, as man's technology *weeds out* the survivors in the plant and animal world, those that will *thrive* are hardly the most biologically diverse, or necessarily the most beneficial. Cockroaches, rats, raccoons, bats, and weeds are far from endangered.

What is wrong with the current rate of extinction is its *chilling* acceleration. According to the World Wildlife Fund, thousands of existing species may be extinct by the end of this century. Such extreme dying-off *portends* the disruption of widespread, complex habitats, key players in the planet's ecological balance. With more and more of those players missing in action, such essentials as clean air and water, productive soil, and many *harvestable* products will increasingly be things of the past. And extinction only breeds more, and faster, extinction.

One especially frightening aspect of the endangerment to wild plants and animals is not what we know for a certainty will happen but what we cannot predict. Our knowledge of earth's biological fabric and its mysteries is, at best, incomplete, uneven. Thus the consequence of man's continued alteration of nature's diversity cannot be forecast with any real degree of accuracy. It is the unknown that has even the experts *scared stiff*.

By Jon Bowermaster. From *Rolling Stone*, May 3, 1990. By Straight Arrow Publishers, Inc. 1992. All Rights Reserved. Reprinted by permission.

B   READING FOR FACT VS. OPINION

In developing critical thinking skills, it is necessary to distinguish facts from opinions. (Refer back to Unit 2, p. 31 for an explanation of the difference between fact and opinion.) In Bowermaster's article, both facts and opinions are used to support the author's main idea. Read the following statements. Next to each statement write F if it is a fact, or O if it is an opinion. Compare your answers with another student.

_____ 1. Ever since man came busting out of the last ice age 11,000 years ago, armed with sharpened sticks, traps, and snares, he has had a nasty habit of wreaking havoc on plants and animals.

_____ 2. The first time he swept across North America, man wiped out saber-toothed cats, mastodons, mammoths, huge ground sloths, short-faced bears, and dire wolves.

_____ 3. Needless to say, the newcomers wasted little time in wasting them, too.

_____ 4. The winning of the West that followed included the butchering of the buffalo, along with varieties of bears, wolves, foxes, and cougars.

_____ 5. Tropical forests are slashed and burned at the rate of 100 acres a minute.

_____ 6. By the middle of the next century, according to the Nature Conservancy, one-half of all the earth's present species may be lost, largely as a result of man's greed, cruelty, and vanity.

_____ 7. On one hectare of any rain forest live countless species of plants and insects that exist nowhere else.

_____ 8. But there's a big difference between natural and unnatural death.

_____ 9. Already the Tasmanian wolf, the laughing owls of New Zealand, the Caribbean monk seals, and many more are history.

_____ 10. While much of the public handwringing over . . . endangered species is done in the name of the "glamour" animals—like blue whales and bald eagles . . . —the unparalleled horror of today's carnage lies more in the sheer number of plants that are disappearing.

_____ 11. When dinosaurs were killed off 65 million years ago, flowering plants survived.

_____ 12. Unfortunately, as man's technology weeds out the survivors in the plant and animal world, those that will thrive are hardly the most biologically diverse, or necessarily the most beneficial.

_____ 13. What is wrong with the current rate of extinction is its chilling acceleration.

C   **WORD SEARCH**

Find boldfaced words in the essay that have similar meanings to the following and write them below.

Nouns

complete destruction: _____

great power: _____

causing damage: _____

medicinal drugs: _____

thoughtless killing: _____

worrying: _____

complexes of stores: _____

10,000 square meters: _____

insignificant amount: _____

short woody stemmed trees: _____

Verbs

eliminates: _____

is a sign of: _____

became extinct: _____

grow strong and healthy: _____

Adjectives

cut: _____

(continued on next page)

leveled to the ground: _____

innumerable: _____

removed: _____

shocking: _____

destroyed: _____

no longer in existence: _____

capable of being cut and used: _____

hard to believe: _____

V. SYNTHESIZING TWO OPINION PIECES

A ✔ DISTINGUISHING OPINIONS

Authors can have different viewpoints, but their opinions can sometimes be similar. Review opinion 1 on pages 75–77 and opinion 2 on pages 78–79.

Work in groups. Read the statements below. Discuss whether Trefil and/or Bowermaster would agree with them. Put a check (✔) in the box if you think they would agree. Leave the box empty if they would disagree or if there is no evidence to support the statement in their opinion.

Discuss how and why the two opinions are the same or different. (In the first statement, for example, Trefil would probably not agree, especially since he states that people may be overselling their case about the dangers of extinction and that dying is just another part of life. Bowermaster, on the other hand, would agree, as he states that man has been wreaking havoc on plants and animals for thousands of years.)

	Trefil: Commentator (Opinion 1)	Bowermaster: Author (Opinion 2)
Mankind is primarily responsible for the destruction of other living things.		✓
It is best to examine the arguments of extinction like a scientist, without feelings.		
The death of a species is part of life.		
Too much attention has been paid to the cute, attractive animals that are endangered rather than the less attractive species that are most endangered.		
The media needs to give more attention to the extinction of species.		
It's hard to be concerned about the extinction of species we've never seen or never knew existed.		
No one really knows how dangerous the situation for animals and plants is.		
Man's survival on this planet is of most importance in the extinction question.		

B   GIVING YOUR OPINION

After you have distinguished the opinions of the commentator and the author, express your own opinions on the above statements. Discuss them with the other students in your group.

C   VOCABULARY REINFORCEMENT: WORD RELATIONS

Work in small groups. The words on the next page come from the commentary and the article. Look at the relationship among the words. For each set of words, cross out the word that is not related to the other three. Compare your answers with those of the students in your group. Discuss the relationships among the words in each set. Then write a word or phrase in the space below that categorizes the relationship. The first one has been done for you.

(continued on next page)

1. *eradicated*   died~~off~~   butchered   wiped out
   eliminated in a destructive manner

2. *impending*   endangered   portending   diverse

3. *habitat*   dam   species   shrubs

4. *vacated*   weeded out   deforested   endangered

5. *slashed*   harvested   cut   razed

6. *annihilation*   havoc   demise   mall

7. *overselling*   countless   drop in the bucket   innumerable

8. *chilling*   schizophrenic   somber   doom

9. *dying off*   extinction   thriving   death of a species

10. *fuss*   mind-boggling   crying wolf   handwringing

VI.   SPEAKING

A ✔ CASE STUDY: THE SPOTTED OWL

The following reading presents a true case that raises the issue of how far protecting endangered species can or should go.

Study the case.

A few years ago, the Fish and Wildlife Service listed the northern spotted owl as a threatened species, thereby protecting it under the Endangered Species

Act. Classified as "threatened," this cute little bird is considered likely to become endangered in the foreseeable future; today, an estimated 6,000 spotted owls live in the Pacific Northwest. Because of heavy timber harvesting in the region, the owl's habitat, the old-growth forests from southwestern British Columbia to northern California, has become severely threatened. Ninety percent of the original forests have already disappeared because of the logging industry.

After the Fish and Wildlife Service listed the spotted owl as a threatened species, the U.S. District Court of Seattle ordered a habitat plan, setting aside 11.6 million acres of federal and private old-growth forest as habitat for the spotted owl, thus severely limiting the number of acres that could continue to be harvested for timber. This protection represented an attempt by Congress and the American people to preserve the biological diversity upon which all humans depend. According to the Fish and Wildlife Service, no more than 2,000 jobs would be lost as a result of these new logging bans. Yet some conservationists say that this new protection is still not enough to save the spotted owls, because the law allows for continued tree cutting.

Needless to say, the timber industry's reaction to this imposed protection for the owl has not been favorable. The industry believes that the plan will result in the loss of up to 100,000 jobs in the area. Officials feel that the lumber industry will die and that the region's timber towns will soon vanish, similar to the old textile towns and mining towns of years ago. A "humans-first" movement has developed, expressing the desire to make a living. Residents who live and work in the timber towns are angry about the fact that political decisions are being made in favor of a small owl that most of them have never even seen rather than in favor of the thousands of workers who have lost and will lose their jobs. For example, in the small logging town of Forks, Washington, unemployment increased by 10 percent in the year after the plan went into effect. One man, a 31-year-old logger with three children, committed suicide when he learned that he would lose his job. Crime is on the rise in Forks, with a recent attempt to burn down the Olympic National Park's headquarters. Many social problems have developed with the loggers' loss of jobs: Children are attempting to commit suicide and more cases of drunken driving and domestic violence have been reported.

People in Forks admit that they have probably harvested too many trees, but they feel that the environmentalists—outsiders—are driving them out of their homes and cherished way of life. The young son of a logger recently posted a sign in the town asking, "An owl needs 2,000 acres to live. Why can't I have room to live?"

Meanwhile, the U.S. government is looking into revising the Endangered Species Act to make it more compatible with national economic goals. The nation is struggling to determine how far it can go to protect endangered species without creating a new endangered species: human beings.

Prepare for a role play. Read the situation and the roles and follow the procedure.

The Situation

The United States House of Representatives has appointed a committee to reconsider the issue of the spotted owl and the future of the U.S. timber industry. The committee is considering a proposal to make the Endangered Species Act more compatible with national economic goals. Before any proposal is made, however, it will hold an open meeting with all those concerned with the case of the ʃpotted owl.

The Roles

1. *Loggers and their families:* You are angry about the fact that people are losing their jobs. Your community is falling apart because of the social problems related to new limitations on the timber industry. Your families have worked in the timber industry for years and you don't have any other options for work. You want to convince the committee to reconsider the protection of the spotted owl.

2. *Environmentalists:* You are shocked by the fact that 90 percent of the original forests have already disappeared. You favor the Endangered Species Act but feel that even it is not enough. You want to convince the committee that tree cutting should be stopped completely to save the spotted owl and to save the earth.

3. *Members of the House of Representatives committee:* You will question both the loggers and the environmentalists about their concerns. After hearing the facts and opinions, you will make a recommendation to either revise the Endangered Species Act in some way or keep it intact.

The Procedure

1. Form three groups for the three roles.

2. The loggers and their families prepare arguments in favor of revising the Endangered Species Act to allow the timber industry to continue. The environmentalists prepare arguments in favor of limiting the timber industry to protect the spotted owl's habitat. The members of the committee prepare questions for both groups.

3. The committee members ask each group to present its position. (Each group should take no more than five minutes.)

4. The committee members ask specific questions of each group.

5. The committee meets separately to create a proposal: Either continue or revise the Endangered Species Act.

6. The decision is presented to the whole group.

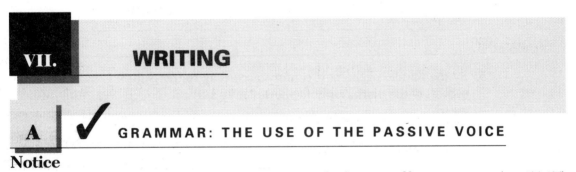

B   DISCUSSION QUESTIONS

In groups, discuss your answers to the following questions.

1. Go back to the questions in the values clarification exercise (p. 73). Do you have the same opinions now, or have you changed your opinions in any way after examining the views of others?

2. It is said that species will only be saved if public behavior is changed. Do you agree? If not, why? If so, describe what changes would be necessary.

3. In your opinion, what are the politics involved in saving endangered species? How might industrial and developing countries see the problem differently?

VII.   WRITING

A   ✓ GRAMMAR: THE USE OF THE PASSIVE VOICE

Notice

Notice the use of the passive voice in both Jim Trefil's commentary (pp. 75–77) and Jon Bowermaster's essay (pp. 78–79). Why do you think these authors make frequent use of the passive voice?

Explanation

The English passive voice is very common in scientific or objective writing. It is the form used when a writer wants to make a statement sound objective or when he or she wants to vary the writing style.

Exercise

The following statements were made in either Jim Trefil's commentary or Jon Bowermaster's article. Each uses the passive voice to describe a situation.

Rewrite each of the statements in the active voice (you may have to supply a subject in the new sentence). Then, with another student, discuss how usage of the active voice changes the feeling or meaning of the original statement. Discuss why you think the writers chose to use the passive voice.

1. My experience has been that when people learn that all this fuss **is being made** over bugs and not large animals, they feel cheated and lose interest in the whole extinction question.

_____

_____

(continued on next page)

2. In fact, most of the tropical species that **are being wiped out** today are insects that live in very restricted locations.

_____

_____

3. Grasslands and wetlands **are increasingly replaced** by subdivisions and malls. Trees and lakes **are poisoned** by acid rain.

_____

_____

4. Occasionally the annihilation was unintentional, as when predators **were introduced** by early explorers to remote locales—such as the dodo on the island of Mauritius.

_____

_____

5. By the middle of the next century, according to the Nature Conservancy, one-half of all the earth's present species **may be lost,** largely as a result of man's greed.

_____

_____

6. Things like the destruction of the tropical rain forest **are described** in somber tones. The destruction of a habitat, we **are told,** is equivalent to the destruction of all the species that live in that habitat.

_____

_____

7. And yet, I've **been trained** as a scientist.

_____

_____

8. . . . if that hectare of hardwood **is razed**—whether to make cardboard packing boxes for VCRs or disposable chopsticks—the species **are gone** forever.

_____

_____

9. The beetles in one mountain valley may look just like their neighbors in the next valley. But they're **counted** as separate species because of very fine technical differences between them.

_____

_____

B   WRITING STYLE: ARGUMENT

Notice

Notice the style of writing James Trefil uses in his commentary (pp. 75–77). His style of writing is argumentative. In what ways does Trefil build his argument against his colleagues?

Explanation

Generally, there are four ways to help a reader or listener understand why you are taking a particular position in an argument. A writer can use: statistics (*numbers and opinion polls*), personal testimony (*the writer's own experience*), factual reference (*facts cannot be argued, but they must be accurate*), or appeal to authority (*the "experts'" opinions can support your argument*).

Trefil uses a combination of evidence to support his argument: *personal testimony* (he mentions his own experience as a family man and as a scientist), *factual reference* (he notes that most of the tropical species becoming extinct are insects and that there are fine technical differences between species), and *appeal to authority* (he cites paleontologists' estimates on the rate of extinction).

Exercise

Go back to Bowermaster's article, "All Creatures Great and Dying." Which of the four ways described above does he use to argue his position on the issue of endangered species? From his article, list three examples of each type he uses. Compare your examples with those of another student and discuss any differences you may have.

Statistics:

_____

_____

_____

Personal Testimony:

_____

_____

_____

Factual Reference:

_____

_____

_____

(continued on next page)

Appeal to Authority:

_____

_____

_____

C ESSAY QUESTIONS

Choose one of the following topics and write an essay. Try to integrate ideas, vocabulary, and writing techniques that you have studied in this unit. In this essay, try to incorporate the following:

- an introductory paragraph that presents both sides of the argument and clearly states your thesis on protecting the environment;

- paragraphs (at least three) that develop your argument with supporting evidence;

- a conclusion that reinforces the position you have taken. It should also end with a new idea (a warning, prediction, value judgment) that has not been mentioned before.

1. T. H. Watkins writes in an article on endangerment:

   If we cannot live in harmony with other forms of life, if we cannot control our hostility toward the earth and its creatures, how shall we ever learn to control our hostility toward each other?

   Do you agree that there is a relationship between human aggression toward the earth and aggression toward other human beings? Write an essay in which you express your views.

2. Nature used to be viewed as a force to which humans reacted or with which they fought for survival. Today it is nature's survival that is threatened.

   Write an essay in which you define the relationship between humankind and nature in today's world.

"JUST SAY 'NO' TO DRUGS"?

5

Cartoon by Jeff Danziger, the Christian Science Monitor

1

I. ANTICIPATING THE ISSUE

Discuss your answers to the following questions.

1. Look at the title. Look at the cartoon. What do you think the issue of this unit will be?

2. What is the message or humor of the cartoon?

3. What do you know about the problems of drug abuse?

II.

BACKGROUND READING

Read the following text.

Opinion polls have shown that Americans view the widespread use of drugs as the number one problem in the United States, where drugs are illegal. Every year the United States spends $8 billion on its war on drugs, mostly on the cost of law enforcement and prohibition, such as the recently imposed **mandatory** drug testing of athletes and state and federal employees. Because drugs are illegal, they have become very expensive. **Black market** prices for heroin and cocaine, for example, are estimated to be 100 times greater than the cost of production. With such prices, drug **pushers** can earn more than $20 billion each year by **pushing their wares** in even the poorest neighborhoods. Most people agree that the so-called "drug war" is far from being won in the United States. Consequently, it has become an **obsession** for many Americans to find some solution to the drug problem.

One proposal is to fight the problem by making drugs legal. This proposal has, in fact, been the cause of a lengthy, unresolved debate. Ever since the 1970s, Americans have argued whether taking the extreme **measure** of legalizing drugs would, in fact, decrease drug use. People who support this proposal believe that the current policies of prosecution and punishment are a waste of money. They feel that more money should be spent on education and treatment, arguing that the black market drives the prices of drugs too high, providing an incentive to get into the drug business. They point to the gangsters of the 1920s and 1930s who disappeared with the end of the prohibition of alcohol in America. If drugs were made legal, they say, drug dealers would lose their big incomes, and drug-related crime would decrease. Advocates of legalization see drugs as a health problem rather than as a criminal justice problem. As it is now, they say, anyone who is caught using drugs is treated as a criminal, not as an addict who needs help. This proposal for legalization has been supported by a variety of leaders, from the most conservative to the most liberal, from secretaries of state to federal district judges who advocate the sale of drugs at prices resembling their costs. These supporters also favor the legalization of **soft drugs**, such as marijuana and hashish. Baltimore Mayor Kurt Schmoke has been a leader in advancing the policy of legalization. For years Schmoke worked as state prosecutor and had to deal with the many deaths of law-enforcement officials from drug-related crimes. Frustrated by the unsuccessful policies to control drugs, and responding to the requests of his **constituents** to take a more aggressive position in dealing with the drug problems of his community, Schmoke decided to take a **hard-nosed** approach to changing the current drug policies: He proposed the legalization of drugs.

The proposal to legalize drugs has not been accepted easily by all

Americans, however. In fact, it has taken a lot of *flak* over the years. Those who oppose the legalization of drugs feel that *decriminalizing* drugs would be a surrender in a drug war that has not really even begun. For them, the solution is not to decriminalize drug crime but to make laws more severe. They point out that legalization would lead to greater drug use, explaining that, with drugs such as *crack* being so common in our cities, there would be an increase in cases of crime and child abuse and an even greater spread of AIDS. Crack is known to cause people to become violent and, when used with dirty needles, spreads disease. Opponents of legalization also point to China. When drugs there were made legal, the selling of opium increased and fanned the drug trade rather than slowed it down. Those who oppose legalization also raise important questions such as: Which drugs would be legalized? Would the state or the individual administer the drugs? Would the government have to support facilities that sell the drugs with tax money? Would the black market really disappear with the legalization of drugs?

So, is it time to recognize that the current war on drugs is not working and accept that legalization may be the only solution? Every few years, voters are asked to *cast their votes* for politicians who claim to have answers to this question. But as of yet, Americans have not chosen legalization as a solution to their country's drug problems.

A   VOCABULARY

Look at the boldfaced words and phrases in the following sentences. From the context of the background reading, determine the best meaning. Circle your answer.

1. Every year the United States spends $8 billion on its war on drugs, for programs such as the recently imposed *mandatory* drug testing of athletes and many state and federal employees.

   a. required   b. extensive

2. *Black market* prices for heroin and cocaine, for example, are estimated to be 100 times greater than the cost of production.

   a. illegal sale   b. lowest sale

3. With such prices, drug *pushers* can earn more than $20 billion each year by pushing their wares in even the poorest neighborhoods.

   a. makers   b. sellers

4. With such prices, drug pushers can earn more than $20 billion each year by *pushing their wares* in even the poorest neighborhoods.

   a. producing supplies   b. aggressively selling their products

5. Consequently, it has become an *obsession* for many Americans to find some solution to the drug problem.

   a. fixed idea that takes over all thought   b. fear

(continued on next page)

6. Ever since the 1970s, Americans have argued whether taking the extreme ***measure*** of legalizing drugs would, in fact, decrease drug use.

    a. distance   b. plan

7. These supporters also favor the legalization of ***soft drugs***.

    a. addictive drugs   b. mildly habit-forming drugs

8. Frustrated by the unsuccessful policies to control drugs, and responding to the requests of his ***constituents*** to take a more aggressive position in dealing with the drug problems of his community, Schmoke decided to take a hard-nosed approach.

    a. voters   b. supporters

9. Schmoke decided to take a ***hard-nosed*** approach to changing the current drug policies: He proposed the legalization of drugs.

    a. tough   b. liberal

10. The legalization of drugs has taken a lot of ***flak*** over the years.

    a. rejection   b. criticism

11. Those who oppose the legalization of drugs feel that ***decriminalizing*** drugs would be a surrender in a drug war that has not really even begun.

    a. making legal   b. making illegal

12. With drugs such as ***crack*** being so common in our cities, there would be an increase in cases of crime and child abuse and an even greater spread of AIDS.

    a. an inexpensive addictive drug   b. an expensive nonaddictive drug

13. Every few years, voters are asked to ***cast their votes*** for politicians who claim to have answers to this question.

    a. throw their votes away   b. vote in favor of

B   **SUMMARIZING THE ISSUE**

Work in small groups. Summarize the issue presented in the background reading. Take notes to complete the following outline:

1. The issue (*state in your own words*):

    _____

    _____

    _____

2. Proponents' (of legalization) arguments:

_____

_____

_____

3. Opponents' (of legalization) arguments:

_____

_____

_____

C   VALUES CLARIFICATION

Work in small groups. Discuss your answers to the following questions.

1. In your country, is there a problem of drug abuse? Are there government policies to control the sale of drugs? Do the policies work well, in your opinion?

2. What is your reaction to the proposal to legalize drugs in the United States? Do you share the proponents' views or the opponents' views on this proposal?

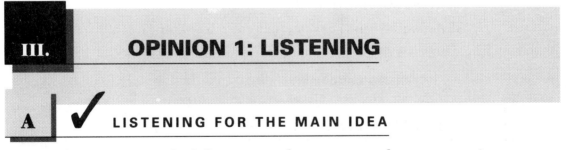

III.   OPINION 1: LISTENING

A ✓ LISTENING FOR THE MAIN IDEA

Listen to the commentary. Check the statement that summarizes the commentator's viewpoint.

☐ 1. Linda Chavez favors the legalization of drugs in the United States.

☐ 2. Linda Chavez opposes the legalization of drugs in the United States.

☐ 3. Linda Chavez has mixed feelings about the legalization of drugs in the United States.

B   LISTENING FOR DETAILS

Read the following questions and answers. Listen to the commentary again and circle the best answer. Then compare your answers with those of another student. Listen again if necessary.

1. What has Congress been willing to do this year?

    a. decriminalize drugs

    b. debate proposals to control drugs

    c. say "no" to the legalization of drugs

2. Which proposal was included in the House bill on drugs?

    a. to punish drug-related murderers by death

    b. to make mandatory drug testing illegal

    c. to refuse the use of illegally gathered evidence in criminal trials

3. What is the Senate trying to do?

    a. fight the House bill

    b. speed up the voting process

    c. establish a committee before the vote

4. What are politicians eager to do, according to the commentator?

    a. change their constituents' minds about drugs

    b. delay a decision on the drug problem until November

    c. find a way to make the drug problem disappear

5. What policy is favored by conservatives?

    a. the death penalty for drug-related murders

    b. decriminalization of drugs

    c. reducing the profit made from drugs

6. What policy is favored by liberals?

    a. longer prison sentences for drug-related crimes

    b. legalization of drugs

    c. stronger law enforcement

7. What argument does the commentator have against Schmoke's approach?

    a. We would be giving in to the drug war.

    b. Drug use would increase.

    c. More children would be born drug addicts.

8. According to the commentator, what will happen to the drug market if we legalize drugs?

    a.   The hard truth about drugs will finally be faced.

    b.   Drug dealers won't be able to sell drugs so easily.

    c.   Pushers may make more money.

9. How do most Americans deal with the drug problem?

    a.   They generally support the "just say no" drug policy.

    b.   They really try to face the drug problem.

    c.   They only talk about it.

C   TEXT COMPLETION AND DISCRETE LISTENING

Read the text of the commentary. Try to fill in the missing words in the text as you remember them. Use your knowledge of text structure, vocabulary, and grammar to help you. Then listen again to the commentary to check your answers, stopping the tape as you fill in the blanks. If you have different answers than the original text, check with your teacher to see if they are acceptable alternatives.

Introduction

This year Congress has been willing to debate almost any _____ in the

war against drugs. Commentator Linda Chavez says the _____ "just

can't say no."

Commentary

Drugs have become a political _____ this election year. The House

recently passed a _____ that would impose a federal death

_____ for drug-related murder. The House bill also calls for widespread

_____ drug testing and would permit the use of illegally gathered evi-

dence in criminal trials. The Senate is considering ways to bring the House bill

to a quick vote, without going through the normally lengthy committee process.

Every politician is eager, it seems, to _____ a tough antidrug

vote before his _____ cast their votes in November. It's as if politicians

feel they have to _____ up with some new and drastic _____

that hasn't been tried before, in the hopes it will make the drug problem

_____ . The death penalty for drug _____ or those who commit

drug-related murders seems to be the favorite of conservatives this year.

(continued on next page)

Now, a _____ of liberals, led by Baltimore Mayor Kurt
13
Schmoke, have come up with a radical approach at the other extreme:

_____ drug use in the hopes that it will take the _____ out of
14   15
drug sales. Schmoke built a reputation as a _____ - _____ state
16
prosecutor before he was _____ mayor of Baltimore. But like most law-
17
_____ officials, he faced frustration in his own _____ on drugs
18   19
in Maryland.

But the alternative that he and others propose would amount to a

_____ . And what's worse, drug use would not diminish. It hasn't in
20
countries like the Netherlands or England, which have similar policies. Lives
would continue to be lost to the ravages drugs inflict on the bodies and

_____ of those who take them.
21

There aren't any easy answers to the drug problem in America. And
election years certainly aren't _____ to discussions about the
22
_____ truth of drug use. Drug dealers _____ their wares be-
23   24
cause there is a market for them in this country. Legalizing drugs won't affect
that market and, _____ , might increase it by removing the penalties.
25

Nancy Reagan took a lot of _____ when she proposed a pro-
26
gram to "just say ' _____ ' to drugs." But is there really any other answer?
27
Americans are going to have to _____ up to some hard questions about
28
ourselves and our values if we're really going to eliminate drugs. Most of us,
unfortunately, would rather talk tough or redefine the problem.

IV.   OPINION 2: READING

A   ✓ READING FOR THE MAIN IDEA

Read the editorial. Check the statement that summarizes the author's viewpoint.

☐   1. Drug legalization could begin to control the U.S. drug problem.

☐ 2. The legalization of drugs is a surrender to the drug war.

☐ 3. Drug legalization is an imperfect solution to a difficult problem.

To Control Drugs, Legalize

by Frederick B. Campbell

The idea of legalizing addictive drugs *conjures up* images of crack being sold like cigarettes at corner newsstands or heroin like whiskey at local bars.

But legalization need not be anything like those frightening images. Indeed, a carefully controlled legalization could be the *key* element in a strategy to put drug pushers out of business.

Legalization would not mean that addictive drugs would be legally available to everyone.

The purpose of legalization would be to place better controls on access to such drugs. *Addiction* would be recognized as a disease or physical *affliction.* For people who have that disease, the substance would be legal.

Licensed clinics would be allowed to provide drugs to such addicts—and only to them—in the same way that many addictive prescription drugs now are legally provided to specific categories of patients. For nonaddicts, the *substances* would remain illegal in the same way that it now is criminal to sell or use prescription drugs without a *prescription*.

Legalization would not mean that pushers would be given free rein.

The basic strategy of controlled legalization would be to *deprive* pushers of their steady and most *lucrative* customers—namely, addicts. If the strategy could be executed successfully, there would be far fewer pushers, because the smaller market would not support so many.

At the same time, police and other law enforcement officials could concentrate on reducing availability to nonaddicts. (Curing addicts of addiction is a medical problem, not a law enforcement one.)

Legalization would not have to work perfectly in order to be beneficial.

Even if some addicts continued to seek drugs from pushers rather than licensed clinics, controlled legalization could have great benefits. If a large portion of addicts used clinics rather than pushers, the number of pushers would decline.

Moreover, in the long term, fewer pushers would mean fewer new users starting and, thus, ultimately fewer addicts.

Legalization would reduce drug-related problems, not increase them.

Opponents of legalization often emphasize emotionally laden tragedies, such as infants born of addicted mothers, often with severe physical and mental problems. These opponents seldom ask the relevant questions.

For example, are there likely to be more "crack babies" if addicts get their drugs from licensed clinics that would take all possible steps to ensure that users do not become pregnant? Or is it likely that there will be more crack babies under the current system in which addicts get no advice or assistance with birth control?

*Legalization would not condemn addicts to **oblivion**.*

Controlled legislation would be the best way to ensure that addicts get all possible assistance to help them get off drugs. It is unlikely that anyone can give up any addictive substance, whether it is cigarettes or alcohol or heroin or crack, unless he or she first decides to do so.

Until that time, however, addicts would be better off getting drugs from licensed clinics, in the safest possible form and under circumstances in which they would be encouraged to try to quit and helped to do so.

*Legalization would not **condone** use of addictive drugs.*

Controlled legislation would amount to a recognition that addiction is a disease, rather than a crime. Under the current system, in which addicts are regarded as criminals, the drug culture attracts people who are **alienated** by mainstream society. This is an especially severe problem among the inner city poor, but

it also strikes suburban youth of the middle and upper classes. Many adolescents pass through rebellious stages in which **petty** criminality may seem desirable. Very few, however, aspire to be diseased.

Controlled legalization of addictive drugs would not be a **panacea** for America's **epidemic**. But it would offer the hope of putting drug pushers out of business.

It may be that this kind of controlled legalization would not work. But the policy debate should not be based on so many false assumptions. Legalization is not necessarily "surrender."

Copyright © 1990 by The New York Times Company. Reprinted by permission.

B   READING FOR AUTHOR'S INTENDED MEANING

Read the following statements. Do you think the author would agree (A) or disagree (D) with them? Write A or D next to each statement. Compare your answers with those of another student. If your answers differ, go back to the text to find out why.

_____ 1. Legalizing drugs means crack will be sold like cigarettes.

_____ 2. Legalizing drugs would begin to end the drug pushers' business.

_____ 3. Addictive drugs should be legally available to addicts.

_____ 4. With legalization, drug pushers would disappear.

_____ 5. If drugs were legalized, police officers would be able to spend more time stopping drug pushers.

_____ 6. Drug legalization will be beneficial only if no addicts continue to buy their drugs from pushers.

_____ 7. If there were fewer drug pushers in the world, there would be fewer drug addicts in the world.

_____ 8. There would be more crack babies if drugs were legalized.

_____ 9. Drug addicts should be allowed to get drugs to help them overcome their addiction.

_____ 10. Drug addiction should not be treated as a crime.

_____ 11. Adolescents may get involved in drugs because the idea of crime is attractive.

_____ 12. The legalization of drugs will solve most of our drug problems.

_____ 13. Even though we don't know whether legalization will work, we should try it.

C   WORD SEARCH

Find boldfaced words in the essay that have similar meaning to the following and write them below.

Nouns

remedy for all troubles or diseases: _____

doctor's written order for medicine: _____

state of being forgotten: _____

drugs:_____

suffering: _____

disease spreading rapidly among many people at the same time and in the same place: _____

great freedom: _____

dependency on a drug: _____

Adjectives

profitable: _____

most important: _____

(continued on next page)

small and unimportant: _____

estranged; cut off from society: _____

Verbs

creates a picture in the mind: _____

overlook; forgive: _____

prevent from enjoying: _____

V. SYNTHESIZING TWO OPINION PIECES

A ✓ DISTINGUISHING OPINIONS

Authors can have different viewpoints, but their opinions can sometimes be similar. Review opinion 1 on pages 97–98 and opinion 2 on pages 99–100.

Work in groups. Read the statements below. Discuss whether Chavez and/or Campbell would agree with them. Put a check (✓) in the box if you think they would agree. Leave the box empty if they would disagree or if there is no evidence to support the statement in their opinion.

Discuss how and why the two opinions are the same or different. (In the first statement, for example, Chavez would agree. She states that the drug dealer market might even increase if penalties are removed with legalization. Campbell would also agree, because he says he believes legalization would have great benefits even if some addicts continued to seek drugs from pushers; he assumes that some probably would.)

	Chavez: Commentator (Opinion 1)	Campbell: Author (Opinion 2)
Some drug addicts will probably continue to buy drugs from pushers after legalization.	✓	✓
The death penalty seems to be an appropriate punishment for drug pushers.		
If drugs were legalized, it would amount to a surrender in the drug war.		

With the legalization of drugs, drug use will increase.		
Drug use must be viewed as a disease rather than a crime.		
Legalization may not be the answer to America's drug problems.		

B   GIVING YOUR OPINION

After you have distinguished the opinions of the commentator and the author, express your own opinions on the above statements. Discuss them with the other students in your group.

C   VOCABULARY REINFORCEMENT: VOCABULARY/CONCEPT GRID

In this activity, you will review some of the vocabulary you learned in the commentary and in the editorial by relating it to important concepts. This will help you to understand and use the words more effectively in discussions on this topic.

Work in groups. For each vocabulary item, discuss its relationship to the concepts written at the top of the grid. How are they related?

If the group thinks there is a positive relationship between the vocabulary item and the concept (one causes the other; one is an example of the other; one supports the other; etc.), put a "+" in the box. If the group thinks there is a negative relationship between the two (one defeats or contradicts the other; one is not an example of the other; one does not support the other; etc.), put a "−" in the box. If your group is unsure of the relationship or cannot agree, put a "?" in the box.

The first one has been done for you (this is just a suggestion; people will sometimes have different opinions on some of the relationships between the vocabulary items and concepts). Here's an explanation for the first example:

> ***affliction*** *. . .is positively related (+) to Drug Addiction because*
>
> - *people suffer physically and psychologically when they take drugs.*
>
> *is positively related (+) to Drug Pushing because*
>
> - *if people didn't buy and use illegal drugs, they wouldn't suffer physically, emotionally, or economically from their addictions to them.*

is unclearly related (?) to the Legalization of Drugs because

- *some might say that it may decrease with legalization because addicts will get better treatment;*

- *others might say that it will increase because more people will buy and use drugs.*

	DRUG ADDICTION	DRUG PUSHING	LEGALIZATION OF DRUGS
affliction	✔	✔	?
black market			
condone the use of drugs			
crack babies			
decriminalizing drugs			
devastation			
epidemic			
hard drugs			
law enforcement			
lucrative market			
oblivion			
panacea			
petty criminality			
push their wares			
soft drugs			

VI.   SPEAKING

A ✔ CASE STUDY: THE HOLLAND MODEL

The following reading presents a true case that raises the issue of whether or not legalization would be an appropriate solution to the drug problem in the United States. Study the case.

Work in small groups. Discuss the implications of Holland's policy for the United States. Present your conclusions to the rest of the class.

In Holland, the drug policy is administered by the Minister of Welfare, Health, and Cultural Affairs. The policy takes a different view of drug problems:

Rather than *wage a war* on drugs, the Dutch have chosen to employ an approach called *Harm Reduction*. Essentially, what this approach assumes is that no country will ever be able to become "drug free," so the best approach to solving drug problems is to use methods that minimize the damage drugs do. How does this contrast with other countries that fight *drug wars*? For one, a drug war philosophy believes more arrests and more severe prison sentences will control drug use, whereas the Harm Reduction philosophy believes that criminalizing drug use only creates more black markets, more crime, and more health problems. In addition, drug war approaches use more police officers, whereas the Harm Reduction approach uses more health and social workers. The Dutch government's policy "tries to ensure that drug users are not caused any more harm by prosecution and imprisonment than by the use of drugs themselves." The Dutch don't claim to have found all the answers to the drug problem, but they do point out that their policy saves more lives than the policies of other countries.

In the 1970s, many young people were drawn to the city of Amsterdam because it was so easy to get marijuana and hashish there; Holland's attitude toward use of these drugs was quite relaxed. In the late 1970s, Holland went even further in relaxing its drug policies by eliminating criminal proceedings against hard-drug users. They also established clinics to administer methadone, a drug used as a substitute for heroine in drug treatment. The idea behind this policy was to treat addiction as a medical problem rather than a criminal one.

Today there are approximately 5,000 drug addicts registered in Amsterdam. About 4,000 are participating in the methadone programs. The average age of drug addicts is thirty-two, an indication that the age of drug addicts has risen in Holland over the years. Between the years 1981 and 1987, for example, the registered users younger than 22 years of age had already decreased from 14.4 percent to 4.8 percent. What's more, between the years 1981 and 1986, the number of people requesting drug-free treatment doubled.

The Dutch believe that the methadone clinics help to reduce their crime rate. If the 4,000 people using the clinics had to buy heroine to support their habit, they would be paying at least $78 a gram, which is only worth two doses of the drug. They say that crime would increase if all these people were not receiving the methadone.

In addition to reducing crime in Holland, Dutch policies have probably reduced the number of AIDS cases in Holland. Amsterdam administers approximately 7,000 injections each year to ensure clean needle use. In 1989, only about 80 of 884 AIDS cases were narcotics users. This figure is significantly lower than that of most countries: In Europe it is generally 23 percent, and in the United States it is 26 percent. The national health-care system supports a needle-exchange program in 52 cities in Holland. Buses cross the city districts giving out methadone and advice about AIDS. There are even machines on the street that will exchange needles for addicts. If a person puts a used needle into the machine, a new, sterile, wrapped needle comes out.

One of the key elements to Holland's drug policy is the distinction they make between soft drugs (marijuana and hashish) and hard drugs (heroine, cocaine, amphetamines, LSD, etc.). The Dutch policy holds that, if the two worlds of drug use don't get mixed up, there will be less tendency for young people to move into hard drugs after experimenting with soft drugs. Actually, the selling and using of soft drugs is illegal in Holland, but the police, prosecutors, and judges have developed a tolerant attitude toward them, as long as they are not done excessively. This attitude has been referred to as "flexible enforcement" in Holland. In Amsterdam, there are coffee shops with eight kinds of "illegal" marijuana on the menu. The Dutch believe that if people can freely buy and smoke the drug in such establishments, they will be less likely to try more dangerous drugs. Of course, if these coffee shops are caught selling hard drugs, the owners will be prosecuted and the coffee shop will be closed. Since the shops opened, marijuana and hashish consumption has declined, the Dutch say. Less than one percent of the population uses these drugs on a daily basis. Only 4 percent of teenagers have ever used them in their lifetime. According to statistics, American teenagers are three times more likely to smoke these drugs than Dutch teenagers.

Of course, critics of the Dutch model have pointed out that Holland is different from other countries, so their drug policies may not be so easily adopted in other contexts. The drug policies in Holland, which encourage forms of treatment that do not necessarily end addiction but do improve addicts' physical and social well-being, may not be most appropriate to other countries' situations. The Dutch like to use the analogy of their relationship to the sea in describing their drug policies: Holland is surrounded by water, a means of livelihood, but at the same time a threat. Though the Dutch have never conquered the sea, they have succeeded in controlling this "enemy." This realistic and matter-of-fact relationship with nature is how they like to approach many aspects of social life.

B   DISCUSSION QUESTIONS

Work in groups. Discuss your answers to the following questions.

1. Go back to the questions in the values clarification exercise (p. 95). Do you have the same opinions now, or have you changed your opinions in any way after examining the views of others?

2. Many people believe that the money used to punish drug users or drug pushers should be used for education instead. Do you think this change in spending would decrease drug use in the United States? Why or why not?

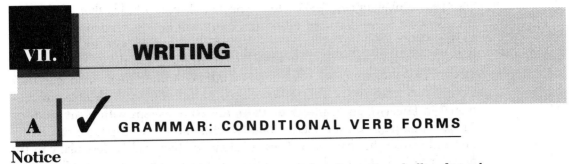

VII.   WRITING

A ✔ GRAMMAR: CONDITIONAL VERB FORMS

Notice

Notice the conditional statement taken from Campbell's editorial:

> *If a large portion of addicts **used** clinics rather than pushers, the number of pushers **would decline**.*

What is the author suggesting about the current situation? What suggestion is he making about changing the situation?

Explanation

The Present Unreal Condition

In the above example, a hypothetical idea was expressed. Campbell expresses an idea that is not yet true: The number of pushers declining. He proposes a condition that would make it true: Large portions of addicts using clinics rather than pushers to buy their drugs.

In these conditional sentences, the following pattern is used:

SUBORDINATE CLAUSE	MAIN CLAUSE
If + past tense	would could } + base verb might

The Real Condition

Imagine that Campbell saw the possibility of the number of pushers declining as a more real, immediate possibility because, for example, drugs had already been legalized. In this case, his sentence would read:

> *If a large portion of addicts **uses** clinics rather than pushers, the number of pushers **will decline**.*

In this example, the possibility of addicts using clinics is real. Clinics exist, and addicts have the choice to use them.

In these conditional sentences, the following pattern is used:

SUBORDINATE CLAUSE	MAIN CLAUSE
If + present tense	will + base verb

The Past Unreal Condition

In addition to present unreal and real conditions, we can express an idea about past events or situations, imagining different outcomes. In other words, if something other than what was true had happened, then something else would have been the result. For example, Campbell's sentence could read:

> *If a large portion of addicts **had used** clinics rather than pushers, the number of pushers **would have declined.***

This sentence implies that clinics had already been available but that addicts had chosen not to use them; they had used pushers to get their drugs instead. Consequently, the number of pushers did not decline.

In these conditional sentences, the following pattern is used:

SUBORDINATE CLAUSE	MAIN CLAUSE	
If + past perfect tense	would might } could	+ have + past participle
If + past perfect tense	would + base verb	

A past unreal condition can either be written with a past result or with a present result, depending on whether the result would be completed in the past or would still be true today.

Exercise

For each of the following, choose the appropriate conditional form to express an idea on the current drug legalization debate.

1. Some critics of legalization claim that if drugs were legalized, there

   _____ (be) more crack addicts.

2. If crack _____ (never, enter) the drug market, more U.S.

   lawmakers _____ (consider) decriminalization as a solution

   to the drug problem.

3. Both proponents and opponents of legalization agree that addicts

   _____ (probably, buy) more drugs, at least initially, if drugs

   are legalized.

4. If the U.S. government _____ (decriminalize) drugs, won't

   kids get the message that drugs are OK?

5. If the drug war _____ (be) more successful in the United States, government leaders _____ (never, propose) the legalization of drugs.

6. Some people believe that there _____ (be) fewer cases of alcoholism today if the prohibition of alcohol _____ (continue) after the 1930s.

7. Drug pushers _____ (not, be able) to make so much money if drugs are sold legally.

8. If the laws _____ (restrict) legal drug sales to adults, pushers will concentrate on selling drugs to kids.

9. Polls have shown that many Americans believe that even if we _____ (spend) more money on drug education than on law enforcement, drug use _____ (not, decrease).

10. If a prominent mayor such as Kurt Schmoke _____ (not, call for) the legalization of drugs in America, journalists _____ (not, pay) as much attention to the proposal.

B

WRITING STYLE: REFUTATION IN ARGUMENTATIVE WRITING

Notice

Notice the way Frederick B. Campbell, the author of "To Control Drugs, Legalize," develops his argument for the legalization of drugs.

What technique does Campbell use to try to convince his readers of the appropriateness of this policy?

Explanation

Campbell organizes his ideas according to arguments that have been presented by the opposition, those who are against the legalization of drugs. He then refutes the arguments of the opposition by offering evidence to show that they are wrong.

Exercises

1. For each of the arguments Campbell chose to discuss, paraphrase his refutation in one sentence. Be sure to use your own words. (The first one has been done for you.)

Arguments of (the people who oppose drug legalization)

Campbell's refutation

1. Legalization would mean that addictive drugs would be legally available to everyone.

Drugs would only be legal for people who are addicted to them.

2. Legalization would mean that pushers would be given free rein.

3. Legalization would have to work perfectly in order to be beneficial.

4. Legalization would increase drug-related problems.

5. Legalization would condemn addicts to oblivion.

6. Legalization would condone use of addictive drugs.

2. In her commentary, Linda Chavez refutes the arguments of those who advocate the legalization of drugs, but she does not always state directly what those arguments are. Imagine the arguments that have been presented to her. Refer to her commentary (pp. 97–98) and write a statement for each argument that she appears to be refuting. (The first one has been done for you.)

Arguments of those in favor of legalization

Chavez's refutation

1. *The best way to win the war on drugs is to legalize them.*

Legalizing drugs would amount to a surrender.

2.

Drug use would not diminish.

3.

Drug use hasn't diminished in countries such as the Netherlands or England.

4. _____   Lives would continue to be lost to
   _____   the ravages drugs inflict on the
   _____   bodies and spirits of those who
                               take them.

5. _____   Legalizing drugs might increase
   _____   the drug market by removing the
   _____   drug penalities.

6. _____   There's really no other answer
   _____   than "just say 'no' to drugs."
   _____

C   ESSAY QUESTIONS

Choose one of the following topics and write an essay. Try to integrate ideas, vocabulary, and writing techniques that you have studied in this unit. In this essay, try to incorporate the following:

- an introductory paragraph that presents both sides of the argument and clearly states your thesis;

- paragraphs (at least three) that develop your argument with supporting evidence;

- a conclusion that reinforces the position you have taken. It should also end with a new idea (a warning, prediction, value judgment) that has not been mentioned before.

1. Chavez states that drug legalization would amount to a surrender in the drug war. Campbell, however, believes that legalization is not necessarily a "surrender," and that it might begin to control the business of drug pushing.

   In your opinion, should drugs be legalized in the United States? Argue either for or against this proposal.

2. Think about these facts:

   - Legalization did not contain or even moderate the opium drug trade in China.

   - Decriminalization of drugs has proven to contain or moderate both soft-drug and hard-drug use in Holland.

   What determines whether legalization is an appropriate solution to the drug problems of a particular country? Write an essay in which you express your opinion.

BRIDGING AN UNCOMMON PAST WITH A COMMON FUTURE

6

"No Hablo Ingles" by
Frank Cotham.

" NO HABLO INGLÉS. "

I. ANTICIPATING THE ISSUE

Discuss your answers to the following questions.

1. Look at the title. Look at the cartoon. What do you think the issue of this unit will be?

2. What is the message or humor of the cartoon?

3. What do you know about the English-language movement in the United States?

BACKGROUND READING

Read the following text.

There is a new movement in the United States: the official-English movement. Although most Americans speak English, U.S. lawmakers have never proclaimed English the official national language. Today there are many people who would like to make that proclamation official.

In the early nineteenth century, many immigrants of different lands and tongues arrived in the United States; they were expected to learn English right away. Parents sent their children to American schools, where students were immersed in the English language. It was only by learning English that they could get an education and find a job in their new world. Yet, although people were expected to learn English (and generally did), English was never an official language.

With the more recent growth of a multicultural, multilingual society in the United States, as in other nations of the world, the question of whether or not its population should be required to share a common language has arisen. In order to accommodate the many language groups living in the U.S., government agencies, schools, and businesses often offer their services in other languages. For example, when Florida residents go to vote for local or national candidates, they can read their **ballots**₁ in Spanish. Non-English-speaking schoolchildren, often Hispanic or Chinese, may study in bilingual education programs, in which they are taught in their native language until they master English. In this way, the children are presumed to gain a sense of identity and self-confidence, which will help them succeed in the future.

Believing that the American people have become **disparate**₂ with multilingualism and that their common tongue, English, is the only thread that still binds Americans together, many people have proposed making English the nation's official language. In fact, many states have already passed legislation making English their official language. They feel that a common language is the only way to encourage people who have been ***lumped together*** to partici-pate fully in the country's democracy. They argue that immigrants cannot be ***woven*** into the culture of the American society without a ***common thread***, in this case "language," and they support their argument by pointing to history: the ***ancestors*** of many Americans came to the U.S. knowing no English but learned it quickly because it was ***indispensable*** for their integration; as a result, they became successful and "American." Supporters of making English an official U.S. language also refer to the examples of Canada and Belgium, countries that have been divided emotionally and politically into two language and cultural groups because of bilingualism.

Opponents of the official-English movement maintain that requiring all U.S. citizens to speak English deprives non-English-speaking Americans of their basic rights and is a violation of free speech. The opposition feels that offi-cial English would not lead to harmony in the United States but rather would promote xenophobia, the fear of foreigners and their cultures. Moreover, they see America as a more ***vibrant,*** interesting society because of its multilingual, multicultural composition. Ethnic pluralism, they say, is what has strengthened the United States.

With greater influxes of immigrants coming into the United States, the official-English movement has gained more support. Recently, many illegal immigrants were ***granted amnesty***. Since they have been given permission by the government to legally continue their residence in the United States, they are now freer to find jobs. This raises concerns about the role they will play in the American society. Some lawmakers fear an even greater tolerance toward multilingualism as a result of amnesty and have begun to ***enlist*** the support of American citizens to amend the country's Constitution, making English the official language.

Demographers predict different ethnic distributions in the U.S. popula-tion of the twenty-first century. An official language may or may not bind that population together. In a sense, the debate is not over a national language but over a national identity. Whether official English represents an attempt to preserve the nation's unity or a desire to return to an America in which all citizens resemble each other remains to be determined.

A   VOCABULARY

Look at the boldfaced words and phrases in the background reading. Try to determine their meaning. Match them with the synonyms or definitions below. Write the number next to the matching word or phrase.

_____ pardoned or forgiven by an authority, such as the government

_____ persons from whom one has descended

_____ put together without a common purpose

_____ essentially different

_____ something in common; something to hold people together

_____ people who study population trends

_1_   pieces of paper with lists of candidates, used in voting

_____ assimilated

_____ thrilling; exciting

_____ obtain or get (help or support)

_____ absolutely necessary

B   SUMMARIZING THE ISSUE

Work in small groups. Summarize the issue presented in the background reading. Take notes to complete the following outline.

1. The issue (*state in your own words*):

_____

_____

_____

2. Proponents' (of official English) arguments:

_____

_____

_____

(continued on next page)

3. Opponents' (of official English) arguments:

_____

_____

_____

C | VALUES CLARIFICATION

Work in small groups. Discuss your answers to the following questions.

1. Is there an official language in your country? Are immigrants to your country required to speak one language? What do you think of your nation's policies?

2. What is your reaction to the official-English movement in the United States? Do you see it as something that will bind or separate the nation?

III. OPINION 1: LISTENING

A ✓ LISTENING FOR THE MAIN IDEA

Listen to the commentary. Check the statement that summarizes the commentator's viewpoint.

☐ 1. All immigrants to America should be required to learn English.

☐ 2. We are a nation of immigrants with no common past or language.

☐ 3. The changing demographics of the United States will be beneficial to American society.

B | LISTENING FOR DETAILS

Read the following questions and answers. Listen to the commentary again and circle the best answer. Then compare your answers with those of another student. Listen again if necessary.

1. According to the commentator, what should hold true for new immigrants to the United States?

   a. They should learn English before they immigrate to the United States.

    b.   They should establish their place in America.

    c.   They should have similar language goals to those of early immigrants.

2. What do many of today's immigrants have in common?

    a.   They are of Hispanic origin.

    b.   They used to live in Mexico.

    c.   They live near Plymouth Rock.

3. What is changing in America?

    a.   the number of people in the United States

    b.   the expression on people's faces

    c.   the way Americans sound

4. What is required by law in some places?

    a.   neighborhoods where Spanish is spoken

    b.   voting in Spanish

    c.   Spanish classes for all schoolchildren

5. What happened in one school district in Texas?

    a.   Hispanic parents tried to get their children to speak only English at home.

    b.   Hispanic parents tried to get their children to speak only English at school.

    c.   Hispanic organizations objected to encouraging children to speak only English at school.

6. According to the commentator, why has the United States succeeded in becoming a nation with its own identity?

    a.   Its population is disparate but unique.

    b.   Its population speaks a common language.

    c.   Its population stems from ancestors who spoke English.

7. What will add to the richness of American society?

    a.   Americans must use their common past to build for the future.

    b.   America must increase its Hispanic population.

    c.   All Americans must speak the same language.

TEXT COMPLETION AND DISCRETE LISTENING

Read the text of the commentary. Try to fill in the missing words in the text as you remember them. Use your knowledge of text structure, vocabulary, and grammar to help you. Then listen again to the commentary to check your answers, stopping the tape as you fill in the blanks. If you have different answers than the original text, check with your teacher to see if they are acceptable alternatives.

Introduction

Mastering the English language once was considered _____ for immigrants seeking their place in America. Commentator Linda Chavez says this should hold true for the country's _____ immigrants as well.

Commentary

America is a nation of immigrants. Every once in a _____ , we're reminded of that simple fact. We were reminded of it last summer, when we celebrated the one hundredth anniversary of the Statue of Liberty. And we were reminded of it again in recent days as we watched thousands of illegal immigrants apply to live here legally under a new law that grants them _____ .

Many of these immigrants are Hispanics. They come from Mexico but also from _____ and South America and the Caribbean. And they join millions of other Hispanics, some of _____ trace their roots in what is now the United States to a time before the Pilgrims landed at Plymouth Rock.[1]

_____ tell us that by the year 2050, one out of every three persons living in the United States will be of Hispanic origin. The _____ of America is changing. So too, some warn, will the sound of America change. Already it is common in many parts of the country to encounter neighborhoods where little English is spoken, even in public. In some places, _____ are required by federal law to be printed in Spanish and other languages in addition to English. Many schools teach Spanish-_____ children in their native language, and all schools are required _____ law to allow

[1] Place where Pilgrims first landed in America in 1620.

such children to speak Spanish among themselves, on the playground or in lunchrooms, for example.

One school district in Texas that recently tried to _____ parents'
12
help in encouraging their children to speak only English while at school _____ the plan when Hispanic organizations objected, even though the
13
proposal had received early support from the parents themselves, who _____ thought it would help their children learn English more quickly.
14

One of the _____ that the United States has succeeded in becom-
15
ing a nation with its own identity and culture, despite the _____ nature
16
of its population, is that it has been bound by a common language. Many Americans—in fact, if _____ together, perhaps a majority of
17
Americans—did not have _____ whose original language was English.
18
Nonetheless, English is our language now.

We are a nation of immigrants with no _____ past, but with a com-
19
mon future. The bridge between the two has been and should continue to be our common English language. The United States is a richer and more _____ society because of its immigrant heritage. The increase in the
20
proportion of Hispanic Americans can add to the richness and vibrancy of this nation, but it can do so only if Hispanics, as all other ethnic groups, decide to be _____ into the culture of our society by the common _____
21   22
of the English language.

IV.   **OPINION 2: READING**

A   ✔   **READING FOR THE MAIN IDEA**

Read the editorial. Check the statement that summarizes the author's viewpoint.

☐   1.   Today, too many people are growing up not learning English in the United States.

(continued on next page)

☐ 2. Bilingual programs only hinder children's learning English.

☐ 3. The official-English movement is taking the wrong approach to language policy in the United States.

---

by Anna Quindlen

Argue, Don't Amend

I've heard so much about the good old days that I feel as if I've lived through them, even though I never walked five miles through the snow to school.[1] People left their doors unlocked. Everyone said "good morning" to everybody else. Women baked. Occasionally, a *naysayer* comes along and suggests that the Depression and segregation had their downside, but folktales have it that those were the days when the sun shone on the U.S. of A.

I got a letter mentioning the good old days not long ago from Alistair Cooke,[2] a handsome man with silver hair and tongue. Mr. Cooke is a *spokesman* for a group called U.S. English, which is shopping for a constitutional amendment declaring English our official language.

I was a little surprised that Mr. Cooke was a spokesman for U.S. English because I've never actually heard him speak U.S. English. I speak U.S. English. Mr. Cooke speaks English English, *mellifluous*, grand, and spoken in the U.S. only in those British Raj movies in which people ride on elephants.

But I was not at all surprised about the constitutional amendment, because the constitutional amendment has become the ne plus ultra[3]—pardon my French—of public discussion. Now that civil liberties and free speech have *proliferated* faster than *gerbils* in the seventh-grade science room, there's only one officially *sanctioned* way to tell the opposition that it's stupid, un-American, and should shut up. Amend the Constitution; end of discussion.

The good old days are always a part of these discussions. Show me an argument about gun control, and I'll show you a hunter who remembers when women were women, men were men, and a *musket* over the *mantel* made a design statement that said Liberty and Justice for All. U.S. English likes the good old days, too. Mr. Cooke says in his letter that he remembers visiting a public school in the Bronx in 1937 and sitting in on classes at which immigrants were learning English.

Those are not exactly the good old days I remember. I remember entire neighborhoods where people spoke Italian or Polish or Greek. Children often served as translators, so that if an encyclopedia salesman came to the door, he was told to go away by a very serious nine-year-old. There was no need for bilingual ballots; the *shop steward* told you who to vote for, if you voted at all.

The children of those immigrants grew up to read and speak English, to work and *prosper*, even to *sponsor* constitutional amendments. The folks at U.S. English are concerned that this will not happen today, and for good reason. Unfortunately, any study of our schools shows you that while

---

[1] Years ago, many school children lived in rural communities and walked long distances to school.

[2] A British historian, well known in the U.S.

[3] Highest point.

there are children who are not **conversant** with English, some of them are kids whose families have been in America for 100 years.

I have my own bilingual **bugaboos**. I think all French restaurants should be required by law to print menus only in English, so no one gets sweetbreads by mistake, and I'd like to knock all the Latin out of legal papers.

I like a good constitutional amendment as well as the next person (loved the First and the Nineteenth), but you can't **take them lightly**. Look at Amendments 18 and 21[4] if you want to see an entire nation caught with its reactions down.[5] Liquor is

prohibited; liquor is allowed. That should have been a fight in the kitchen, not an **incursion** into the **bedrock** of democracy.

I'm all in favor of fights in the kitchen. U.S. English can insist that some bilingual programs exist only to support bilingual administrators and may actually **hinder** children from learning English, and they would be right. Bilingual advocates can argue that learning initially in a native language helps assimilate immigrants and that there's no real danger of America becoming a bilingual nation, another Quebec. They would be right, too. The question can be settled on a case-by-case compromise basis, and no one will be satisfied. That's the American way—a good old-fashioned fight.

[4] Amendments to the Constitution: Eighteen prohibited alcohol use, Twenty-one repealed the prohibition.

[5] From the expression "caught with his pants down," meaning "in an embarrassing situation."

"Argue, Don't Amend," by Anna Quindlen, February 11, 1990. Copyright © 1990 by The New York Times Company. Reprinted by permission.

B   READING FOR AUTHOR'S INTENDED MEANING

Read the following statements. Do you think the author would agree (A) or disagree (D) with them? Write A or D next to each statement. Compare your answers with those of another student. If your answers differ, go back to the text to find out why.

_____ 1. The olden days must have been better than today.

_____ 2. Alistair Cooke would like the U.S. Constitution to be amended.

_____ 3. Alistair Cooke is arguing for a language he has never spoken.

_____ 4. Cooke speaks English beautifully.

_____ 5. Civil liberties and free speech have gone too far.

_____ 6. The good old days represent sexism and nationalism.

_____ 7. More people spoke English in the good old days.

_____ 8. Immigrants were less likely to make individual choices in the good old days.

_____ 9. The fact that there are children today who do not speak English is a problem.

_____ 10. French restaurants in the United States should be required by law to print their menus in English.

_____ 11. The U.S. Constitution should not have had to concern itself with liquor laws.

(continued on next page)

_____ 12. Some bilingual programs are corrupt and ineffective.

_____ 13. A case-by-case compromise is an unsatisfactory way to settle the question of bilingual education.

C WORD SEARCH

Find boldfaced words in the essay that have similar meaning to the following and write them below.

Nouns

structure above and around a fireplace: _____

basis: _____

union leader at the workplace: _____

a person who doubts or denies something: _____

attack on: _____

small rodents (animals) kept as pets: _____

a person speaking on behalf of a group: _____

firearm used by foot soldiers (now replaced by rifle): _____

concerns: _____

Verbs

delay: _____

succeed: _____

to present and support a proposal: _____

avoid recognizing their importance: _____

spread rapidly; increased: _____

Adjectives

adopted/approved: _____

familiar with or knowledgeable about: _____

sweet sounding: _____

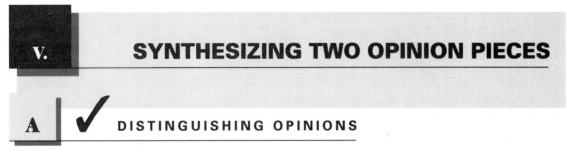

V. **SYNTHESIZING TWO OPINION PIECES**

A ✔ **DISTINGUISHING OPINIONS**

Authors can have different viewpoints, but their opinions can sometimes be similar. Review opinion 1 on pages 118–119 and opinion 2 on pages 120–121.

Work in groups. Read the statements below. Discuss whether Chavez and/or Quindlen would agree with them. Put a check (✔) in the box if you think they would agree. Leave the box empty if they would disagree or if there is no evidence to support the statement in their opinion.

Discuss how and why the two opinions are the same or different. (In the first statement, for example, Chavez would probably agree. She states that one of the reasons the United States has succeeded in becoming a nation with its own identity and culture is that it was bound by a common language. She is fearful that bilingualism will break that bond. Quindlen, on the other hand, would disagree. She points out that in the olden days, entire neighborhoods spoke other languages and that people couldn't even vote properly because they didn't speak English.)

	Chavez: Commentator (Opinion 1)	Quindlen: Author (Opinion 2)
America was bound together more strongly by English in the olden days.	✔	
The Constitution should be amended to make English the official language of the United States.		
Bilingual education may not help immigrants assimilate into the American culture.		
Allowing immigrants to speak their native language gives them more freedom and independence.		
The fact that many children will not learn English well is a legitimate concern.		
The United States is in danger of becoming a bilingual nation.		
Differences in heritage make the U.S. population more interesting.		

B GIVING YOUR OPINION

After you have distinguished the opinions of the commentator and the author, express your own opinions on the above statements. Discuss them with the other students in your group.

C VOCABULARY REINFORCEMENT: NOUNS

The following nouns come from the commentary and the editorial. Look at the nouns, then read the sentences. Complete the sentences with one of the nouns.

amnesty	ancestor	ballot	bedrock
common thread	demographer	incursion	musket
naysayer	spokesman		

1. The _____ of American democracy is found in the first ten amendments to the U.S. Constitution.

2. A _____ for U.S. English has called for an amendment to the Constitution.

3. A _____ of the effectiveness of bilingual programs will say that they only hinder children's learning of English.

4. A _____ can show us that the face of America is changing.

5. Many political refugees have been granted _____ around the world.

6. Opponents of the amendment feel that declaring English the official language of the United States would be an _____ into the multicultural society.

7. If a _____ is written in Spanish as well as English, it allows many non-English-speaking Hispanics to vote.

8. Many Americans can trace their roots to an _____ who immigrated to the United States from a European country.

9. Without the _____ of the English language, America may look like a disparate nation.

10. In the olden days, a soldier used a _____ rather than a rifle.

VI.   **SPEAKING**

A   ✔   **CASE STUDY: QUEBEC'S LANGUAGE POLICY**

The following reading presents a true case that raises the issue of whether an official-language policy is the best solution for a bilingual nation.

Work in small groups. Study the case to determine the strengths of the various proposals that have been made for Quebec's future. Discuss the various issues. Then present your own proposals for a redefinition of Quebec to the rest of the class.

Canada has been divided linguistically and culturally ever since British forces defeated the French on the Plains of Abraham in 1759. Despite the fact that Canada has been a partnership between French and English Canadians for a long time, French Quebec has never accepted that historical conquest.

For 115 years, Canada's constitution remained under the control of the British Parliament. In 1982, however, after a number of failed attempts, the constitution was finally "Canadianized," when the British gave up their control. Quebec, Canada's second largest province, did not sign the new document because it did not protect Quebec's distinct French linguistic and cultural heritage. Today, Quebecers are particularly concerned about this missing element of the constitution, as immigration has changed the face of Quebec and there is a current drop in Quebec's birthrate: In 1842, half the people in Canada were of French origin, but by 1990 that half had been reduced to a quarter. Quebecers fear that they could one day become a minority in their own province.

Since 1982, there has been great concern about Quebec's unique situation, and attempts have been made to bring the French-speaking Canadian province into the constitution. The most famous attempt was known as the Meech Lake Accord, in which five constitutional amendments were designed to accommodate Quebec's special demands. Those demands were the following: 1) the constitution should recognize Quebec as a "distinct society" within Canada; 2) Quebec should be given a veto over constitutional amendments; 3) Quebec should be given power over immigration into its territory to help maintain its French-speaking character; 4) provinces should be allowed to "opt out" of federal spending programs if they establish comparable programs that meet "national objectives"; and 5) provinces should be given a role in nominating senators and Supreme Court justices (who are currently appointed by the prime minister).

Two of Canada's ten provinces, Manitoba and Newfoundland, refused to ratify the Meech Lake Accord; consequently, it failed. The most controversial of Quebec's demands was the first: its demand for special status. To many

Canadians, this request was unreasonable. Quebecers, on the other hand, interpreted the failure of the Meech Lake Accord as Canada turning its back on Quebec. The ultimate failure of the accord represents two incompatible views of Canadian federalism: The view of many Quebecers that their province deserved special recognition and particular powers because of its French-speaking identity; and the view by most English-speaking Canadians that all provinces in Canada must be constitutionally equal. In addition, the failure of the Meech Lake Accord brought up a new issue of debate: Canada's natives had objected to the accord because it failed to acknowledge that they, like the Quebecers, were made up of a "distinct society." Their refusal to support the accord reminded Canadians of the country's unfair treatment of its 700,000 aboriginal people.

If the accord had been signed, many believe that the Quebec provincial government would have used its constitutional guarantees to further the interests of Quebec, in particular, its language policy. Several laws have already been passed to maintain, or as some see it, "impose," the French language in Canada. For example, all new immigrant children to Quebec must attend French schools, regardless of their country of origin. All national institutions in Canada are obliged to offer services in both French and English. Another law, known as Bill 178, prohibits outdoor signs and billboards in Quebec to advertise in any language but French; only indoor signs can be in English. The language laws of Quebec have not been received favorably by all Canadians, particularly English-speaking Quebecers. In fact, many English-speaking residents of Quebec have moved to other provinces.

Tensions remain high, and it is still unsure whether Quebec will be brought into Canada's constitution or go as far as breaking away from the confederation in favor of a separate nationhood. Ten years ago, a minority of residents of Quebec favored the idea of making Quebec a sovereign, independent province. But by the time the Meech Lake Accord failed, polls had shown that 63 percent of French-speaking Quebecers supported some form of separation from the rest of Canada, though it is not clear what form that separation would take: full independence; sovereignty inside an economic union; or simply a further loosening of Canada's confederation, similar to the goals of the European Community. Those who argue for separation point to Switzerland as a successful example of a sovereignty-association. Quebec's success in developing multinational business firms based in the province has given Quebecers confidence that they can succeed economically and politically on their own. Many Canadians have expressed the feeling that if Quebec really wants to leave, it should be allowed to do so and then survive on its own—without association to Canada. Other Canadians argue that every attempt should be made to preserve Canada's bilingual multicultural society and agree on a constitution that will unite Quebec with the rest of Canada as a federation. Still others suggest that the provinces could simply "agree to disagree" and allow Quebec's nonsigning of the constitution to persist.

Many issues must be considered for the future of Quebec: the preservation of its people's language and culture; the United States government's hope that Canada will stay together; a developing global economy; the many anglophones who have left Quebec for other provinces (e.g., since 1976, 14,000 of Montreal's management jobs have been lost to Toronto); the aboriginal Canadians and their demands for special status; the negotiations for dividing Canada's assets and liabilities if Quebec does separate; recent resistance of English-Canadians to support Quebec's demands; and economists' predictions that Quebec's sovereignty would *not* create a financial crisis.

B **DISCUSSION QUESTIONS**

In groups, discuss your answers to the following questions.

1. Go back to the questions in the values clarification exercise (p. 116). Do you have the same opinions now, or have you changed your opinions in any way after examining the views of others?

2. Discuss the meaning behind Anna Quindlen's statement: "Show me an argument about gun control, and I'll show you a hunter who remembers when women were women, men were men, and a musket over the mantel made a design statement that said Liberty and Justice for All." What point is she making with this statement? Explain how, for her, this is an analogy for the U.S.-English movement.

3. In what ways is the language problem in Canada similar to the official English movement in the U.S.? In what ways is it different? Discuss the similarities and differences between the two movements to enforce a language policy.

VII.   WRITING

A ✔ **GRAMMAR: ADJECTIVE CLAUSES**

Notice

Notice the structure of the underlined adjective clauses in these sentences taken from the commentary:

*a.   And they join millions of other Hispanics, **some of whom** trace their roots in what is now the United States to a time before the Pilgrims landed at Plymouth Rock.*

*b.   Already it is common in many parts of the country to encounter neighborhoods **where** little English is spoken, even in public.*

*c.   One school district in Texas **that** recently tried to enlist parents' help in encouraging their children to speak only English while at school dropped the plan when Hispanic organizations objected, even though the proposal had received early support from the . . .*

> d. . . . *parents themselves,* **who** *presumably thought it would help their children learn English more quickly.*
>
> e. *Many Americans—in fact, if lumped together, perhaps a majority of Americans—did not have ancestors* **whose** *original language was English.*

Discuss what each of the relative pronouns and relative adverbs (in bold print) refers to in each clause.

Which of the adjective clauses are introduced by a comma and which ones are not? Can you explain why?

Explanation

Like adjectives, adjective clauses give us information about nouns. They can be used effectively to combine two simple ideas into one, making sentences more complex and more sophisticated.

Adjective clauses are subordinate clauses that are linked by the relative pronouns: *who, whom, that, which, whose* or the special adjunct forms for time and place: *when* and *where.*

The above examples illustrate two types of adjective clauses: restrictive and nonrestrictive. In adjective clauses *b, c,* and *e,* the information that follows the relative pronoun or relative adverb cannot be taken out of the sentence. It is necessary in order to identify or explain the meaning of the noun in the sentence. In these restrictive adjective clauses, the clause is *not* separated by commas.

In adjective clauses *a* and *d,* however, the information that follows the relative pronoun *can* be taken out of the sentence; it provides extra information. It is not necessary in order to identify or explain the meaning of the noun in the sentence. In these nonrestrictive adjective clauses, the clause is separated by commas.

(Note: Avoid using the relative pronoun *that* in nonrestrictive adjective clauses; instead, use *who* to describe a person or *which* to describe a thing.)

Notice the special case of *a,* in which the quantifier *some* is used with the relative pronoun *whom.* This is a variation in the use of the nonrestrictive adjective clause. Other variations include: *none of whom, one of whom, both of whom, none of which, most of which, a little of which,* etc.

Exercise

Complete the sentences with the correct relative pronoun or adverb. Add commas where necessary.

1. Alistair Cooke _____ is a spokesman for U.S. English speaks English English.

2. Immigrant children _____ first language is not English may study in bilingual education programs before being mainstreamed into the English-speaking school system.

3. In the 1930s, there were entire neighborhoods in _____ only Italian, Polish, or Greek was spoken.

4. There are many children in the United States today _____ families have been in the country for more than 100 years and still don't speak English well.

5. The constitutional amendment _____ is being proposed by the group U.S. English would have an impact on schools and ballots.

6. Hispanic parents _____ originally thought their children could learn English more quickly if they spoke it at school objected to a proposal to make English the school's only language.

7. Some people remember a time _____ all immigrants were expected to learn English in the United States.

8. Many immigrants to the United States are Hispanics most of _____ come from Mexico, Central and South America, and the Caribbean.

9. Some Americans fear that the multilingual nature of their country will result in another Quebec _____ is a province with its own distinct language and culture.

10. Some people say that there is no proof that a constitutional amendment _____ makes English the official language of the United States would bind Americans together.

B   **WRITING STYLE: DICTION AND TONE OF VOICE**

Notice

Notice the way Anna Quindlen tries to convince her readers that a constitutional amendment is not a good idea.

How does her choice of words help to express her ideas in an exact way?

How does her attitude help to express her ideas in an exact way?

Explanation

Quindlen chooses words to mean exactly what she intends. Notice her diction (choice of words) in the following examples:

> Mr. Cooke speaks English English, **mellifluous, grand,** and spoken in the U.S. only in those British Raj movies in which people ride on elephants.

By choosing the words *mellifluous* and *grand* to describe Cooke's English, Quindlen purposefully separates his language from American English and makes a stronger point that he does not speak the same language as Americans.

> That should have been a fight in the kitchen, not an **incursion** into the **bedrock** of democracy.

Incursion is normally used in the language of combat. It is much stronger than if she had said *change*. *Bedrock* implies a strong base that cannot be destroyed because it is so firmly held in the ground. This word choice is stronger than if she had said *basis* or *foundation* of democracy.

Notice also that Quindlen changes her *tone of voice* (attitude) throughout her editorial to express different feelings toward the proposed official-English amendment.

She uses six different tones of voice:
1. Anger
2. Humor
3. Irony
4. Nostalgia
5. Resignation
6. Sadness

Exercise

Go back to Quindlen's editorial (page pp. 120–121). Look at her use of diction and tone. Refer to specific paragraphs of her editorial to answer the following questions.

Paragraph 1:

    a. Which expression does Quindlen use to express the negative consequences of the Depression and segregation?

    b. Which tone of voice is expressed by those who talk about "the good old days"?

Paragraph 2:

    a. Which words does Quindlen use to describe Alistair Cooke?

    b. Which verb does she choose to describe his interest in a constitutional amendment?

Paragraph 3:

    a. Which tone(s) of voice does Quindlen use when she describes where Cooke's English is spoken?

Paragraph 4:

    a. Explain the effectiveness of Quindlen's use of *ne plus ultra* in this paragraph. Why has she used a Latin phrase here?

    b. Which tone(s) of voice does she use at the end of this paragraph, when describing the attitudes of those who want to amend the Constitution?

Paragraph 5:

    a. Which tone of voice does Quindlen use in describing the good old days?

Paragraph 6:

    a. Which tone of voice does Quindlen use to describe her own perception of "the good old days"?

Paragraph 7:

    a. Which tone of voice does Quindlen use to describe the U.S. English people's concern that immigrant children will not grow up to work and prosper?

Paragraph 8:

    a. Which word does Quindlen use to describe her personal difficulties with the use of other languages?

    b. Which tone(s) of voice does she use in giving examples of these?

Paragraph 9:

    a. Which words describe Quindlen's preference for where discussions of language policy should take place?

    b. Which tone(s) of voice does she use in describing the Eighteenth and Twenty-first amendments to the Constitution?

C   ESSAY QUESTIONS

Choose one of the following topics and write an essay. Try to integrate ideas, vocabulary, and writing techniques that you have studied in this unit. In this essay, try to incorporate the following:

- an introductory paragraph that presents different sides of the argument and clearly states your thesis;

- paragraphs (at least three) that develop your argument with supporting evidence;

- a conclusion that reinforces the position you have taken. It should also end with a new idea (a warning, prediction, value judgment) that has not been mentioned before.

1. It has been argued that the official-English movement in the United States is a nationalistic movement, which, taken further, will promote xenophobic attitudes toward people of different language backgrounds, cultures, races, and religions.

   Do you agree with this argument, or do you share the opinion of those who feel that America has reached the point where a common language must be endorsed? Write an essay in which you express your opinion.

2. Several years ago, there was an effort to create an international language, known as Esperanto, in which all countries of the world could communicate efficiently. The movement never really caught on; few people ever really learned or spoke Esperanto. Instead, English seems to have become the language of international affairs.

   Write an essay in which you discuss your view of the use of English as an international language.

HAVE ALL THE HEROES DIED?

From: ELEMENTARY:
THE CARTOONIST
DID IT by Robert
Mankoff. Copyright ©
1980 by Robert Mankoff.
Published by arrange-
ment with Avon Books,
a division of the Hearst
Corporation.

"Very good, Gary: 'A hero is a celebrity who did something real.'"

I. ANTICIPATING THE ISSUE

Discuss your answers to the following questions.

1. Look at the title. Look at the cartoon. What do you think the issue of this unit will be?

2. What is the message or humor of the cartoon?

3. What do you know about heroes and/or role models?

BACKGROUND READING

Read the following text.

A hero, it is said, is someone who is "larger than life," whom we can admire for great qualities or abilities that we may never have. Our heroes reflect the values, hopes, and beliefs of a particular time. Heroes have included political and religious leaders, athletes, movie stars, and musicians.

In the United States, for example, political leaders who led the country to greater freedom and democracy have been heroes to many. George Washington, the nation's first president, John Kennedy, the vibrant young president who inspired hope, and Martin Luther King, the civil rights leader who fought for racial equality, all attained hero status among Americans. Sports was, and still is, the first source of heroes for many American children. Picture, for example, the 1930s sports stadium: a red-haired, ***freckled***-faced boy sits in the stands, magnetized by the style, grace, and actions of the larger-than-life athlete, Lou Gehrig, the famous baseball player who died of a nerve disease that was later named after him. That young boy was a true believer.

Today, however, many people say they do not have heroes. It is difficult to find an equivalent of Washington, Kennedy, King, or Gehrig. Political figures in today's world of leaders rarely, if ever, appear larger than life to us. In today's world of ***prying*** journalists and a television-age public, it seems difficult for anyone to attain heroic stature. What is worse, we now ***dredge up*** information about our past heroes, only to take away their heroism: we now know that John Kennedy ran around with other women; there appears to be evidence that Martin Luther King did, too. And today, more and more of our heroes have been forced to ***abdicate*** their hero status as new discoveries of their real lives have been made.

For athletes, the days of hero worship may be over as well, as more and more sports figures have been discovered breaking the rules of the game, exhibiting violent behavior in competition, using steroids to intensify muscle development, and abusing alcohol and drugs. Like political leaders of the past, heroic athletes of the past have fallen under the ***umbrella*** of "heroes with feet of clay," heroes with human frailties or weaknesses. Even the famous baseball hero, Babe Ruth, has fallen to shame in our modern world. Considered a hero for his outstanding record of home runs, overall excellence as an athlete, and generous contribution to the community, he was a model for many young boys. Today, however, his "model personality" is considered a ***sham***, and he is ***put down*** by many people. They now focus on his failures. Because he ate and drank too much, he had a ***potbelly,*** something that would never be tolerated in a baseball player today. And, like John Kennedy, he is criticized for having chased women, another unacceptable behavior in a modern-day hero.

With the loss of our heroes, then, what is left for us to **look up to?** The **buzzword** in today's language is "role model," someone whose behavior is "imitated," but not necessarily "courageous" or "heroic." Sports players continue to be regarded as role models by their fans and by the baseball team owners, who have an interest in "selling" the heroic quality of their players. Business leaders who have **stood up to** economic pressure to save American industry from failure have also been considered role models. Take, for example, Lee Iacocca, chief executive officer of Chrysler Corporation, who saved his corporation from bankruptcy and perhaps even prevented a **fatal** outcome to the American car industry. He persuaded American consumers to buy Chryslers for the good of America; consequently, many considered him a successful business role model.

But even being a role model in today's world is not easy. In fact, anyone daring to enter public life must have an ego big enough to survive the daily investigations into his or her personal affairs. Much of the public, critical of their poor behavior and drug use, has rejected ballplayers as role models. Players' unions, who represent the rights of ballplayers to be treated fairly and paid equitable salaries, will argue that baseball players are just normal people like everybody else, denying any special treatment of them. The business world has also shared in the loss of role models. In another example within the car industry, Roger Smith, chief executive officer of General Motors, is a man who could have, or should have, served as a role model in American business. Yet, he, like so many other public figures, allowed his ego to get in the way. Reports indicate that through bad management and selfishness he allowed his company to fail while his pension was raised; he retired from his position a millionaire.

If our heroes have died and our role models are scrutinized, what can be said about our society? Perhaps the **crux** of the issue lies in the fact that Americans have always looked to heroes and role models to exemplify traditional American values. Yet today's public has become ungrateful and ungenerous toward its public figures. It doesn't want to let them **get away with** having fame and fortune if they are not perfect human beings. Perhaps the public knows too much about them and has become too demanding, or perhaps today's role models are too self-possessed. But is living without heroes and role models a satisfactory state of affairs?

A   VOCABULARY

The following sentences are taken from the background reading. Try to determine the meaning of the boldfaced words and phrases. Write a synonym or your own definition of the word. Then check the answer key for suggested synonyms or definitions.

1. Picture, for example, the 1930s sports stadium: a red-haired, **freckled**-faced boy sits in the stands, magnetized by the style, grace, and actions of the larger-than-life athlete. . . .

(continued on next page)

2. In today's world of *prying* journalists and a television-age public, it seems difficult for anyone to attain heroic stature.

_____

3. What is worse, we now *dredge up* information about our past heroes, only to take away their heroism.

_____

4. And today, more and more of our heroes have been forced to *abdicate* their hero status as new discoveries of their real lives have been made.

_____

5. Like political leaders of the past, heroic athletes of the past have fallen under the *umbrella* of "heroes with feet of clay," heroes with human frailties or weaknesses.

_____

6. Today, however, his "model personality" is considered a *sham,* and he is put down by many people.

_____

7. Today, however, his "model personality" is considered a sham, and he is *put down* by many people.

_____

8. Because he ate and drank too much, he had a *potbelly,* something that would never be tolerated in a baseball player today.

_____

9. With the loss of our heroes, then, what is left for us to *look up to?*

_____

10. The *buzzword* in today's language is "role model," someone whose behavior is "imitated," but not necessarily "courageous" or "heroic."

_____

11. Business leaders who have *stood up to* economic pressure to save American industry from failure have also been considered role models.

_____

12. Take, for example, Lee Iacocca, chief executive officer of Chrysler Corporation, who saved his corporation from bankruptcy and perhaps even prevented a *fatal* outcome to the American car industry.

_____

13. Perhaps the ***crux*** of the issue lies in the fact that Americans have always looked to heroes and role models to exemplify traditional American values.

_____

14. It doesn't want to let them ***get away with*** having fame and fortune if they are not perfect human beings.

_____

B   **SUMMARIZING THE ISSUE**

Work in small groups. Summarize the issue presented in the background reading. Take notes to complete the following outline.

1. The issue (*state in your own words*):

_____

_____

_____

2. Examples of past heroes:

_____

_____

_____

3. Examples of present-day role models:

_____

_____

_____

4. Problems with heroes/role models today:

_____

_____

_____

C   **VALUES CLARIFICATION**

Work in small groups. Discuss your answers to the following questions.

1. Do you have any heroes or role models? Who are they, and why do you look up to them?

(continued on next page)

2. Do you consider athletes to be heroes/role models? What about corporate leaders? Why or why not?

3. In your opinion, have we lost our heroes? Do people need heroes? Why or why not?

III. OPINION 1: LISTENING

A ✓ LISTENING FOR THE MAIN IDEA

Listen to the commentary. Check the statement that summarizes the commentator's viewpoint.

☐ 1. There are no heroes in today's world, only role models.

☐ 2. Ballplayers should be considered heroes, in spite of their flaws.

☐ 3. There are no heroes anymore because no one can be perfect.

B LISTENING FOR DETAILS

Read the following questions and answers. Listen to the commentary again and circle the best answer. Then compare your answers with those of another student. Listen again if necessary.

1. Why was Lou Gehrig considered a role model?

    a. He was a lucky ballplayer.

    b. He made a lot of money.

    c. He died with courage.

2. What factor primarily contributes to the difference between owners and players in sports, according to Frank Deford?

    a. drugs

    b. the definition of the game

    c. the players' image to the public

3. What opinion does the commentator hold about players?

    a. The word *hero* should not be used to describe them.

    b.   They have a choice in whether or not they are role models.

    c.   They are role models to children.

4. What seems to irritate the commentator about players?

    a.   Ballplayers get paid more than most people.

    b.   Union people won't admit that the players are special.

    c.   Players like Babe Ruth chased women.

5. What excusable mistake did John Kennedy make, according to the commentator?

    a.   He had an affair.

    b.   He worked with the Mafia.

    c.   He argued with Khrushchev.

6. Why is it tougher to be a role model in today's world?

    a.   People are interested in other people's business.

    b.   It's a better world now.

    c.   The world has become more civilized.

7. Why are players wrong, according to the commentator?

    a.   They are too selfish to have children.

    b.   They don't assume their role as models for kids.

    c.   They allow themselves to replace saints, statesmen, educators, and preachers as kids' role models.

8. Who else do kids choose as their role models?

    a.   musicians

    b.   horse racers

    c.   car racers

9. What does the commentator think about ballplayers as role models?

    a.   They make good ones.

    b.   They are used too much as role models by the unions.

    c.   They can't be role models for adults.

10. Why does the commentator believe we live in a healthy society?

    a.   Our heroes can be like gods.

    b.   Heroes are human.

    c.   We let ballplayers be heroes.

C   TEXT COMPLETION AND DISCRETE LISTENING

Read the text of the commentary. Try to fill in the missing words in the text as you remember them. Use your knowledge of text structure, vocabulary, and grammar to help you. Then listen again to the commentary to check your answers, stopping the tape as you fill in the blanks. If you have different answers than the original text, check with your teacher to see if they are acceptable alternatives.

Introduction

"Today's the day I consider myself the luckiest man on the face of the earth" . . . Lou Gehrig saying good-bye to the _____ **1** at Yankee Stadium on July 4th, 1939. A hardworking ballplayer, dedicated to his family, Gehrig was courageous in his battle against a _____ **2** disease. He was a role model, the type of athlete that commentator Frank Deford says you don't hear much about these days.

Commentary

While drugs remain, and surely will so, the _____ **3** of the issue separating owners and players in all sports—the _____ **4** of dispute—involves the question of definition: how are players perceived?

Curiously, it's upside- _____ **5** . The players' unions—and this is a matter that crosses all sports lines—the unions maintain that players are just like everybody else while the owners argue that players are very special folks. Crazy, isn't it?

The _____ **6** is *role model*. For some reason, people are embarrassed to even use the word *hero* anymore. So ballplayers are, well maybe they are, role models. Unfortunately, being a role model is like being tall, or bald, or _____ **7** . You don't have any control over it. And, like it or not, kids are always going to make ballplayers their _____ **8** , their role models. This is one of the reasons that ballplayers get paid much more than most other folks.

So, I'm getting very tired of players and the players' _____ **9** people saying "they don't want to be role models; they're just like everybody else." I'm also getting very tired of people _____ **10** up poor Babe Ruth's name and then putting him _____ **11** . Babe Ruth was a terrific hero in his time.

People say, "See! What a _____ it all is! Babe Ruth drank too much, he
                                    12
ate too much, and he chased women." Yeah, but who knew? What they knew
was he hit home runs. John Kennedy was a terrific hero. OK, OK, he was committing adultery in the White House with a _____ mistress. But who
                                                        13
knew? What they knew was he _____ up to Khrushchev.
                                          14

Unquestionably, though, it's tougher all the time to be a totally successful
role model. It's a very _____ world. And you can't get _____
                                15   16
with the same stuff nowadays. Maybe this is good. It's a different world now.
Babe Ruth wouldn't have a _____ if he were a star today. Civilization
                                    17
marches on.

I think ballplayers, in their _____ and their self-centered escape
                                        18
mode, miss the point. Of course children should choose saints and statesmen
and educators and preachers as their role models, but you know very well that
they're not going to; that's why they're children, and also why they grow up to
be grown-ups.

Do you know who children also choose as their role models? Well, rock
singers, disc jockeys, anybody older who drives a red _____ car, come-
                                                                19
dians who say very dirty words out loud. These, by and large, are today's role
models for today's children. And, by comparison, ballplayers, I think, make very
good role models, indeed. I think the _____ ought to recognize that and
                                                20
make the players aware of it, too.

I have no idea where the idea grew up that sports was _____ to be
                                                                21
perfect. And just because it isn't, then everyone can go around talking about
Babe Ruth's failures of the flesh and _____ all personal reponsibility
                                                22
themselves. Children are going to _____ up to ballplayers, and so, for
                                            23
that matter, will some adults. And in a very honest way, this shows what a
_____ society we really are. Heroes have never been gods. Heroes, OK,
        24
"role models," are very _____ , and what is more human than a young
                                25
man with a number on his back able to deal with curveballs better than temptation? We're in a sorry _____ if we can't relax and let ballplayers be
                                26
heroes, the way they're supposed to.

IV.   **OPINION 2: READING**

A   ✔   **READING FOR THE MAIN IDEA**

The following editorial is written by Russell Baker, a humorist. He writes ironically about heroes and role models. (Notice, for example, how he plays with words in his title: He changes the normal spelling of "roll," describing movement, to "role," refer-ring to "role models.") Read the editorial. Check the statement that summarizes the author's viewpoint.

☐   1.   Society is obliged to provide role models.

☐   2.   Roger Smith is America's best role model in industry.

☐   3.   Today's role models have many failings.

by Russell Baker

Merrily We Role Along

First, you had to have a hero. Then all the heroes died, and those that didn't came down with terminal feet of clay. What a *pickle*.

For a while you could still find *bush-league* heroes in the newspaper business. These were reporters who specialized in exposing the old heroes.

Fearlessly, they lifted the old heroes' *trouser cuffs*, pulled aside their socks, ripped off their shoes, and showed the world the shame underlying the heroism: feet of clay.

Rot was *rampant* in the social fabric, however. Soon the reporter heroes were eating $50 lunches with two great wines and cognac in the coffee.

After lunch they raised their lecture fees to $15,000 per *yak*[1] and notified pub-lishers that bidding on their next book would start at $3 million.

They were so busy getting rich and famous they no longer had time to rip off any shoes but their own, which they did with decreasing frequency after discover-ing the clayey tale within.

---

[1] To talk too much; in this context, the author is humorously referring to a lecture.

With the hero's passing, America was ready for the role model, a burdensome job. At first some role models did not want to be role models, but there was no getting out of it.

Some baseball players who had used illegal narcotics, for instance, were given unusually *harsh* sentences because judges declared them to be role models.

This said that society was entitled to collect an especially *onerous* debt when feet of clay were discovered on a role model. The theory was that Americans were entitled to role models.

This was a drastic change from the age of heroes. Nobody had ever said the country was entitled to heroes. Now, though, not only were role models springing up everywhere, but serious people were also making serious arguments that society was obliged to provide them.

Just the other day, for example, a distinguished black professor of the Harvard Law School criticized the place for not having a *tenured* black woman on the faculty. Black female students, he reasoned, require a black female professor as a role model.

This astonished me. I have always thought that anybody lucky enough to get into the Harvard Law School *has the world handed over on a plate of solid silver* and can need nothing more in this life.

Apparently it is not so. Even these *blessed* few standing on the *threshold* of all the money, power, and glory that naturally accrue to the kids from Harvard Law—even these darlings of destiny now require role models.

Well, to make a long story short, I concluded that I had better take a role model, too. When matters reach a stage where even Harvard people need role models, it's obviously foolish to hang back.

So I am playing it safe. I have taken a role model. He is Roger B. Smith, the chairman of General Motors.

This was not a *hasty* choice. I considered a long roster of corporation giants under whose management American industry *has gone down the tubes* in recent years.

What I admired was the skill with which these captains of industry's decline were able year after year to collect multimillion-dollar salaries, bonuses, and stock handouts, and, when caught out in some egregious incompetence, to bail out unblushingly in golden parachutes[2] providing them with lifetimes of *lush* living.

I finally chose Mr. Smith as my personal role model not because General Motors has failed any more alarmingly than many others you could name, but because, as he retires, his pension is about to be raised from $700,000 to $1.25 million per year.

Suppose he had built a Cadillac that made Americans sneer at Mercedes-Benz and a Chevrolet that made them abandon their Hondas on the Cross Bronx Expressway. They would probably have *put him out to pasture* with a Timex[3] and a rocking chair. Where nothing succeeds like failure—that's where a man can feel almost as safe as a kid at Harvard Law.

[2] From "the golden handshake," often used when referring to big business deals.

[3] Traditionally, American companies have given workers a watch, such as a Timex, on retirement as a token of appreciation.

B   READING FOR AUTHOR'S INTENDED MEANING

Read the following statements. Do you think the author would agree (A) or disagree (D) with them? Write A or D next to each statement. Compare your answers with those of another student. If your answers differ, go back to the text to find out why.

_____ 1. Americans feel they need heroes.

_____ 2. Journalists can be considered heroes because they so skillfully exposed other heroes' failings.

_____ 3. Reporter heroes have feet of clay.

_____ 4. Americans create their role models.

_____ 5. Baseball players who used narcotics shouldn't have been sentenced so severely for their crime because they were role models.

_____ 6. Americans are entitled to role models.

_____ 7. Black female students at Harvard Law School need a black female role model.

_____ 8. Students at Harvard Law are destined for comfortable life.

_____ 9. Corporate leaders can be admired for their wealth.

_____ 10. Corporate leaders have not cared about the nation.

_____ 11. Mr. Smith built quality cars.

C   WORD SEARCH

Find boldfaced words in the article that have similar meaning to the following and write them below.

Nouns

difficult situation: _____

entrance or beginning: _____

bottom of men's pants: _____

bad stuff: _____

Adjectives

made too quickly: _____

luxurious: _____

widespread: _____

given a permanent teaching position: _____

mediocre: _____

burdensome: _____

fortunate: _____

severe: _____

Verbs (idiomatic expressions)

forced him to retire from a job: _____

has everything one could possibly ask for: _____

has failed: _____

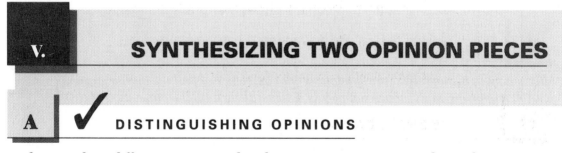

V. **SYNTHESIZING TWO OPINION PIECES**

A ✓ **DISTINGUISHING OPINIONS**

Authors can have different viewpoints, but their opinions can sometimes be similar. Review opinion 1 on pages 140–141 and opinion 2 on pages 142–143.

Work in groups. Read the statements below. Discuss whether Deford and/or Baker would agree with them. Put a check (✓) in the box if you think they would agree. Leave the box empty if they would disagree or if there is no evidence to support the statement in their opinion.

Discuss how and why the two opinions are the same or different. (In the first statement, for example, Deford would agree. He states that players say they don't want to

(continued on next page)

be role models and are like everybody else. Baker would also agree. He states that some role models did not want to be role models but that there was no way of their getting out of it.)

	Deford: Commentator (Opinion 1)	Baker: Author (Opinion 2)
Role models don't necessarily choose to be role models.	✓	
The use of drugs has affected the perception of role models in sports.		
Old heroes have been destroyed by the media.		
What people don't know about heroes is OK.		
It may be a good thing that we look for the failings of our heroes.		
There *are* still role models in today's world.		
We could be choosing better role models.		
Heroes are only human.		

B   GIVING YOUR OPINION

After you have distinguished the opinions of the commentator and the author, express your own opinions on the above statements. Discuss them with the other students in your group.

C   VOCABULARY REINFORCEMENT: CATEGORIZATION

Work in small groups. The following list of adjectives comes from vocabulary (or related forms of vocabulary) in the commentary and editorial. Discuss the meaning of each adjective and write it under the most appropriate category on the next page.

adulterous	burdensome	onerous	rotten
bald	freckled	potbellied	selfish
blessed	lush	prying	upside-down

Categorize adjectives from the list on the previous page that describe:

People's physical appearance:

_____

_____

_____

Something very positive:

_____

_____

_____

Antisocial behavior:

_____

_____

_____

Something changed from its normal condition:

_____

_____

_____

A difficult and weighty task:

_____

_____

_____

VI.   SPEAKING

A   ✔   CASE STUDY: JULIA ANNE MCGEE

The following reading presents a true case that was originally broadcast on the radio by Frank Deford, the commentator you listened to earlier in this unit. The case describes a situation in which heroism interferes with professionalism and raises the issue of whether or not special consideration should be given to a high-school hero.

Study the case.

Julia Anne McGee was, in the 1986–1987 school year, a tenured English teacher at the Campbell County Comprehensive High School. In her first period class, one of her students was a young man named John Garner. Not only did Garner often fail to show up for class, but he would not do makeup work, which Ms. McGee leaned over backwards to assign him. Finally, on January 12, 1987, and in strict accordance with the rules, Ms. McGee gave young Garner an "F."

(continued on next page)

The following things happened in short order: A considerable hue and cry arose. Certain elements in Campbell County threatened and intimidated Ms. McGee. A petition was prepared by another member of the faculty and passed around school, calling for Ms. McGee's dismissal. The principal himself contacted her father and asked him to bring pressure upon his own daughter to fix Garner's grades. He also suggested that if she did, he, the principal, would give her a good evaluation. A bullet was fired through Ms. McGee's automobile windshield as she returned from a psychiatrist's office, for by now Ms. McGee was under treatment for stress and depression occasioned by these events. And then buttons were sold on school property and at school events where board of education members were present, the buttons celebrating the shooting. One button said, "I didn't shoot Anne McGee . . . I tried but missed."

At one point, Ms. McGee was too emotionally upset to complete her teaching assignments, and even though she was under care of the psychiatrist by now, the superintendent of schools ordered her back to school. When she didn't return, the superintendent suspended her. The board of education supported the superintendent, finding Ms. McGee guilty of abandonment of her position, refusal to return to work, insubordination, and dereliction of duties. The board then fired Ms. McGee. There is no testimony that she had been subject to dismissal before she gave the one "F" to the one student.

Probably it will come as no surprise to you at this stage to learn that that student, John Garner, was the star of the Campbell County basketball team. The "F" Ms. McGee gave him, you see, made him ineligible. Ms. McGee took her case to the County Chancery Court, which found for her, ordering her reinstated to teaching with all stature and benefits. But still not satisfied, the superintendent of schools, Kenneth Smiley Miller, filed an appeal, seeking that her dismissal be approved.

Prepare for a role play. Read the situation and the roles, and follow the procedure.

The Situation

After the bullet was fired through Ms. McGee's car windshield, a local television station considered broadcasting an interview program in which the various people involved in Ms. McGee's case could express their views of the situation. Television journalists will interview the various people involved in the story on tomorrow evening's news program.

The Roles

Group A:

Julia Anne McGee
Other teachers at the school
The psychiatrist

Group B:

John Garner
Students from Campbell County Comprehensive High School
Campbell County basketball team players

Group C:

The school principal
Members of the board of education
Kenneth Smiley Miller, superintendent of schools

Group D:

The newspaper journalists

The Procedure

1. The class divides into four groups. Each group prepares its view of Ms. McGee's case. (Individuals can prepare arguments based on their particular roles.)

2. The television journalists prepare specific questions for each of the groups and individuals involved in the case.

3. The journalists ask specific questions of each group, trying to balance the views in their interview.

4. The journalists thank everyone for appearing on the program.

B   DISCUSSION QUESTIONS

In groups, discuss your answers to the following questions.

1. Go back to the questions in the values clarification exercise (p. 137). Do you have the same opinions now, or have you changed your opinions in any way after examining the views of others?

2. Is the obsession with heroes and role models typically American? If so, what is it about the American culture that makes people need heroes or role models?

3. Do heroes reflect the values of a culture? What areas of life should role models be drawn from?

WRITING

A ✔ GRAMMAR: CONJUNCTIONS OF CONCESSION

Notice

Notice the use of "while" in each of the following statements that were made by the commentator:

> **While** *drugs remain . . . the crux of the issue separating owners and players in all sports—the umbrella of the dispute—involves the question of definition: How are players perceived?*

In this sentence, does the commentator have an opinion? If so, what is it? What is the meaning of "while" in the preceding sentence?

> *The players' unions maintain that players are just like everybody else,* **while** *the owners argue that players are very special folks.*

In this sentence, does the commentator have an opinion? If so, what is it? What is the meaning of "while" in the preceding sentence?

Explanation

Concession is used when a speaker or writer wants to acknowledge a commonly held point of view but make a point stronger or present an opposite point of view.

Concession is useful in both speaking and writing. Acknowledging another or more commonly held view strengthens a speaker's or writer's own argument. The following conjunctions are commonly used to concede a point:

though
even though
although
while   }   + a clause
even if
regardless of the fact that
in spite of the fact that
despite the fact that

Examples

> **<u>Even though our heroes have died,</u>** *role models still provide an example for many people.*

> **<u>Despite the fact that our heroes have died,</u>** *role models still provide an example for many people.*

Exercise

Combine the following sentences to incorporate phrases of concession. Use the information you heard in the commentary or read in the editorial to help you decide which sentence is concession and which sentence is the commentator's or author's point of view. Then write one sentence. You may have to make minor changes. (The first one has been done for you.)

1. Babe Ruth was a terrific hero in his time.   Babe Ruth ate and drank too much.

    (Commentator's viewpoint)

    _Babe Ruth was a terrific hero in his time_____, regardlesss

    of the fact that   _he ate and drank too much_____ .

2. Children will always look up to ballplayers.   It is an unfortunate fact that children make ballplayers their heroes.

    (Commentator's viewpoint)

    Although _____

    _____ .

3. A ballplayer should be considered a hero.   People are embarrassed to use the word *hero*.

    (Commentator's viewpoint)

    Even though _____

    _____ .

4. Reporter heroes tried to show the world the shame underlying old heroes.   Reporter heroes had feet of clay, too.

    (Author's viewpoint)

    In spite of the fact that _____

    _____ .

(continued on next page)

5. John Kennedy was a heroic president.

   (*Commentator's viewpoint*)

   While _____

   _____.

   It is said that John Kennedy had affairs.

6. Children choose ballplayers and rock singers as their heroes.

   (*Commentator's viewpoint*)

   _____

   even if _____.

   Children should choose saints and educators as their heroes.

7. The public chooses who it wants as role models.

   (*Author's viewpoint*)

   _____

   even though _____.

   Some role models do not want to be role models.

8. Players have failures or shortcomings.

   (*Commentator's viewpoint*)

   Though_____

   _____.

   Players make very good role models.

9. Harvard Law students want to have role models.

   (*Author's viewpoint*)

   Despite the fact that _____

   _____.

   Harvard Law students have the world handed over on a plate of solid silver.

B   WRITING STYLE: ILLUSTRATION

Notice

Reread the fourth paragraph of the commentary on page 140. How does commentator Frank Deford support his idea that role models of the past could be role models because no one knew about their behavior?

Explanation

In the fourth paragraph of his commentary, Deford supports his opinion about past role models through illustration. He cites both Babe Ruth and John Kennedy as two examples of past heroes who have lost their heroic status.

The use of such examples makes ideas more concrete and lends support to generalizations. We have seen two ways to support a main idea through illustration:

a.   A series of examples:

Do you know who children also choose as their role models? Well, **rock singers, disc jockeys, anybody older who drives a red sports car, comedians who say very dirty words out loud.** *These, by and large, are today's role models for today's children. And, by comparison, ballplayers, I think, make very good role models, indeed. I think the unions ought to recognize that and make the players aware of it, too.*

b.   One extended example:

What I admired was the skill with which these captains of industry's decline were able year after year to collect multimillion-dollar salaries, bonuses, and stock handouts, and, when caught out in some egregious incompetence, to bail out unblushingly in golden parachutes providing them with lifetimes of lush living.
     I finally chose Mr. Smith as my personal role model not because General Motors has failed any more alarmingly than many others you could name, but because, as he retires, his pension is about to be raised from $700,000 to $1.25 million per year.
     Suppose he had built a Cadillac that made Americans sneer at Mercedes-Benz and a Chevrolet that made them abandon their Hondas on the Cross Bronx Expressway. They would probably have put him out to pasture with a Timex and a rocking chair. *Where nothing succeeds like failure—that's where a man can feel almost as safe as a kid at Harvard Law.*

Exercise

Each of the following is a topic sentence that could be developed into an interesting paragraph with illustration. Choose one or two and write a complete paragraph for each. Develop the main idea with either a series of examples or one extended example, as indicated.

1. Today's role models are not the same as yesterday's heroes. (Use several examples.)

2. Without heroes to emulate, children have no sense of what they should try to become. (Use one extended example.)

3. The only reason our heroes have disappeared is that today we expect them to be perfect. (Use several examples.)

4. Because of the media's influence, no person is able to become a hero anymore. (Use several examples.)

5. Sports heroes are totally appropriate role models for children. (Use one extended example.)

C — ESSAY QUESTIONS

Choose one of the following topics and write an essay. Try to integrate ideas, vocabulary, and writing techniques that you have studied in this unit. In this essay, try to incorporate the following:

- an introductory paragraph that clearly states your thesis;

- paragraphs (at least three) that develop your argument with supporting evidence;

- a conclusion that reinforces the position you have taken. It should also end with a new idea (a warning, prediction, value judgment) that has not been mentioned before.

1. Heroes vary greatly from one culture to another. Consider the differences between the heroes in your country/culture and those in America. Write an essay in which you compare and contrast the two types.

2. It has been said that no one remains a hero if you get to know him or her well enough. What does this mean? Do you agree or disgree? Is it impossible to find a true hero today? Was it ever possible? Write an essay in which you discuss your opinion.

THE RIGHT TO DIE VS. THE RIGHT TO LIFE

I. ANTICIPATING THE ISSUE

Discuss your answers to the following questions.

1. Look at the title. Look at the cartoon. What do you think the issue of this unit will be?

2. What is the message or humor of the cartoon?

3. What do you know about the right-to-die vs. the right-to-life controversy?

BACKGROUND READING

Read the following text.

With unprecedented advances in medical technology, a debate has developed over whether or not a person on life support has the right to die. On one side of the debate are those who say that withdrawing a feeding tube or turning off a *respirator* gives doctors the power to take another's life. On the other side is the view that fundamentally personal decisions about whether to continue living in an irreversible coma should be left to an individual or a family. This debate over *euthanasia*, the painless death of persons suffering from a disease, involves conflicting *ethics:* moral, religious, and even political. As we advance toward the future, these ethics will involve the lives, deaths, and destinies of more and more people.

Possibly the most widely reported case in the euthanasia debate was the Nancy Cruzan case, which involved a thirty-two-year-old woman from Missouri who existed for many years in a "persistent *vegetative* state" after a car accident. Her parents lived with the *trauma* of their daughter's *coma* for years before deciding to do something. Although she had rested in a *serene* state in her hospital bed for seven years, they did not want her to continue treatment that would keep her in the state they knew Nancy would not want to be in. But when her parents *petitioned the court* to disconnect the feeding tube that was keeping their daughter alive, their request was ultimately denied. The lower-court ruling was later supported by the Supreme Court. Without "clear and convincing evidence" that Nancy Cruzan would have wanted her life-sustaining treatment to end, the Court held that the state is free to carry out its interest in "the protection and preservation of human life." Right-to-life activists have used the Court's decision to support their cause.

A less known case involved an eighty-eight-year-old woman from New York whose sister had obtained legal permission to remove her feeding tube, but that permission was later withdrawn. The woman's doctors had given the *prognosis* that the woman would remain in a hopeless state with no chance of recovery. However, before the feeding tube was removed, she improved and began talking and eating on her own. The doctors could not explain how the woman had *revived,* and defined her improvement as a *miracle.* Later, when the woman was asked what she would wish to have done in her case, she responded, "These are difficult decisions," and went back to sleep. The next day she said that she wanted to wait on a decision. Right-to-life activists have pointed to this case, too, to support their defense of, whom they call, "vulnerable people."

Right-to-die activists, in contrast, contend that decisions about treatment for the dying should belong to the patients and their families. Other court cases have, in fact, ruled in their favor. When Paul Brophy, a fire fighter, lapsed into a vegetative state, his wife managed to get hospital officials to remove his feeding tube, as he had stated that he would never want to live in a coma. Many people now write "living wills" stating their wish for euthanasia, in case they ever end up in a vegetative state. Patients who can make their wishes known are also being granted the right to end their lives. Larry McAfee, who was paralyzed from the neck down in a motorcycle accident, said that he did not want to exist in his present state. A judge ruled that he could **unhook** his respirator and die, supporting McAfee's belief that it was not prolonging his life but prolonging his death. In still another case, Dr. Jack Kevorkian assisted an Alzheimer's[1] patient in dying with his "suicide machine," a machine he had created to help terminally ill patients end their lives. The machine caused the woman to die of a **massive heart attack.** The court did not find the doctor guilty of murder, as the patient had clearly chosen and administered her own death. Many people, in fact, found the patient to be a courageous pioneer, as she had taken control of the circumstances of her own death before it was too late.

The debate over euthanasia will only become more complex as medical technology continues to grow and improve. There are those who contend that it will soon become just part of medical treatment, others who believe that its potential power of eliminating people will prevent it from becoming a solution for human suffering. Most people hope neither they nor their family members will ever have to confront this issue.

[1] A serious disease that causes the deterioration of mental ability.

A   VOCABULARY

Look at the boldfaced words and phrases in the background reading. Try to determine their meaning from the context. Then, complete the following sentences to show you understand their meaning. Compare your sentences with those of another student. Check a dictionary if you disagree about the meanings.

1. A **respirator** is used to help someone _____

   _____

2. **Euthanasia** has not yet been accepted for humans, but it has been for _____

   _____

3. One place that children might learn **ethics** is in _____

   _____

4. If someone is in a **vegetative** state, he or she can't _____

   _____

5. If you experience a **trauma,** you probably feel _____

   _____

(continued on next page)

6. A **coma** is often described as a deep _____

_____

7. If someone has a **serene** look on her face, she probably looks _____

_____

8. You might have to **petition the court** if you _____

_____

9. If a doctor's **prognosis** is not good for a terminally ill patient, it usually means

_____

10. If a person becomes unconcious but is then **revived,** he can _____

_____

11. An example of a **miracle** is _____

_____

12. Something that you might **unhook** is _____

_____

13. If a person has a **massive heart attack,** he _____

_____

B   SUMMARIZING THE ISSUE

Work in small groups. Summarize the issue presented in the background reading. Take notes to complete the following outline:

1. The issue (*state in your own words*):

_____

_____

_____

2. Proponents' (of euthanasia) arguments:

_____

_____

_____

3. Opponents' (of euthanasia) arguments:

_____

_____

_____

C | VALUES CLARIFICATION

Work in small groups. Discuss your answers to the following questions.

1. Do you tend to agree with the arguments of the "right-to-die" or "right-to-life" advocates? Who do you think is the best to decide the future of a comatose or terminally ill person: family, lawyers, the court, religious leaders, or someone else? Why?

2. Is the situation of a person who is not in a coma but who knows that he or she will soon die or deteriorate from a disease different from that of a comatose person? Should people who can make clear decisions about their destiny be allowed to choose death?

III. | OPINION 1: LISTENING

A | ✓ LISTENING FOR THE MAIN IDEA

Listen to the commentary. Check the statement that summarizes the commentator's viewpoint.

☐ 1. To allow someone to die takes courage.

☐ 2. The right to die cannot be accepted until we answer specific ethical questions.

☐ 3. Keeping people alive on life-support systems can be cruel.

B | LISTENING FOR DETAILS

Read the following questions and answers. Listen to the commentary again and circle the best answer. Then compare your answers with those of another student. Listen again if necessary.

1. What is often argued?

    a. Who should end a life

    b. When a life should be ended

    c. Why a life was ended

(continued on next page)

2. What happened to Gerard's mother?

    a. She was diagnosed with Parkinson's disease.

    b. She was admitted to the hospital.

    c. She lived through a heart attack.

3. What difficult choice did Gerard's father have to make?

    a. Whether or not to use a respirator in his wife's treatment.

    b. Whether or not to let his wife die

    c. Whether or not to pressure the doctors to save her

4. The doctor's prognosis was that

    a. Gerard's mother would probably come out of her coma.

    b. his mother would suffer more brain damage.

    c. his mother would always be in a vegetative state.

5. Why wasn't the family allowed to let her die?

    a. Under state law, once she was on a respirator, she must stay on it.

    b. A court order refused the family the right.

    c. She had the chance to live for ten more years.

6. Gerard's mother's coma can be best described as

    a. serene.

    b. convulsive.

    c. nervous.

7. Why didn't Gerard turn off his mother's machine?

    a. He was afraid she wouldn't die in peace.

    b. Someone would have found out within a few hours.

    c. He wasn't courageous enough.

8. Why did the hospital wean his mother off the life-support system?

    a. She could only breathe through a tube in her throat.

    b. She had lost too much weight to continue full treatment.

    c. State law required a gradual reduction.

9. What conclusion does Gerard reach about this experience?

    a. Euthanasia is an ethical issue that needs far more discussion and argument.

    b. Human beings are basically cruel.

    c. The prolonging of his mother's life was inhumane.

C   TEXT COMPLETION AND DISCRETE LISTENING

Read the text of the commentary. Try to fill in the missing words in the text as you remember them. Use your knowledge of text structure, vocabulary, and grammar to help you. Then listen again to the commentary to check your answers, stopping the tape as you fill in the blanks. If you have different answers than the original text, check with your teacher to see if they are acceptable alternatives.

Introduction

It is often argued that no one on _____ is equipped to judge the proper
                                    1
moment to end a life. But, in fact, people make those decisions every day. And

commentator Philip Gerard found sometimes they live to _____ their
                                                          2
choices.

Commentary

Just over a year ago, after fighting Parkinson's disease for almost ten years, my

mother suffered a _____ heart attack. She survived it only because she
                       3
was already in the hospital. She stopped breathing for at least eight minutes,

possibly as long as half an hour, before she was _____ by extraordinary
                                                       4
means: defibrillator, adrenaline, the whole crash-cart, Code-Blue scene.[1] My

father got a phone call demanding that he make an immediate choice: Put my

mother on a _____ or let her die right then. Under pressure and unpre-
                 5
pared for the awful circumstances, my father made the instinctive, human

choice: Try to save her.

At the hospital, the doctors gave us their _____ . For my mother to
                                                6
come out of her coma would be a _____ and a hideous one. The mas-
                                     7
sive brain damage would leave her in a persistent _____ state. Then,
                                                        8
the family decided, unhook the machine and let her die. Impossible, the doc-

tors said. Under state law, once my mother was _____ up to the
                                                      9
machine, she could not be unhooked without a court order. She might live for

as long as a decade. My father would have to _____ the court to allow
                                                   10
his wife of forty years to die.

When I first heard the word "coma," I imagined _____ catatonia.[2]
                                                     11

[1] A hospital emergency; in a hospital, a call for immediate medical assistance.

[2] Total lack of movement; maintaining one position over a long period of time.

But my mother's coma began as constant convulsions. With each _____
12
the respirator shoved into her lungs, her body shuddered. She frothed at the
mouth. Her eyeballs rolled back, white, into her head. She was _____
13
down to the bed or she would have fallen to the floor. This lasted day and night
for three days. After that, her nervous system virtually destroyed by the unrelieved _____ , she quieted. My sisters and I took turns sleeping on a cot
14
in my mother's room. We didn't want her to be _____ when she died.
15

After a week of that, I recall lying awake into the small hours of a snowy
morning, listening to the _____ of the monitors and the "suff'ing" of the
16
respirator. I prayed for the _____ to turn off the machine and let her
17
die in peace. It would have been easy—just click off the toggle. No one would
have _____ for hours.
18

I didn't have the courage.

My mother _____ three months. In the end, she was breathing
19
through a tube permanently inserted in her throat. She _____ almost
20
nothing. The doctors were keeping tissue alive, but the woman was long gone.
Honoring state law, the doctors _____ her off the respirator a little each
21
day, forcing her to labor for every breath. They said she was in no pain, but her
face contorted and her body convulsed. Then she died.

You can argue the fine medical _____ of the thing. All I can add is
22
this: I'd whip any man who treated a dog so cruelly.

IV. **OPINION 2: READING**

A ✓ **READING FOR THE MAIN IDEA**

Read the editorial. Check the statement that summarizes the author's viewpoint.

☐ 1. It is costing society a great deal of money to keep people alive at
any cost.

☐   2.   Living wills may be the best solution for unreasonable life support.

☐   3.   We must work toward respecting life, as we don't know the consequences of euthanasia.

MORE ON WHEN TO DIE

by William F. Buckley, Jr.

NEW YORK, JULY 11

I had at school a most *provocative* professor who liked mean questions, meanly formulated, because he liked to make his students think—"an agonizing alternative in your case," he might have said. One day it was announced that medical science had come through with a cure for, I forget what it was: some form of pneumonia. "What," the professor said, "are we supposed to die of?" And indeed if it were all an abstract game, and we counted 977 *extant* terminal diseases for each one of which medical science in due course came up with a cure, that would leave us nothing to die from save just plain decomposition of the flesh. It is generally agreed, if I read science correctly, that this is the one process that cannot be *arrested*. Inevitably, human beings being rational animals, thought is given to such questions as: Are there preferable ways to die than through biological decomposition?

A provocative book was published last year. It is called *Setting Limits*, with the explanatory subtitle, *Medical Goals in an Aging Society*. Its author, Daniel Callahan, is what one calls a bioethicist, someone who considers the ethical implications of biological developments. Mr. Callahan is the director of the Hastings Center, which he founded, and which inquires into such questions as—well, setting "limits" to *viable* lifetimes.

Callahan tells us that at the current rate of increase in *longevity*, the cost of maintaining the most senior population in America will by the end of the century (which is not very far away) come to $200 billion a year. Mr. Callahan is not a penny-pincher, but his point is that we may be engaged in *subsidizing* a great deal of agony as the result of our *preoccupation* with keeping people alive at any cost.

Most Americans are familiar with the *creeping* availability of what the lawyers call "*living wills*." These vary from state to state but have in common their search for a legal instrument by which an individual can, with *forethought*, specify the conditions under which he desires to be permitted to die. What Callahan uniquely advances is the idea of a living will in effect generally accepted by society at large, and one that focuses on a particular age. For instance, how would one greet the proposal that no publicly funded nursing home or hospital could finance a costly operation (say a heart bypass) for anyone over the age of 85?

The prospect of a corporate position on the right age to die is properly horrifying. Callahan goes so far as to include as an acceptable *stratagem* the removal of food and water from old people who are *insensate* and would not feel the pain of their *mortal* deprivation. Such a proposal is shocking to moralist Nat Hentoff of *The Village Voice*, who comments, "If an old person is diagnosed as being in a *chronic* vegetative state (some physicians screw up this diagnosis),[1] the Callahan plan *mandates* that the feeding tube be denied or removed. No one is certain whether someone actually in a persistent vegetative state can *feel* what's going on while being starved to death. If there is sensation, there is no more horrible way to die." And then medical experts tell you that the cost of feeding insensate people is about the most inexpensive thing in medicine. True, it costs $20,000 a year to maintain someone in a nursing home. But to feed such a person through tubes costs only $10 per day.

The root question—here Hentoff wins the argument, I think—is moral, not *empirical*. If life is a divine gift, as Christians are taught to believe it is, then interruptions of it by acts of commission (suicide) or omission (a refusal to accept medical aid) are wrong. What the bioethicists search for is the ground in between. And the influence here of Pope Pius XII's exhortation in 1957 is critical for many Catholics and non-Catholics. What he said was that although no one may *collude* in any act of suicide, neither is the Christian required to take "extraordinary measures" to maintain life. In the famous case of Karen Ann Quinlan in New Jersey, the priest and the courts authorized the removal of the respirator from the comatose patient (ironically, she lived on for nine years).

The whole business *torments*, especially since more and more people have come into personal contact with the dying patient who comes to look upon medicine as a form of *torture*, given that its effect is to prolong life, and to prolong life for some is to prolong pain. No doubt, in the years to come, a working formula of sorts will emerge. It is critically important that it accept the moral implications of the question. If a society is ready for euthanasia, it has rejected the primary attribute of life: namely, that it is God-given.

Taken from the "On The Right" column by William F. Buckley, Jr. Copyright © 1988, Dist. Universal Press Syndicate. Reprinted with permission. All rights reserved.

---

[1] Do incorrectly.

B READING FOR THE AUTHOR'S OPINION

Read the following statements. All of the statements refer to ideas expressed in the article, but only some of them support the author's opinion. The others refer to what people who oppose his views have said. Decide which statements support Buckley's (B) opinions and which statements refer to the opposition's (O) opinions. Write B or O next to each statement. Compare your answers with those of another student. If your answers differ, go back to the text to find out why.

_____ 1. There may be preferable ways to die than through biological decomposition.

_____ 2. We may need to explore the idea of setting limits to viable lifetimes.

_____ 3. We are spending too much money to keep people alive.

_____ 4. A "living will" for society may be necessary in the future.

_____ 5. It is acceptable to remove food and water from old people who are
      insensate.

_____ 6. We can't know whether someone in a chronic vegetative state can feel what's
      going on.

_____ 7. It's not expensive to feed a person through tubes.

_____ 8. Euthanasia is a moral, not an empirical, question.

_____ 9. Life is a divine gift.

_____ 10. No one should collude in any act of suicide.

_____ 11. To prolong life for some is to prolong pain.

_____ 12. Society must be ready for euthanasia.

C   WORD SEARCH

Find boldfaced words in the article that have similar meaning to the following.

Nouns

suffering: _____

state of mind in which something takes up all thoughts:_____

long life: _____

careful planning: _____

trick; device to deceive: _____

legal documents indicating conditions under which patient can be permitted to

die: _____

Adjectives

still in existence: _____

(continued on next page)

continual: _____

causing death: _____

able to exist: _____

relying on observation and experiment: _____

likely to cause interest or argument: _____

without the power to feel or experience: _____

coming on gradually: _____

stopped: _____

Verbs

causes severe suffering: _____

granting money for: _____

conspire; plot: _____

orders; requires: _____

V. SYNTHESIZING TWO OPINION PIECES

A ✓ DISTINGUISHING OPINIONS

Authors can have different viewpoints, but their opinions can sometimes be similar. Review opinion 1 on pages 161–162 and opinion 2 on pages 163–164.

Work in groups. Read the statements below. Discuss whether Gerard and/or Buckley would agree with them. Put a check (✓) in the box if you think they would agree. Leave the box empty if they would disagree or if there is no evidence to support the statement in their opinion.

Discuss how and why the two opinions are the same or different. (In the first state-
ment, for example, Gerard would probably agree. His family was not allowed to
unhook the machine, which caused his mother even greater suffering. Buckley would
probably not agree, however. He rejects euthanasia and feels that a refusal to accept
medical aid is wrong. He would probably not agree with a family having this power.)

	Gerard: Commentator (Opinion 1)	Buckley: Author (Opinion 2)
Families should have the ultimate power to decide the fate of a family member in a persistent vegetative state.	✓	
Extraordinary measures should be taken if it means keeping a person alive.		
Modern medicine can be torture.		
Euthanasia may be the least cruel treatment for a patient.		
We need to set limits to viable lifetimes, especially in an aging society.		
"Living wills" are a good solution to the problems posed by modern technology.		
It is costing society too much money to keep people alive at all costs.		

B   GIVING YOUR OPINION

After you have distinguished the opinions of the commentator and the author, express
your own opinions on the above statements. Discuss them with the other students in
your group.

C   VOCABULARY REINFORCEMENT: WORD FORMS

Work in small groups. In the following chart you will find vocabulary from the commentary and the editorial. Fill in the chart with the appropriate word forms for each vocabulary item. (An "X" has been placed in the box if there is no related word form.) Use a dictionary to help you if you are not sure.

NOUNS	VERBS	ADJECTIVES	ADVERBS
X	X	chronic	
coma	X		X
ethics	X		
miracle	X		
preoccupation			X
		provocative	
		revived	X
	X	serene	
torture			
trauma			
		vegetative	X
	X	viable	X

Read the following sentences. Complete the sentences with a word from the chart. Be sure to use the correct form of the word you choose.

1. To decide whether euthanasia should be made legal is one of the most difficult _____ decisions of the decade.

2. Doctors can now _____ patients by extraordinary means when they suffer from heart attacks.

3. As we continue to develop technology that keeps people alive through artificial means, there is a greater chance that they will live as _____.

4. The _____ we observe in most comatose patients may be misleading, as we cannot know what they feel.

5. The concept that corporations might decide what constitutes a

   _____ lifetime is alarming to many people.

6. Making life/death decisions is a _____ experience for families of

   terminally ill patients.

7. Buckley _____ us into thinking about the appropriateness of

   mercy killing by stating that if a society is ready for euthanasia, it has rejected

   the primary attribute of life.

8. _____ ill patients spend much of their time in doctors' offices

   and hospitals.

9. The only way doctors could explain the eighty-eight-year-old woman's recovery

   after her feeding tube had been removed was that her revival was

   _____.

10. Many people have come to believe that prolonging a terminally ill patient's life

    is more _____ than generous.

11. Some people say that it is only in industrialized countries that people can afford

    to have a _____ with the right-to-die issue.

12. Some _____ patients have lived in hospital beds for many

    years.

VI.   SPEAKING

A ✓   CASE STUDY: DR. DEATH

*The following reading presents a true case that raises the issue of whether or not sui-
cide, as an active form of euthanasia, should be legalized. Study the case.*

Patients who once simply asked their doctors to help cure their diseases are
now asking for more: aid in managing their deaths.

On the afternoon of June 4, 1990, Janet Atkins, a diagnosed victim of

Alzheimer's disease, sat with Dr. Jack Kevorkian in his 1968 Volkswagen van. He had connected her to his home-built death machine, which would give her a means to end her life. Kevorkian told his patient to "have a good trip," as she pushed the button that would activate a powerful barbiturate and deadly potassium chloride into her bloodstream. She then died of a massive heart attack, her death reactivating an age-long debate over euthanasia and the right of terminally ill patients to end their own lives.

Janet Atkins was fifty-four when she decided to end her life. Even though her doctor had told her she could still live a good life for another year, and in spite of the fact that she was still playing tennis, she made up her mind to die before Alzheimer's "peeled her away, layer by layer," as her husband, who supported his wife's decision, described it. Janet, a vital and active woman, chose to die before her disease made life unbearable. At her death, she had already lost her ability to read books and play music.

Kevorkian, as a result of assisting Janet's death, was ostracized by the medical community. His colleagues consider his death machine a "moral cop out," a way to get around responsibility. What is more, they say, his act was contrary to the Hippocratic Oath, the oath taken by doctors to observe the medical code of ethics in the medical profession. Critics also worry about "assisted suicides" eventually leading to "pressured suicides," in which those whose lives are not valued by society are considered too expensive to sustain. In Michigan, where Kevorkian performed his act, there were no laws against assisting suicides. But authorities there debated his prosecution, as did the public. Was Kevorkian a murderer or a humanitarian?

Kevorkian's response to the criticism was the following: "If I go to jail," he said, "remember that I am not immoral. Society is." He claimed that he was not the agent of Janet's death, but rather an assistant. Stripped of his medical practice, Kevorkian was left to pursue his business with his suicide machine. He has since helped others in their pursuit of death.

In fact, to the terminally ill who resent the medical care that prolongs their suffering, Kevorkian has become a hero. And some right-to-die activists, who advocate a person's right to a quick and dignified death, have even called him a "saint" or a "man of the decade."

Meanwhile, lawmakers and the public continue to debate whether Kevorkian's suicide machine is an instrument of murder or a service to humanity. And while this debate persists, many people wait in line to be hooked up to his machine.

The Debate

Now divide the class into two groups for a debate. The debate will focus on whether doctor-assisted suicide should be legalized. Use the information in the case to help you plan your arguments.

The Teams

Team A will argue in favor of doctor-assisted suicide. You believe Dr. Kevorkian is a hero and that he has offered a service to humanity. You are right-to-die advocates who support active euthanasia. You think doctors should be allowed to assist their patients in ending their lives.

Team B will argue against doctor-assisted suicide. You believe Dr. Kevorkian is a murderer and that he has created a climate for pressured suicides. You are right-to-life advocates who cannot accept suicide as a means to end one's life. You think doctors should not be involved in their patients' desire to end their lives.

Prepare your arguments. Select a moderator to lead the debate.

The Procedure

1. Teams A and B prepare their arguments in small groups, citing evidence from the case and from the readings.

2. Teams A and B face each other for a debate.

3. Team A begins with a three-minute presentation.

4. Team B then gives a three-minute presentation.

5. Team A responds to Team B's presentation for three minutes.

6. Team B responds to Team A's presentation for three minutes.

After the debate, the moderator evaluates the strength of both arguments.

B   DISCUSSION QUESTIONS

In groups, discuss your answers to the following questions.

1. Go back to the questions in the values clarification exercise (p. 159). Do you have the same opinions now, or have you changed your opinions in any way after examining the views of others?

2. In your opinion, what role should doctors take in advising patients and/or their families in these cases? What is their responsibility?

3. Derek Humphry is the executive director of the Hemlock Society, an organization that promotes public awareness and acceptance of euthanasia. He predicted that active euthanasia will be a standard part of American medicine within a decade. If this is true, what effect will it have on society?

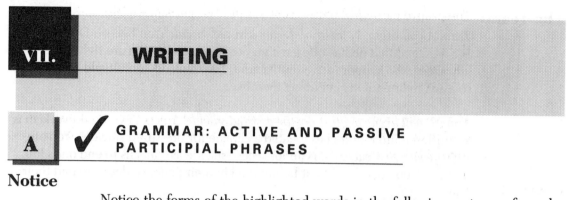

VII. WRITING

A ✓ GRAMMAR: ACTIVE AND PASSIVE PARTICIPIAL PHRASES

Notice

Notice the forms of the highlighted words in the following sentences from the commentary:

> *Honoring* state law, the doctors weaned her off the respirator a little each day, *forcing* her to labor for every breath.

> *Under pressure and* **unprepared** *for the awful circumstances, my father made the instinctive, human choice: Try to save her.*

Which of the verbs is an active participle? Which of the verbs is a passive participle?

In what type of writing do we generally see these verb forms?

Explanation

Participles tend to occur more frequently in descriptive prose and less frequently in factual, scientific writing. They tend to evoke a visual image in the mind of the listener or reader.

Active Participles

In the example, *honoring* and *forcing* are both active participles. They both describe what the doctors are doing.

The present participial phrase contains the present participle of the verb.

In the active voice, the present participial phrase indicates that the action in the phrase and the action in the main clause take place at the same time. In the first quote, the *honoring* and *forcing* both occurred at the same time as the verb in the main clause, *weaning*.

When the action in the participial phrase happens before the action in the main clause, whether the main clause is past or present, the perfect participial phrase (*having* + past participle) is used. For example: **Having weaned her off the respirator**, the doctors allowed her to die.

Passive Participles

In the example, *unprepared* is a passive participle. It gives a reason for the result expressed in the main clause.

The passive participial phrase contains the past participle of the verb.

Unlike the active participial phrases, the time relationship in these phrases is not always significant. This is because the passive participle usually functions as an adjective and is descriptive in nature.

The perfect progressive participle (*having* + *been* + past participle) may also be used in descriptive cases in the passive voice. For example: ***Having been pressured by doctors,*** *my father made the instinctive human choice.*

Exercise

Fill in the blanks with the active or passive participle of the verb in parentheses. Choose the correct form (present, past, perfect, or perfect progressive). Each sentence refers to Philip Gerard's story (the commentary).

1. _____ (fight) Parkinson's disease for almost ten years, his mother suffered a massive heart attack.

2. _____ (be) in the hospital, she could be revived by extraordinary means.

3. The doctor called his father, _____ (demand) that he make a choice.

4. _____ (confuse) and _____ (shock), his father made the instinctive, human choice to save her.

5. _____ (give) the prognosis, the family decided to unhook the machines.

6. _____ (respect) state law, the hospital told the family that they could not unhook the machine without a court order.

7. _____ (hear) the word *coma* the first time, Gerard pictured a state of serenity.

8. Her nervous system, _____ (destroy) by unrelieved trauma, finally broke down.

9. _____ (lie) awake into the small hours of a snowy morning, Gerard listened to the hum of the monitors and the "suff'ing" of the respirator.

(continued on next page)

10. _____ (hope) for the courage, Gerard thought of turning off the machine.

11. She had to breathe independently, _____ (wean) off the respirator.

B WRITING STYLE: NARRATION

Notice

Notice the writing style of Philip Gerard's commentary. Without discussing the issue directly, he gets us to think about euthanasia. How does he do this?

Explanation

Through a personal account of his mother's illness and subsequent death, Gerard describes the difficulty of keeping a person alive through artificial means. He narrates his own story and, through his story, provokes us into thinking about euthanasia.

Most brief narrative essays focus on a single experience that changed the writer's outlook on something. This is the case for Gerard's commentary.

In essay writing, the purpose of narration is to inform, support your thesis, and help your essay arrive at its conclusion. A well-told story is hard to forget, which is why narration is especially effective for communicating an idea.

Effective narration should contain several things:

1. *A consistent point of view:* Narration should be delivered from the same point of view throughout the story. The most common points of view are first person ("I"), in which we experience an event through the writer's eyes and ears, and third person ("he/she"), in which the writer is not a participant in the action being described. The first person is more subjective; the third person is more objective.

2. *A chronological organization:* There should be a clear beginning, middle, and end to a story. Effective narration proceeds chronologically because time order helps establish what happened and when. With narration there should be a clear past, present, and future.

3. *A clear context:* Readers/listeners should know what, to whom, where, when, and how things happen.

4. *Effective details:* If details are well chosen, they will help the reader/listener envision the situation being described. Details can provide enough information to help set the scene, but there should not be so many details so as to confuse or overwhelm the reader/listener.

5. *A thesis:* There should be a clear idea that provokes thought or discussion about why you wrote your narration. There should be a point behind the story.

6. *Sophisticated transitional devices:* When we tell a story in speaking, we tend to use informal connectors such as "and then . . . ," "and so . . . ," etc. In writing, however, we use more sophisticated connectors. Here are some common transitional devices to show the sequence of time:

---

a. Sequence of events: *first, second, third; then, next, later, finally; yesterday, today, tomorrow*

b. Reference to the past: *sometime before; earlier that day; some years ago; just last week/month/year; the year Tom moved away; on April 14th*

c. Forecast the future: *afterward; much later; after many years; in the hours/days/weeks/years to come*

d. Two things happening at the same time: *meanwhile; at that moment; at the same time*

e. Causation: *since; because*

f. Explanation of a result: *accordingly; as a result; consequently; as a consequence; thus*

Exercise

Look at Philip Gerard's commentary (pp. 161–162). Using the above list as a reference, analyze his narration. Take notes to answer the following questions. Then compare your answers with those of another student to see if you agree. Discuss your answers with the class.

1. From what point of view does Gerard tell his story? Is this point of view consistent?

   _____

   _____

   _____

2. Describe the chronology of Gerard's narration.

   Beginning: _____

   Middle: _____

   End: _____

(continued on next page)

3. Describe briefly the context that he has set for his narration.

What?_____

To whom? _____

Where? _____

When? _____

How? _____

4. List some of the effective details Gerard uses in his narration.

_____

_____

_____

5. Although Gerard does not state his thesis directly, there is a clear idea being presented. What point is there behind his story?

_____

_____

_____

6. What transitional devices does Gerard use in his essay to show time sequence?

_____

_____

_____

Essay Questions

Choose one of the following topics. Try to integrate ideas, vocabulary, and writing techniques that you have studied in this unit. For question 1, try to incorporate the following:

- an introductory paragraph that presents both sides of the argument and clearly states your thesis (whether you support euthanasia or not);

- paragraphs (at least three) that develop your argument with supporting evidence;

- a conclusion that reinforces the position you have taken. It should also end with a new idea (a warning, prediction, value judgment) that has not been mentioned before.

1. Do you believe life-support systems, respirators, and feeding tubes are devices that sustain life or prolong dying? Write an essay in which you express your opinion.

2. Write about a time when you had to make a decision that was a matter of life and death. Develop a thesis through your narration.

REDUCING INEQUALITY IN EDUCATION

Cartoon by Joel Pett, from the Phi Delta Kappa Journal.

I. ANTICIPATING THE ISSUE

Discuss your answers to the following questions.

1. Look at the title. Look at the cartoon. What do you think the issue of this unit will be?

2. What is the message or humor of the cartoon?

3. What do you know about the problems of integration and/or segregation in education?

BACKGROUND READING

Read the following text.

The Fourteenth Amendment to the U.S. Constitution guarantees each citizen equal protection under the law. However, up until the 1950s, this equal protection was interpreted as "separate but equal" for Americans of European ancestry and Americans of African ancestry. This segregation was most apparent in education. American public schools have not always been racially integrated, but since the 1950s, efforts have been made to integrate American society through the schools. The road to integrating America's schools has been a long and hard one, and the goals of integration have changed along the way.

In the early 1800s, black slaves were not allowed to attend schools in America, so all schools were white. In later years, black and white children both attended public schools, but separately. In 1896, a famous Supreme Court case, *Plessy v. Ferguson*, attempted to attack the "separate but equal" ***doctrine***[1] that had ruled the country for so long. Homer Plessy, the ***plaintiff***[2] in the case, attacked the Louisiana law that required segregation on trains within the state, stating that his rights had been violated under the Constitution. He claimed that legal segregation had created a system in which black citizens were inferior in the eyes of the law. Plessy lost his case, and the Court's 8–1 decision ruled that "segregation by race did not necessarily imply racial inferiority," thus upholding the doctrine of "separate but equal." The decision resulted in the continuation of segregated schooling.

It was not until many years later that the nation officially ***repudiated***[3] its segregation policies. In 1954, the Supreme Court ***overturned***[4] "separate but equal" in the famous *Brown v. Board of Education* case. Linda Brown, a five-year-old girl, had to walk five blocks to a bus stop and then ride two miles each day to her all-black elementary school in Topeka, Kansas, even though there was an all-white school only four blocks from her home. Her parents, believing that the segregated school system deprived their daughter of her constitutional rights, sued the Topeka Board of Education. The Supreme Court then interpreted the Fourteenth Amendment to mean that states had to provide equal educational opportunities to all students and viewed segregated schooling as "inherently unequal." This ***momentous*** decision practically ***banned*** segregation in the public schools—at least in theory.

For several years, however, there was no real attempt made to integrate the schools. Because U.S. education is not nationalized, powerful local school districts were able to continue their old practices. Then in the late 1960s and early 1970s, several court decisions ordered the elimination of segregated schools. Desegregation processes were instituted through mandatory ***busing***, in which children from ***predominantly*** white school systems were sent in buses to black schools, and children from predominantly black school systems were sent in buses to white schools. The focus was on integrating African-Americans into the ***mainstream*** of white America. Many families in busing programs have been satisfied with the results. However, opponents of busing point out that it is ***ironic*** that children must spend so much time traveling to school on buses when avoiding busing was one of the original reasons for the *Brown v. Board of Education* case.

Even advocates of busing concede that busing may have created more problems than expected. Many white parents have protested busing by fleeing the inner city for the suburbs; others have enrolled their children in private schools. This "white flight" has caused cities and schools to ***resegregate***, forming even more racially isolated ***ghettos*** within many American cities.

And while the physical separation of children by race is far less common than it was in 1954, there is evidence that the number of racially segregated schools is now on the rise. In fact, in some areas of the United States, particularly in the Northeast, the degree of racial separation in the schools is even greater than it was in 1954.

Some African-Americans as well have left their own communities, in order to live in safer areas with better schools. This has left inner-city children with fewer successful, well-educated black **role models,** and instead has allowed the negative example of drug **pushers** to take their place. Many black parents have also come to oppose school busing, insisting instead on better quality educational programs in neighborhood schools. The famous *Brown v. Board of Education* case had officially registered the nation's distaste for discrimination, yet many parents now see the results of the 1954 case as a **mixed blessing**.

In recent years, educators and governments have sought new ways, other than busing, to deal with segregation. In a recent case, the Supreme Court softened its position, ruling that school systems could be freed from mandatory busing if they complied "in good faith" with desegregation orders.

Alternative plans for integrating schools have been offered, many of them focusing on curriculum improvement and teacher training. These plans are often referred to as "choice," because parents gain the right to choose their children's school, public or private. Many believe that giving parents the right to choose a school will lead to "voluntary" desegregation and that a free-market approach to schooling is one of the only ways to improve the quality of American education and give equal opportunity to all students. Critics of this approach claim that many schools will be left abandoned as students and their families **vie over** the better schools.

One example of a choice program is the "magnet schools," designed to draw white students back into inner city schools by offering a specialized curriculum, focusing, for example, on science or art. With quality education incentives, these schools also work toward integration by balancing the ratio of black and white students in each school. Magnet schools have been successful in some areas but not so in others. Although some parents are attracted to the focused curriculum of a magnet school, they remain reluctant to send their children back to inner-city public schools. African-American parents see the emphasis on getting white students to enroll in the magnet schools as an insult.

In some states, an even more extreme concept of schooling has been proposed, and in a few cases, attempted. "Voucher programs" are being advocated, in which each child receives a voucher that can be "spent" on any public or private school of his or her choice, regardless of its location. Critics of this system say that voucher programs may lead to more segregated schooling as the more highly educated parents tend to do the research that is needed to choose the best schools.

The school does seem to be the most appropriate place to ensure that all people have equal opportunity in "one nation under God."[1] So far, it has been the most appropriate place to begin the process of integration. The best method for realizing this goal, however, remains unclear.

[1] From "The Pledge of Allegiance" to the flag (the promise of devotion of a U.S. citizen to the country).

A   VOCABULARY

Look at the boldfaced words and phrases in the background reading. Try to determine their meaning. Match them with the synonyms or definitions below. Write the number next to the matching word or phrase.

_____ a.   rejected as unjust

_____ b.   the main way of thinking or acting

_____ c.   mostly

_____ d.   sections of towns lived in by people who are underprivileged or discriminated against

_____ e.   outlawed; made illegal   6

_____ f.   important; serious   5

_____ g.   transport of children to achieve racial integration

_____ h.   defeated; in law, decided against (to reverse) an earlier ruling (decision)

_____ i.   segregate again

_____ j.   in law, a person who brings action against someone in court

_____ k.   having the opposite result from what is expected

(continued on next page)

_____ l.   drug sellers

_____ m.   something that has both advantages and disadvantages

_____ n.   people who can be respected or admired for what they do

_____ o.   compete for

_____ p.   beliefs of a political system; principles

B   SUMMARIZING THE ISSUE

_Work in small groups. Summarize the issue presented in the background reading. Take
notes to complete the following outline._

   1. The issue (_state in your own words_): _____

      _____

   2. Pros and cons of solutions to segregation in U.S. public education:

	Pros	**Cons**

      a. Busing:

         _____

         _____

      b. Magnet schools:

         _____

         _____

      c. Voucher programs:

         _____

         _____

C   VALUES CLARIFICATION

Work in small groups. Discuss your answers to the following questions.

   1. Has racial segregation been a problem in schools in your country? If so, how
      have people or the government dealt with it?

   2. Study the proposals for integration in the United States presented in your notes
      from "Summarizing the Issue." What are your reactions to these proposals?
      Would they have any significance in your country?

III.   OPINION 1: LISTENING

A ✓ LISTENING FOR THE MAIN IDEA

Listen to the commentary. Check the statement that summarizes the commentator's viewpoint.

☐ 1. The African-American community is losing its identity through integration efforts.

☐ 2. The *Brown v. Board of Education* decision was a mistake.

☐ 3. New integration efforts must be made to ensure equal opportunity for all students.

B   LISTENING FOR DETAILS

Read the following questions and answers. Listen to the commentary again and circle the best answer. Then compare your answers with those of another student. Listen again if necessary.

1. What happened in 1954?

    a. All racial segregation was ended in the United States.

    b. American public schools were integrated.

    c. The Supreme Court ruled on racial segregation.

2. Why isn't it odd that there are no celebrations for this anniversary, according to the commentator?

    a. There is a sense of weariness at court-imposed busing schemes.

    b. Because black children used to have to ride buses past all-white schools.

    c. Because integration has been successful.

3. Why was the *Brown v. Board of Education* decision necessary?

    a. It had to explain the doctrine of "separate but equal."

    b. The 1896 *Plessy v. Ferguson* decision had never been written into law.

    c. The country had proclaimed itself a nation of equality.

(continued on next page)

4. What problem exists in the notion of integration?

    a. It assumes that all black and white children must automatically integrate in schools.

    b. It assumes that black children can't learn well without the presence of white children.

    c. It results in an inferior education for all children.

5. Why wasn't integration so ideal for the black community?

    a. It cost the black community so much money.

    b. Segregation was never really outlawed in some schools.

    c. The well-educated blacks left their communities without role models.

6. What happened to predominantly black neighborhoods as a result of integration?

    a. They expanded into the suburbs.

    b. More ghettos formed.

    c. The pushers controlled them.

7. What did African-Americans give up as a result of the *Brown v. Board of Education* decision?

    a. Equality among whites

    b. A feeling of self-sufficiency

    c. Special help from the government

8. According to Muhammed, what was wrong with the way in which integration was handled?

    a. African-Americans allowed the government to lead integration efforts.

    b. African-Americans never accepted European-Americans.

    c. African-Americans didn't become part of the country's mainstream.

C   TEXT COMPLETION AND DISCRETE LISTENING

Read the text of the commentary. Try to fill in the missing words in the text as you remember them. Use your knowledge of text structure, vocabulary, and grammar to help you. Then listen again to the commentary to check your answers, stopping the tape as you fill in the blanks. If you have different answers than the original text, check with your teacher to see if they are acceptable alternatives.

Introduction

This country's racial segregation in public schools was _____ by the

Supreme Court on this date in 1954. Commentator Askia Muhammed believes

the ruling came as a _____ blessing.

Commentary

It's odd that on this thirty-fifth anniversary of one of the most _____

Supreme Court decisions there are no national celebrations. Or, maybe it's not

so odd.

I think there's a sense of national weariness at various court-imposed

school-integration-by- _____ schemes over the years. So who wants to

celebrate *that* anniversary? It's _____ because the Washington D.C.

_____ , whose case was joined into the *Brown v. Topeka, Kansas, Board

of Education* suit, were parents who complained that their children had to ride

buses _____ an all-white junior high school in their neighborhood. But

the whole concept of integration or _____ is full of ironies, as far as I'm

concerned.

The *Brown v. Board* decision had to be, however. Historically, the

_____ of "separate but equal" from the 1896 *Plessy v. Ferguson* deci-

sion had to be _____ in U.S. law if the country was to refer to itself sin-

cerely as "one nation under God."

My only problem with the notion of integration, though, is having to auto-

matically _____ that, unless white children are around, black children

cannot possibly be learning anything in school. It breeds unacceptable

_____ thinking among blacks, the descendants of slaves in this country.

We paid a dear price for integration. The well-educated blacks were free to move anywhere they chose when segregation was _____ . And they chose, increasingly, to leave the masses of suffering people most in need of their presence, their guidance, their stability, their leadership by example. The black communities' _____ models, once forced to live in _____ black neighborhoods by segregated housing laws, were at last able to flee to the suburbs. They fled, leaving the _____ to be vied over by the _____ and the poor.

As a nation, we gained as much as we lost when the Supreme Court _____ "separate but equal." But I, for one, wish we hadn't so quickly lost the sense of self- _____ , of pride, of self-help, self-government that African-Americans surrendered. We thought, "Let George[1] do it," instead of wanting to do it for ourselves, mostly so we could get along with the majority, the European-Americans, as we integrated into the country's _____ .

[1] George Bush, former U.S. president, representing the country's government.

IV. OPINION 2: READING

A ✓ READING FOR THE MAIN IDEA

Read the editorial. Check the statement that summarizes the author's viewpoint.

- ☐ 1. We must continue to use integrated schooling as a means for ending discrimination.

- ☐ 2. Integration efforts have not been successful in the schools.

- ☐ 3. Choice and excellence may be the best alternatives to integrative schooling.

Defending the Common School

BY MICHAEL D. FORD

Education in a democratic society must equip children to develop their potential and to participate fully in American life. For the community at large, the schools have discharged this responsibility well. But for many minorities, and particularly for the children of the ghetto, the schools have failed to provide the educational experience which could overcome the effects of discrimination and deprivation.[1]

Busing was the principal tool used to *remedy* educational inequality, and it *sparked* controversy and resistance in most of the communities where it was employed. Its proponents saw it as an effective remedy for the problems of racial isolation and inadequate educational resources in black communities. Opposition to busing was expressed as a fear of crime and a protest against government intervention in community affairs; it signaled an unwillingness to *relinquish* the cherished ideal of the neighborhood school. The most *telling* argument against busing was that it was *counterproductive*, because whites would abandon the affected schools, resulting in even greater isolation for blacks.

The phenomenon of "white flight" was and is real. Inner-city school systems have lost significant numbers of white students, thereby increasing the number of predominantly minority schools. But it is equally clear that busing has been effective in reducing or ending school segregation in some com-

[1]The Kerner Commission Report, 1967.

munities. In small cities, some suburban areas, and the rural South, racial isolation has been reduced. Numerous surveys reveal that black and white parents whose children have been bused to eliminate school segregation have been overwhelmingly positive about the experience. However, despite its history of mixed success, busing has lost support even among proponents of educational equality.

Conservatives have reformulated the terms of debate on educational issues following a successful campaign to end busing as a focal point of educational reform. Since the early 1980s, they have led a chorus singing the tune of "excellence" in education. They now argue for programs that will lead to measurable improvements in student performance. The danger they underscore is not the unfair burden imposed on black children by educational inequalities but the loss of American global *preeminence*. In order to ensure that we are producing the ranks of highly skilled, technologically sophisticated students necessary to maintain our nation's competitive advantage, they advocate national achievement exams, a longer school year, periodic assessments of teacher competency, and privatization of education through school voucher programs.

The American common school was created in order to provide a setting in which children from different backgrounds could learn together, free from the constraints or benefits of family background. It was an environment designed to provide the resources for individual development and an appreciation of the common good. Students were expected to become productive citizens, able to contribute to the *polity* as well as to the economy. The radical individualism of conservative privatization[2] schemes would likely cripple public education and erode any sense of *the public good*.

The talk about choice and excellence has *preempted* attempts to focus on quality in education. Some in the black community have directed their attention to other issues, like Afrocentric curriculums and all-male schools. The diminished national concern for equal educational opportunity is responsible in part for this inward turn. All students should experience programs of study that enhance their self-image. However, a curriculum that insists on only one *vantage point* for learning, whether it be European or African, will impose burdens on students by limiting their vision.

Curricular issues are important, but they are no substitute for a well-articulated program that directly confronts racial inequality in education and other social *arenas*. All black children, female and male, deserve good schools; that goal will be realized only if we are willing to press just claims[3] on all appropriate state institutions. Settling those claims will require that we generate a new will—in the words of the Kerner Commission, "a will to tax ourselves to the extent necessary"—to fund programs that target the conditions imposed by racial inequality.

In this vein, one of the most promising developments in American education in recent years is linked to a number of court cases that challenge the disparities in funding among local school districts. Lawsuits seeking redistribution of state funds among local school districts[4] to balance educational resources have been filed in nearly two dozen states, beginning with a suit filed in Texas twenty-three years ago and not settled until 1989.

The intent of these suits is simply to *level* the playing field. The remedies crafted by state legislatures as a response to successful suits vary. Most have adopted measures that provide increased funding to districts with below-average tax bases.[5] Montana also *capped* spending in wealthy districts. However, more significant changes in the funding of education will be necessary to *tackle* the problem generated by the ongoing segregation of our society. Given decreasing state revenues and the lack of support for new taxes, some activists are beginning to talk about a national system of revenue collection and distribution to address educational inequalities.

Efforts to reduce educational inequalities will not in and of themselves end poverty or racism, however well funded they may be; housing and employment discrimination must be eliminated as well. But schools are *crucial* determinants of social mobility and well-being, organized and administered by the state, not the marketplace, and therefore it is

---

[2] The move from a public to a private approach to education. (Private schools are paid for by the individual and are selective. Public schools are paid for through taxes and are open to everyone.)

[3] Fight for a fair amount of money.

[4] In the United States, property is taxed to provide funds for education. This means that wealthier communities provide more money to their schools than poorer communities.

[5] Poorer neighborhoods.

reasonable and *feasible* to insist that the government act to *ensure* that they serve all citizens equally.

Poverty and racism have created specific educational needs in the black community. We know where the substandard schools are, and we can assess the critical shortages in human and material resources. It is right to *press for* more and better teachers in black schools. We should adopt measures that establish more effective links between parents and schools. We should support curriculums that open our children to a world of possibilities, not courses of study that wall them in intellectually and culturally. However, we must continue to insist on desegregation as a critical yardstick by which policies and programs are measured.

Desegregating schooling does not signify that black schoolchildren cannot learn outside the company of white children. It emphasizes our recognition that common schooling can be a focal point for confronting racism and for providing children with equitably shared resources. Our increasingly diverse society will have to contend with the multiplying strains that result from difference. The American school has long been viewed as the best meeting ground for the creation of our civic culture; if we are to *nurture* democratic and egalitarian *impulses*, no other setting is likely to be as *hospitable*.

Source: "Defending the Common School," by Michael D. Ford, from the December 9, 1991, issue of *The Nation*.

B   READING FOR AUTHOR'S INTENDED MEANING

Read the following statements. Do you think the author would agree (A) or disagree (D) with them? Write A or D next to each statement. Compare your answers with those of another student. If your answers differ, go back to the text to find out why.

_____ 1. People who opposed busing had an argument that made sense.

_____ 2. The problem of "white flight" from inner-city schools has been exaggerated.

_____ 3. Busing has been a successful means of reducing segregation.

_____ 4. Conservatives in America are concerned about the educational inequality offered to African-American children.

_____ 5. The loss of America's global preeminence should be the ultimate concern when discussing the country's educational practices.

_____ 6. Increasing the number of private schools will hurt American schooling.

_____ 7. Business firms may be a good model for public schooling in the future.

(continued on next page)

_____ 8. African-American communities have become more focused on their own culture with the loss of interest in equal educational opportunity in America.

_____ 9. An Afrocentric curriculum gives African-Americans an advantage in learning.

_____10. Court cases have been an effective means for equalizing state funds for schools.

_____11. School is the most effective place for the government to combat racial inequalities.

_____12. Schools should adopt free-market, or business, practices with less control by the state.

_____13. A school should not always be evaluated by its success or failure to desegregate.

_____14. The American school is still the best place to integrate society.

C   WORD SEARCH

Find boldfaced words in the essay that have similar meaning to the following and write them below.

Nouns/Phrases

in this respect; regarding this topic: _____

society as a political organization: _____

point of view: _____

scenes of interest or activity: _____

excellence above others: _____

sudden wishes to do something: _____

benefit to society: _____

Verbs

take action about: _____

activated: _____

insist on: _____

further the development of: _____

give up: _____

make certain: _____

make equal: _____

put a limit on: _____

correct: _____

replaced: _____

Adjectives

receptive: _____

extremely important: _____

blocking the way of a goal: _____

showing a person's feelings or opinions: _____

possible (can be done): _____

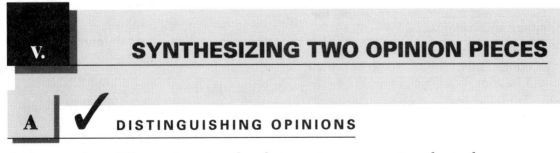

V.   SYNTHESIZING TWO OPINION PIECES

A ✔ DISTINGUISHING OPINIONS

*Authors can have different viewpoints, but their opinions can sometimes be similar.
Review opinion 1 on pages 185–186 and opinion 2 on pages 187–189.*

*Work in groups. Read the statements on the next page. Discuss whether Muhammed
and/or Ford would agree with them. Put a check (✓) in the box if you think they
would agree. Leave the box empty if they would disagree or if there is no evidence to
support the statement in their opinion.*

(continued on next page)

Discuss how and why the two opinions are the same or different. (In the first state-ment, for example, Muhammed would not agree. It bothers him that the notion of inte-gration implies that black children cannot learn without the presence of white chil-dren; this implies that black children might benefit from learning in a black school. Ford, however, would probably agree because he says that we should support curricu-lums that open our children to a world of possibilities, not courses of study that wall them in culturally.)

	Muhammed: Commentator (Opinion 1)	Ford: Author (Opinion 2)
African-Americans are at an educational disadvantage when they study in all-black schools.		✓
Preserving an African-American identity should be an educational goal.		
American schools should be more concerned about their lack of excellence than about segregation.		
Busing has been an effective remedy for integration.		
Integrated schooling implies African-Americans integrating into the mainstream.		
The *Brown v. Board of Education* decision should be celebrated.		
Government should be responsible for educational reforms.		
Taxation is a solution to inequality in education.		

B   **GIVING YOUR OPINION**

After you have distinguished the opinions of the commentator and the author, express your own opinions on the above statements. Discuss them with the other students in your group.

C	**VOCABULARY REINFORCEMENT:** **VOCABULARY/CONCEPT GRID**

In this activity, you will review some of the vocabulary you learned in the commentary and in the editorial by relating it to important concepts. This will help you to understand and use the words more effectively in discussions on this topic.

Work in groups. For each vocabulary item, discuss its relationship to the concepts written at the top of the grid. How are they related?

If the group thinks there is a positive relation between the vocabulary item and the concept (one causes the other; one is an example of the other; one supports the other; etc.), put a "+" in the box. If the group thinks there is a negative relation between the two (one defeats or contradicts the other; one is not an example of the other; one does not support the other; etc.), put a " – " in the box. If your group is unsure of the relationship or cannot agree, put a "?" in the box.

The first one has been done for you (this is just a suggestion; people will sometimes have different opinions on some of the relationships between the vocabulary items and concepts). Here's a possible explanation for the first example:

American global preeminence . . .

is negatively related (–) to **Integration** *because*

- *focusing on the nation's competitive advantage (or "excellence" programs) has meant turning away from integration efforts (such as busing).*

is unclearly related (?) to **Mainstream America** *because*

- *some might argue that the country's mainstream (white) population is more interested in its country's preeminence;*

- *others might argue that the country's mainstream (white) population is more interested in focusing on integration efforts.*

is positively related (+) to **Resegregation** *because*

- *if inequalities of education are no longer the focus in education because of the preeminence concern, it is likely that children from different backgrounds will no longer learn together in the same settings.*

	INTEGRATION	MAINSTREAM AMERICA	RESEGREGATION
American global preeminence	–	?	✦
Brown v. Board of Education case			
busing			
common school			
ghettos			
impoverishment			
low teacher morale			
national weariness			
nurturing of democratic impulses			
Plessy v. Ferguson case			
public good			
pushers			
role models			
school voucher programs			
"separate but equal" doctrine			
"white flight"			

VI.   SPEAKING

A   ✓   CASE STUDY: THE KANSAS CITY SCHOOL DISTRICT

The following reading presents a true case that raises the issue of how to integrate American schools. Study the case.

Work in small groups. Discuss the appropriateness of the Kansas City magnet school program for school integration. Put yourselves in the position of the taxpayers of Kansas City. Write a list of your concerns and/or proposals. Present your conclusions to the rest of the class.

Kansas City, Missouri, has instituted a school desegregation program that is unique in the United States. It is the only urban district that has attempted to desegregate its 74 percent minority school system through a total magnet school approach. Its goal is to achieve a ratio of 60 percent minority and 40 percent white in each of the 78 elementary, middle, and secondary schools involved in the program. In 1986, Kansas City schoolchildren, the plaintiffs, filed suit against the school district and the state, the defendants, claiming that segregation laws that had been in place more than 30 years before were responsible for the deterioration of educational opportunities for all children. As examples, they pointed to the fact that books were being sent to black schools after they had been used by students in white schools and that old manual typewriters were being bought for black schools whereas electric typewriters were being bought for white schools.

Federal Judge Russell Clark ruled in favor of the plaintiffs, recognizing that the state had not done enough to eliminate discrimination in Kansas City public schools. First he ordered the rehabilitation of school buildings and the raising of teachers' salaries. Because classes typically had 30 students, he said it was necessary to hire 1,000 new teachers and build 1,000 more classrooms to improve schooling. Then he ordered the integration of all of Kansas City's public schools. Although Judge Clark knew that he could have integrated Kansas City schools in one day through a busing program, he realized that the district would probably have been 100 percent black by the second day because of "white flight." Instead, he chose to achieve integration through a comprehensive magnet school program, believing that if the entire district were a magnet, all students would have choices and opportunities. In an effort to lure white students back into the city with specialized programs in areas such as business technology, Latin, environmental science, and visual and performing arts, all schools in the district were given a special focus. This plan has turned out to be the country's most expensive and intensive school desegregation effort, and Judge Clark's decision is unique in that it has demonstrated the judiciary's willingness to focus its power on social engineering. Yet, his utopian vision of integrating Kansas City public schools has not been realized without criticism.

To create a comprehensive magnet school program requires money. The cost of this six-year desegregation effort will total approximately $700 million to integrate approximately 35,000 children. New facilities are being built, a marketing program to recruit nonminority students has been developed, and in some cases students are being taken to schools by taxicab. The state is paying for this effort, but the taxpayers must pay between 20 and 25 percent of it. And even though the taxpayers voted against a proposal to raise taxes for this effort, property taxes doubled. Judge Clark overrode the voters' decision, stating that it was unconstitutional; in other words, he interpreted the Fourteenth Amendment to mean that equal opportunities were not being provided to all of Kansas City's children. The Supreme Court upheld Clark's ruling. In addition, Judge Clark proposed an income surtax for *all* people working in Kansas City, as he felt that people working in the city who lived in the suburbs should share in the expenses. This proposal was repealed, however.

The results of Kansas City's desegregation effort are still unclear, but in the first year of Judge Clark's ruling, whites continued to leave the district. This problem has since stabilized. Although the goal of the program was to transfer 1,000 white students by the second year, only 200 or so actually transferred.

(continued on next page)

Test scores have remained the same or even dropped in the high schools and middle schools since becoming magnets, but test scores in the elementary schools have slightly increased. Moreover, quotas have not been filled to reach the 60–40 percent ratio goal. Many magnet school places are being left empty because white students are not filling them and black students are being turned away in an effort to achieve the ratio goal; this angers many African-American parents. A recent survey indicated that only 12 percent of private-school parents and 8 percent of suburban-school parents would consider sending their children to a magnet school. In spite of the curricular specialization offered by these schools, these parents continue to feel reluctant to send their children into the inner city.

Meanwhile, many taxpayers in Kansas City continue to search for a means to put an end to Judge Clark's rule over the school district and their money. They are anxious to see something for their money, for their time, and for their children. Other residents hold the hope that Judge Clark's ruling will be the remedy: reduce educational inequalities and integrate their communities.

B   DISCUSSION QUESTIONS

In groups, discuss your answers to the following questions.

1. Go back to the questions in the values clarification exercise (p. 182). Do you have the same opinions now, or have you changed your opinions in any way after examining the views of others?

2. Michael Ford states that "the talk about choice and excellence has preempted attempts to focus on inequality in education." Do you agree with this statement? Can schools work on both goals simultaneously, or must one goal replace the other?

3. How do the efforts at desegregating American public schools resemble or differ from efforts to create racial balance and harmony in other social arenas, either in your country or in the United States?

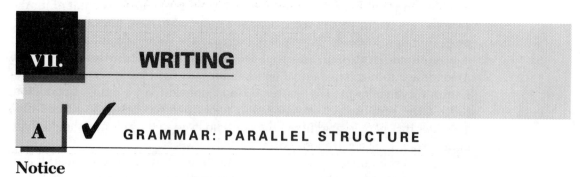

VII.   WRITING

A   ✓   GRAMMAR: PARALLEL STRUCTURE

Notice

Notice the form of the words in bold in the following examples from the editorial:

*a. But it is equally clear that busing has been effective in **reducing** or **ending** school segregation in some communities.*

*b. In order to ensure that we are producing the ranks of **highly skilled, technologically sophisticated** students necessary to maintain our . . .*

*c. . . . nation's competitive advantage, they advocate **national achievement exams, a longer school year, periodic assessments of teacher competency, and privatization of education through school voucher programs.***

What do you notice about the grammatical forms of the various groups of words illustrated above?

Explanation

Parallel structure is a construction that expresses a combination of ideas in similar grammatical form. Most parts of speech can be placed in a parallel construction.

In the above examples, the words in "a" are both gerund verb forms, the words in "b" are both adverb + adjective combinations, and the words in "c" are noun phrases.

Exercise

The following sentences contain errors in parallel structure. Find the error and rewrite the sentence with correct parallel structure.

1. Many white parents enrolled their children in private schools and in schools in the suburbs as a result of busing.

   _____

   _____

   _____

2. The Supreme Court's 1954 ruling came with not only many advantages for African-Americans but also there were many disadvantages.

   _____

   _____

   _____

3. Busing attempted to end segregated schooling, eliminate racism, and creating the common school in America.

   _____

   _____

   _____

(continued on next page)

4. Some people view the *Brown v. Board of Education* case as a mixed blessing, while other view it as momentous.

_____

_____

_____

5. The doctrine of "separate but equal" was supported in the *Plessy v. Ferguson* case, overturned in the *Brown v. Board of Education* case, and people debated it in Kansas City.

_____

_____

_____

6. Because of "white flight," many African-Americans have been left to live in ghettos that are dangerous, drug-infested, and in poverty.

_____

_____

_____

7. Because of their inability to draw suburban children back into the inner cities and they lost money because of empty spaces, some magnet schools may have to close.

_____

_____

_____

8. American public schools have instituted three major policies involving schools and race: segregated schooling, mandatory busing, and choosing schools.

_____

_____

_____

9. Some parents don't want to bus their children outside their communities, but "excellence" programs for their children are what they want.

_____

_____

_____

(continued on next page)

10. The American common school was designed to provide resources for individual development, to teach an appreciation of the common good, and it provided a setting in which children from different backgrounds could learn together.

_____

_____

_____

B   WRITING STYLE: CAUSE AND EFFECT

Notice

Notice the way Askia Muhammed develops his thesis in the commentary. He believes that African-Americans have lost their sense of self-sufficiency, pride, self-help, and self-government as a result of the *Brown v. Board of Education* decision. How does he develop his thesis to show *why* or *how* they lost these things?

Explanation

Muhammed uses a cause-and-effect analysis to show the connections between events and situations. A cause-and-effect analysis can take two different approaches. In either approach, a writer tries to explain reasons for things. When we explore *causes*, we examine a situation or event and try to explain what caused it. We try to answer a question that asks how or why:

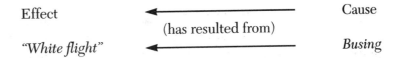

Effect   Cause
                        (has resulted from)

"White flight"   *Busing*

When we explore *effects*, we examine a situation or event and try to look at what has happened as a result of it. We try to answer a question that asks *what*:

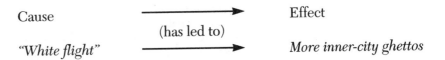

Cause   Effect
                        (has led to)

"White flight"   *More inner-city ghettos*

Sound reasoning and logic are essential to a good cause-and-effect analysis. It is necessary to examine relationships between events and situations carefully.

A cause-and-effect essay can involve complex writing, as there is rarely one cause for an effect, or one effect from a cause. In any given cause-and-effect analysis, there are generally immediate causes (those closest to the effect) and ultimate causes (those more distant or even hidden).

Exercises

1. Work with another student. One helpful way to develop a cause-and-effect essay is to use a graphic organizer to help visualize the connections between events. Look again at the case study on pp. 194–196. If you were to write a cause-and-effect analysis of the case involving the Kansas City School District, you could organize the causes and effects into a graphic organizer that looked something like the following. Study it and then complete the graphic organizer with information from the case study. Attach a blank piece of paper to the bottom of this page to continue your graphic organizer.

2. Work with another student. Use the graphic organizer for the Kansas City School District as a model and create a graphic organizer for Askia Muhammed's commentary (see pp. 185–186).

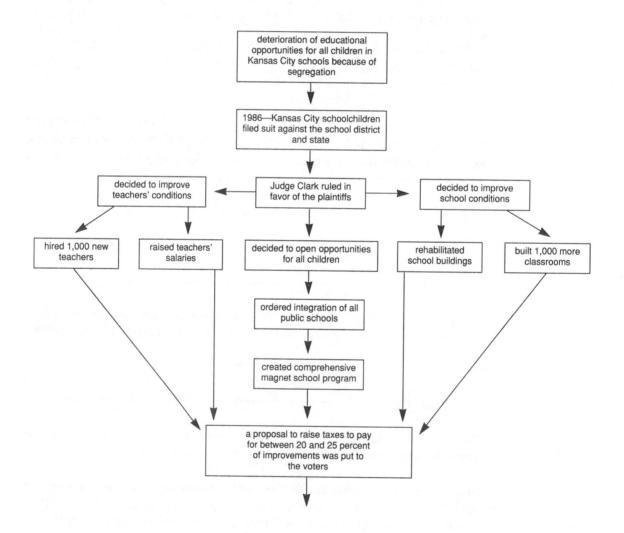

C   ESSAY QUESTIONS

Choose one of the following topics and write an essay. Try to integrate ideas, vocabulary, and writing techniques that you have studied in this unit. In question 1, try to incorporate the following:

- an introductory paragraph that presents the various sides of the argument and clearly states your thesis;

- paragraphs (at least three) that develop your argument with supporting evidence;

- a conclusion that reinforces the position you have taken. It should also end with a new idea (a warning, prediction, value judgment) that has not been mentioned before.

1. Askia Muhammed believes that the 1954 Supreme Court ruling came as a "mixed blessing." What factors contribute to his opinion? Do you agree with his conclusion, based on what you know about American public schooling? Write an essay in which you discuss your opinion.

2. Write an essay in which you describe the causes and the effects of an integration effort in another country. Consider the approaches used in integration, whether through schools or other means, and analyze the cause-and-effect relationships.

ANOTHER FIRST AMENDMENT ISSUE?

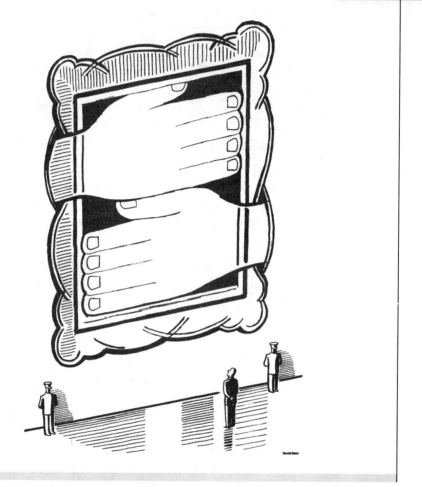

I. ANTICIPATING THE ISSUE

Discuss your answers to the following questions.

1. Look at the title. Look at the cartoon. What do you think the issue of this unit will be?

2. What is the message of the cartoon?

3. What do you know about censorship?

II.

BACKGROUND READING

Read the following text.

The United States is well known for the freedoms protected by its Constitution. The First Amendment, in particular, protects citizens' rights to free speech. Yet, in spite of this amendment, the U.S. has had its share of attempts to **censor** material. This censorship represents a growing intolerance that many Americans have toward their own society. More and more people have expressed **outrage** over what is printed in books, depicted in paintings and photographs, written in songs, or demonstrated at political gatherings. Because of this outrage, many books have been censored from school libraries, art has been denied public funding, musicians have had concerts canceled, and political demonstrations have been limited. Probably the most extreme censorship proposal in the U.S. has been to amend the Constitution to prohibit the burning of the U.S. flag, an act sometimes practiced by those who want to protest against American policies.

A growing number of parents, lawyers, and religious leaders have felt the need to limit free expression. These advocates of censorship range from the politically conservative to the politically liberal. In the South, for example, many conservative communities, while fighting to include time in school for prayer, are fighting to ban particular children's books. In extreme cases, **righteous** religious leaders in those communities have given **sermons** claiming that American towns and cities will soon turn into **Sodom and Gomorrah** if literary standards are not imposed in the schools. In addition, some African-American parents have rejected Mark Twain's *Huckleberry Finn* because of the book's use of "racist" language. Liberal feminists, too, have called for bans on published material containing pornography.

Censorship proposals are not only common in the world of books, but also in the worlds of art and music. Robert Mapplethorpe, for example, drew public attention when people discovered that his work, which had been funded by the NEA (National Endowment for the Arts), included sexually explicit photographs of male couples. Many people saw his photographs as examples of people living in **squalor.** Karen Finley, a performance artist, also drew attention when the NEA denied her public funding because many had claimed her work was **obscene.** In the music world, legal actions were brought against a rap group called 2 Live Crew because the **lyricism** in their new hit album was thought to be too sexual and morally offensive. The record was banned by a federal judge in Florida. Yet, from this case we can conclude that censorship in America is not consistent. While the group was acquitted for the obscenity charges, the record seller *was* convicted for selling the album in the same state. In fact, once the record was censored, it started to **thrive.** With the media's attention on all of these cases, there now seems to be a new connection between being censored and making a ***buck***.

Censorship, of course, is not unique to the United States. Throughout the world, the freedom of expression has often been limited. For years, during the Cultural Revolution, books were burned in China; people had little choice in what to read. Just recently, the China Film Censorship Board banned a new film about an all-powerful master of four mistresses in the 1920s. Israel tried to suppress a book which embarrassed its top-secret intelligence agency, the Mossad. The book presents the Mossad as a ***corrupt*** agency, full of "greed, lust and total lack of respect for human life." Perhaps the most famous case involving censored material was that of Salman Rushdie, who, while living in England, published his famous ***Satanic Verses***, a book that offended the religious sensibilities of many people.

Many people, however, reject any attempt to control the freedom of expression. In the United States, advocates of the First Amendment argue that censorship erodes our free exchange of ideas. Artists who have seen their colleagues ***get burned*** by museums canceling their exhibits or cutting their funding argue that creativity suffers with censorship practices. Others point to the fact that famous works of ***profundity*** have sometimes been censored when first released, but that our concept of what is morally acceptable changes over time. Walt Whitman's *Leaves of Grass* was declared obscene and banned in 1882. James Joyce's *Ulysses* was impossible to obtain in its first decade. Henry Miller's books *Tropic of Cancer* and *Tropic of Capricorn* were banned when they were first published, only to be loved and studied by many in later years.

The question today seems to be whether the current waves of censorship represent a threatening phenomenon and must be stopped, or whether American society has reached the point described in the words of a judge in a recent censorship case, "it's a question between two ancient enemies—'anything goes' versus 'enough already.' "

A VOCABULARY

Look at the boldfaced words and phrases in the following sentences. From the context of the background reading, determine the best meaning. Circle your answer.

1. Yet, in spite of this amendment, the U.S. has had its share of attempts to ***censor*** material.

   a. remove; restrict   b. develop; expand

2. More and more people have expressed ***outrage*** over what is printed in books, expressed in paintings and photographs, written in songs, or demonstrated at political gatherings.

   a. disappointment   b. anger

3. In extreme cases, *righteous* religious leaders in those communities have given sermons claiming that American towns and cities will soon turn into Sodom and Gomorrah if literary standards are not imposed in the schools.

   a. morally correct   b. physically strong

4. Righteous religious leaders . . . have given *sermons* claiming that American towns and cities will soon turn into Sodom and Gomorrah.

   a. lectures   b. suggestions

5. American towns and cities will soon turn into **Sodom and Gomorrah** if literary standards are not imposed in the schools.

   a. cities of holy people   b. cities of sinful people

6. Many people saw his photographs as examples of people living in *squalor.*

   a. secrecy   b. dirt

7. Karen Finley, a performance artist, also drew attention when the NEA denied her public funding because many had claimed her work was *obscene.*

   a. cheaply produced   b. morally offensive

8. In the music world, legal actions were brought against a rap group called 2 Live Crew because the *lyricism* in their new hit album was thought to be too sexual and morally offensive.

   a. style used to apply words   b. rhythm and beat used
      to music   in music

9. In fact, once the record was censored, it started to *thrive*.

   a. die   b. prosper

10. With the media's attention on all of these cases, there now seems to be a new connection between being censored and making a *buck*.

    a. story   b. dollar

11. The book presents the Mossad as a *corrupt* agency, full of "greed, lust and total lack of respect for human life."

    a. rich   b. immoral

12. Perhaps the most famous case involving censored material was that of Salman Rushdie, who, while living in England, published his famous *Satanic* Verses, a book that offended the religious sensibilities of many people.

    a. evil; like the devil   b. poetic

13. Salman Rushdie published his famous *Satanic* **Verses**, a book that offended the religious sensibilities of many people.

    a. writings   b. songs

(continued on next page)

14. Artists who have seen their colleagues ***get burned*** by museums canceling their exhibits or cutting their funding argue that creativity suffers with censorship practices.

a. become famous b. get hurt

15. Others point to the fact that famous works of ***profundity*** have sometimes been censored when first released, but that our concept of what is morally acceptable changes over time.

a. intellectual depth b. sexual explicitness

B SUMMARIZING THE ISSUE

Work in small groups. Summarize the issue presented in the background reading. Take notes to complete the following outline.

1. The issue (*state in your own words*):

_____

_____

_____

2. Proponents' (of censorship) arguments:

_____

_____

_____

3. Opponents' (of censorship) arguments:

_____

_____

_____

C VALUES CLARIFICATION

Work in small groups. Discuss your answers to the following questions.

1. Has art or literature been censored in your country? What kind was censored and why? Who has the authority to censor?

2. What is your opinion of censorship practices?

III.   OPINION 1: LISTENING

A   ✔ LISTENING FOR THE MAIN IDEA

Listen to the commentary. Check the statement that summarizes the commentator's viewpoint.

☐   1.   Many works of art should be censored.

☐   2.   He wants his work to be censored.

☐   3.   Censorship helps people to become famous.

B   LISTENING FOR DETAILS

Read the following questions and answers. Listen to the commentary again and circle the best answer. Then compare your answers with those of another student. Listen again if necessary.

1. According to Jerry Stern, what happens to an author who writes literary or intellectual material?

   a.   His books get outlawed.

   b.   He is viewed as profound.

   c.   He never becomes successful.

2. What does he say he needs someone to do?

   a.   Govern him.

   b.   Arrest him.

   c.   Name him.

3. What kind of statement does he want ministers to make about him?

   a.   Condemning

   b.   Corrupt

   c.   Threatening

(continued on next page)

4. Which of the following is not mentioned as a result of Stern's art?

    a. The nation will go to war.

    b. Institutions will fall apart.

    c. Children will suffer.

5. What will happen if the media attacks Stern's writing?

    a. People will be upset with the media.

    b. People will enjoy the sensational story.

    c. People will change their minds about censorship.

6. What else will happen if his work is censored?

    a. Other artists will lose work.

    b. Money will be made.

    c. Lawyers will not be allowed in court.

7. Why is censorship good?

    a. Everyone learns what is wrong with the art.

    b. Few people are affected by it.

    c. Both the censor and the censored become famous.

C   TEXT COMPLETION AND DISCRETE LISTENING

Read the text of the commentary. Try to fill in the missing words in the text as you remember them. Use your knowledge of text structure, vocabulary, and grammar to help you. Then listen again to the commentary to check your answers, stopping the tape as you fill in the blanks. If you have different answers than the original text, check with your teacher to see if they are acceptable alternatives.

Introduction

Commentator Jerry Stern thinks there's a _____ to be made in all
^{1}
this censorship business.

Commentary

Please, oh please, oh _____ me.
^{2}
Please, someone, outlaw my poetry.

I tried _____ and profundity,
^{3}
but I got ignored completely.

I need a _____ , I need a judge,

4

I'll take a governor, I don't need much.

I just need someone to make me _____

5

by arresting me and calling me names.

I need a minister to write a big _____

6

Saying I'm Satan, worse than vermin.

I need politicians to make their speeches

Saying I'll _____ their Georgia peaches,[1]

7

to claim I'm a threat to civilization,

a malignant blemish on our fair nation.

Tell the _____ , oh tell them please

8

That my kind of art will bring the nation to its _____ .

9

Hospitals will close, children will wail,

Bridges will collapse, banks will fail.

_____ , Gomorrah, and even worse . . .

10

That's what'll happen if you read my _____ .

11

Oh please, oh media, attack my _____ ,

12

The _____ love outrage, and they like to holler,

13

"He's awful, he's _____ , his mind's in the gutter.

14

Slice him to pieces, _____ him in butter."

15

Churches will get filled, _____ get votes,

16

Artists can make statements, critics give quotes,

Records'll sell more, art prices rise,

The courts will be busy, the lawyers _____ .

17

(continued on next page)

[1] A humorous way of talking about young Southern women.

_____ good for all concerned.
18

It's only a few who really get _____ .
19

So, please, oh someone, censor my _____ ,
20

And we both can be on the cover of _Time_.

IV. OPINION 2: READING

A ✔ READING FOR THE MAIN IDEA

Read the editorial. Check the statement that summarizes the author's viewpoint.

- ☐ 1. Demanding community standards is equal to censorship.
- ☐ 2. Our communities have the right to set standards.
- ☐ 3. It's preposterous to amend the Constitution to prohibit flag burning.

What About Our Values?

The U.S. **political arena** is beginning to look like a traveling circus. In center ring, the world-famous American flag-burning controversy. Ring left, we feature a national argument over the sex-drenched lyrics of a rap group called 2 Live Crew. And in the arts circle there's a nonstop pitched battle over the erotic photographs of Robert Mapplethorpe.

The news outlets that describe and in a sense do the promotion for the actors in these controversies tend to define them in the same basic terms. It's always a confrontation between right-wing **zealots** on one side and free thinkers and First-Amendment advocates on the other.

To a great extent, many of these controversies are largely **scams**. They exist because the people who organize them know that the press and the people in the TV business will provide publicity. The Broward County, Florida, legal system hasn't made 2 Live Crew rich and famous; the media have. All such a group has to do is manage to get arrested, and the media **moguls** will descend on them with millions in free advertising. But of course, the newspapers defending the 2 Live Crew lyrics or the Mapplethorpe photographs somehow **desist** from inflicting them on their readers.

It's been fun, but maybe it's time to recognize that something more complex is going on than yet another First Amendment dispute. We'll admit that some of these issues arrive in difficult *shades of gray*, but how did it ever happen that it is now a settled "right" to spend public money to promote Robert Mapplethorpe's photographs, but an indisputable "crime" to spend public money on prayer in a school? Somehow, it seems to us, the country's basic social and political principles have left the tracks.

Or rather, perhaps, the principles of the country's largely self-appointed *elites* have fundamentally diverged from the broader public's. Our sense is that the broader public wants some sense of community; it feels the community has a right to set some standards. As Harlem political leader Basil Patterson said recently: "Everything has gotten so *crude*. You hear it in the streets all the time, and not just there. In some of the music you hear now, and on television." Standards, of course, imply that some are left in and some are left out: some things are allowed, some are not. It is sometimes called

having a sense of judgment.

Against this, elite culture in the United States over the past twenty years has developed the position, and presses it every time one of these *flaps* arises, that community standards equate with majority repression of anything that is individual, *iconoclastic*, experimental, free. What is primarily at work here is an assault on the notion of community standards. It is an attempt to eliminate all the practices and procedures that civil society in the United States has established to define itself.

What's more, this *mind-set* has its own internal censorship. Many common-sense liberals have discovered that they are expected to adhere to a *seamless web* of ideological commitment— flag-burning as politics, Sierra Club environmentalism, the most extremely militant gay rights, militant women's rights, animal rights, sexual display as art, unlimited abortion. Liberals are not only not allowed to deviate from the claims of their most extreme members on any of these matters, they will *be denounced* or driven out if they do.

It is something of a paradox that these are

the people who claim to be defending independent thinking.

Further, it is simply foolish to believe that refusing to give public grants to a Karen Finley is the first step on a *slippery slope* to banning "Ulysses." No one is talking about community standards that legalize oppressions such as separate racial drinking fountains. They are looking for standards that help the community's members with the task of moving forward in a complex world with a moral and political compass. Denying the community's right to press its views on flag burning or public obscenity because it might hamper someone's "individual rights" is to *obliterate* the very ideal of judgment. Just who are the *yahoos* here?

* * *

Sooner or later the political and intellectual leadership of this country has to wake up to the fact that this constant, recurring tension between these extreme positions and the American middle class is about something other than the First Amendment. The flag's man-on-the-street defenders know that their battle is about something larger than just the flag itself. And they know that each time the courts, politicians, and press combine to defeat their claims to mainstream values, civil life in this country somehow ends up more **corrosive** and **antagonistic**.

We agree that there's something preposterous about amending the Constitution to prohibit flag burning, but no more **preposterous** than the mind-set of court rulings that make such lengths necessary. It is in fact a relatively harmless way of telling the courts and the **intelligentsia** they have tilted too far against community standards. A community has *some* rights, and a law against burning the very symbol of community is not a lot to ask.

"The Flag and the Community" (Review & Outlook), 6-18-90. *Reprinted with permission of* The Wall Street Journal © 1990 *Dow Jones & Company, Inc. All rights reserved.*

B   READING FOR AUTHOR'S INTENDED MEANING

Read the following statements. Do you think the author would agree (A) or disagree (D) with them? Write A or D next to each statement. Compare your answers with those of another student. If your answers differ, go back to the text to find out why.

_____ 1. Americans are disagreeing over their values.

_____ 2. Journalists who report these incidences of controversy tend to favor the values of the left.

_____ 3. None of these debates is really about the issues.

_____ 4. Artists who are censored profit from free advertising of their work.

_____ 5. The support of the First Amendment is a good argument for all these disagreements.

_____ 6. Public money for prayer should be withheld from schools.

_____ 7. Those who are interested in protecting all forms of art represent the broader public.

_____ 8. Harlem political leader Basil Patterson's comment is wrong.

_____ 9. The elite culture works against American culture and values.

_____10. Liberals tend to censor themselves.

_____11. Liberals promote independent thinking.

_____12. If money is refused to support art such as Karen Finley's, good literature may also eventually suffer.

_____13. There should be a constitutional amendment that prohibits flag burning.

C   WORD SEARCH

Find boldfaced words in the essay that have similar meaning to the following and write them below

Nouns

groups in society considered to be superior because of the power or intelligence of their members: _____

undefined tangle: _____

scene of public controversy: _____

fanatics: _____

crude or ill-mannered people; people with many vices: _____

states of nervous excitement or confusion: _____

a course of action that may lead to failure or mistake: _____

that part of the community that can be regarded as intellectual and capable of independent thinking: _____

tricks; fake acts: _____

ambiguity: _____

powerful or important people: _____

way of thinking: _____

Verbs

destroy: _____

cease; stop: _____

be condemned or criticized publicly: _____

Adjectives

attacking of popular beliefs or customs: _____

absurd: _____

(continued on next page)

lacking in taste or refinement: _____

destructive: _____

hostile: _____

| V. | **SYNTHESIZING TWO OPINION PIECES** |

A ✔ DISTINGUISHING OPINIONS

Authors can have different viewpoints, but their opinions can sometimes be similar. Review opinion 1 on pages 208–210 and opinion 2 on pages 210–212.

Work in groups. Read the statements below. Discuss whether Stern and/or the author of the editorial would agree with them. Put a check (✔) in the box if you think they would agree. Leave the box empty if they would disagree or if there is no evidence to support the statement in their opinion.

Discuss how and why the two opinions are the same or different. (In the first statement, for example, both Stern and the author would agree. Stern says that if he is censored, he can be on the cover of Time. *The author says the media has made 2 Live Crew rich and famous.)*

	Stern: Commentator (Opinion 1)	"What About Our Values": Author (Opinion 2)
The media helps artists to become famous.	✔	✔
Advocates of censorship tend to be from the religious right.		
American society needs stronger standards.		
Censorship improves the condition of individuals more than of society.		
The First Amendment to the American Constitution is in danger.		
Public money should be spent on art, even if it is controversial.		
Everything has gotten so crude.		

B   GIVING YOUR OPINION

After you have distinguished the opinions of the commentator and the author, express your own opinions on the statements. Discuss them with the other students in your group.

C   VOCABULARY REINFORCEMENT: WORD RELATIONS

Work in small groups. The following words come from the commentary and the editorial. Look at the relationship among the words. For each set of words, cross out the word that is not related to the other three. Compare your answers with those of the students in your group. Discuss the relationship among the words in each set. Then write a word or phrase in the space below that categorizes the relationship. The first one has been done for you.

1. *express outrage*   holler   wail   ~~thrive~~
   cry out loud to express negative feelings
   _____

2. *moguls*   intelligentsia   yahoos   elites
   _____

3. *squalor*   verse   blemish   vermin
   _____

4. *satanic*   righteous   corrupt   sinful
   _____

5. *censor*   outlaw   desist   obliterate
   _____

6. *iconoclastic*   obscene   corrosive   antagonistic
   _____

7. *shades of gray*   slippery slope   political arena   seamless web
   _____

VI.

SPEAKING

A ✓ **CASE STUDY: THE _AMERICAN PSYCHO_ CASE**

The following reading presents a true case that raises the issue of whether creative work should sometimes be censored. Study the case.

Work in small groups. Discuss what you consider to be the best decision for Vintage Books. Present your conclusions to the rest of the class.

When he was just twenty, Bret Easton Ellis published his first book, entitled _Less than Zero_, a novel which explored the world of rich, alienated California teenagers. His second book, _The Rules of Attraction_, was a total failure. But by the time Ellis was twenty-six, he had a contract with Simon & Schuster Publishing Company to publish a book that has caused a lot of flap, _American Psycho_.

The book was viewed as a probable best-seller; consequently, Ellis received a $345,000 advance from the company. But during the editorial process, various Simon & Schuster employees, men and women, took offense at the depictions of violence against women in the book. George Corsillo, a designer who worked on earlier novels by Ellis, refused to work on _American Psycho_ because, he said, "I felt disgusted with myself for reading it." The book had already been promoted in Simon & Schuster's winter catalog as "a black comedy, a disturbing portrait of a psychopath, a subtle send-up of the blatant behavior of the eighties, and a grotesque nightmare of lust and insanity." But as people began to read the novel, its vivid satanic details became criticized. Women, in particular, were outraged by the material. The 366-page book contained shockingly graphic scenes of rape, torture, and dismemberment. "I like to dissect girls," says the main character, who dresses with style and works on Wall Street, but who, in fact, drugs and murders women, butchers them, and hangs their body parts in his apartment; tortures dogs; sets fire to Japanese deliverymen; and kills a child, calling it "extremely painless," because he has "no real history, no worthwhile past." The author defended the content of his book by stating that his intention was to show, symbolically, "how desensitized our culture has become toward violence." He claimed that there was a moral tone to his book and that his work was the result of extensive research in criminology. He called his novel a "parody" about a serial murderer.

Finally, the chairman of Simon & Schuster, Richard Snyder, after seeing advance stories of the novel, stated that because the book contained topics of "such questionable taste," he would have to pull it from the company's projected publications. In November, the company announced that it was canceling the book, a decision that is rarely made in the publishing world. Ellis was allowed to keep his $345,000 advance. Because of the company's decision, Ellis has thrived, in terms of notoriety and cash.

Many applauded Simon & Schuster's decision. But many First Amendment enthusiasts considered this act of cancellation an act of corporate censorship. Artists who have become so scared of losing their right to freedom of artistic expression have rallied to Ellis's defense, even though they might find his work crude or even sinful. Others have claimed that the case is not a question of censorship, as publishing houses are free to decide whether or not to publish a book. No matter what position people have taken, it is clear that people have been asked to determine whether or not there are limits to free expression.

Two days after Simon & Schuster's decision to cancel the publication of the book, Vintage Books, a subsidiary company of Random House, announced that it was considering purchasing the rights to *American Psyc. o*. Many support Vintage's interest in publishing the book. Others criticize the company for its commercial interest in pursuing publication. Some reactions have been extreme: The customs division of revenue in Canada announced that it was considering banning the book from importation, on the grounds that it was squalor. Some women from the National Organization of Women (NOW) have already begun to lobby against the book's publication, proposing a boycott of the book.

Meanwhile, the Vintage Books staff has left for a sales meeting on an island off the coast of Florida. At this meeting, they will decide whether or not to publish the book.

B   DISCUSSION QUESTIONS

Work in groups. Discuss your answers to the following questions.

1. Go back to the questions in the values clarification exercise (p. 206). Do you have the same opinions now, or have you changed your opinions in any way after examining the views of others?

2. Robert Parker, a mystery writer, has stated:

   In general, I believe that writers should be free to write what they wish; and publishers should be free to publish what they wish; and each should be free to do it at any time.

   Do you agree with his opinion? Why or why not?

3. The author of "What About Our Values?" states that "something more complex is going on than yet another First Amendment dispute."

   Do you agree? If so, what is that something that is more complex?

VII.   WRITING

A ✓ GRAMMAR: NOUN CLAUSES IN SUBJECT AND OBJECT POSITIONS

Notice

Notice the structure of the underlined phrases in these two sentences taken from the editorial, "What About Our Values?"

> *What is primarily at work here* is an assault on the notion of community standards.

> The flag's man-on-the-street defenders know *that their battle is about something larger than just the flag itself.*

How do these two phrases function in the sentences? In what way are they the same or different?

Explanation

In both sentences, the underlined phrases are functioning as nouns; they are called noun clauses. The first one is the subject of its sentence; the second one is the object of its sentence.

A noun clause allows a speaker or writer to describe an idea more fully or to give a noun more emphasis. It can give more information than a single noun. (Notice that in both bold phrases above, a single noun could be substituted and the sentence would be grammatically correct.)

To introduce a noun clause, "question words" are often used. However, *question word order is not used*. The same pattern as regular statements is used (subject + verb + object).

The following words typically introduce noun clauses in subject and object positions:

> who
> *Who bought Joe's car?*
> *I don't know __who bought it.__*
> which
> *Which car did he sell?*
> *I don't remember __which car he sold.__*
> why
> *Why did he sell it?*
> *__Why he sold it__ will never make sense to me!*

what
What is he doing now?
<u>What he's doing now is</u> *working for a new company.*

where
Where does he live now?
<u>Where he lives now</u> *is in the city.*

when
When did he move?
I don't recall **<u>when he moved</u>** *exactly.*

how
How does he get to work?
He didn't tell me **<u>how he gets to work.</u>**

whose
Whose office is he working in?
He didn't tell me **<u>whose office he's working in.</u>**

The following words introduce noun clauses related to yes/no questions.

if
Will he continue working with this company?
I don't know **<u>if he will continue working with them.</u>**

whether (or not)
Will he continue working with this company?
<u>Whether (or not) he will continue working with this company</u>
is still uncertain.

The following word introduces noun clauses after verbs such
as *believe, claim, decide, know, say, think.* It can be written optionally.

that
Jon claims **<u>(that) he can win the race.</u>**

Exercise

Answer the following questions. Include noun clauses in either the subject or
object position. Use information from opinion 2, the editorial, to complete your
answers.

1. What does the U.S. political arena resemble?

   What _____

   _____

2. What made 2 Live Crew famous?

   What _____

   _____

(continued on next page)

3. What do the media moguls provide for artists?

   What _____

   _____

4. Is the prohibition of flag burning really a First Amendment issue?

   The author questions whether _____

   _____

5. How did it ever happen that it is now a settled "right" to spend public money to promote Robert Mapplethorpe's photographs?

   The author asks how _____

   _____

6. Why is it an indisputable crime to spend public money on school prayer?

   The author wonders why _____

   _____

7. What does the broader public want?

   What _____

   _____

8. Everything has gotten so crude. You hear it in the streets all the time, and not just there. In some of the music you hear now, and on television.

   Basil Patterson explains where _____

   _____

9. Every time one of these flaps arises, the elite culture presses its position.

   The author observes when _____

   _____

10. A law against burning the very symbol of community is not a lot to ask.

    The author believes that _____

    _____

B WRITING STYLE: THE USE OF IRONY

Notice

Notice the tone Jerry Stern uses in his commentary:

> *Please, oh please, oh censor me.*
> *Please, someone outlaw my poetry.*
> *I tried lyricism and profundity,*
> *but I got ignored completely.*

Describe what is really meant in these lines. The same tone is used in his entire commentary.

How does Jerry Stern's commentary describe the current situation of censorship? What is his message?

Explanation

Irony is a sophisticated style of speaking or writing. When we use irony, we use words creatively to suggest something different from their literal meaning. Irony can sometimes make a point stronger than if it is presented literally.

Jerry Stern's commentary involves two forms of irony:

a. He says something other than what he really means (he does not *really* want to be censored; he does not *really* need a senator, etc.). In this case, what is said on the surface is nearly (or exactly) the opposite of what is meant.

b. The *situation* he describes is ironic: Although we would expect censorship to have a negative impact on writers or artists, it actually makes them more famous. In this case, there is a sharp contradiction between what is expected and what actually happens.

Irony can involve many different uses of language. Here are three additional types of irony:

c. Humorous, gentle, or affectionate use of language (play on words, puns):

Tomorrow it will be partly Wednesday.

d. A simple understatement or an overstatement:

I think the president knows a few people. He should be able to get someone to support this proposal.

e. Sarcasm:

He's a writer for the ages—for the ages of four to eight.

Exercise

Work in groups. The following ironic statements were made in either the commentary or the editorial. For each, discuss which elements of irony are used. Refer to the forms of irony listed above and write the corresponding letter(s). (In some cases, you may find different elements of irony in the same example.) Then, discuss the literal message of the statement (i.e., what is the writer really *saying, in your opinion?).*

_____ 1. "... but how did it ever happen that it is now a settled 'right' to spend public money to promote Robert Mapplethorpe's photographs, but an indisputable 'crime' to spend public money on prayer in a school?"

(continued on next page)

_____ 2. "Or rather, perhaps, the principles of the country's largely self-appointed elites have fundamentally diverged from the broader public's."

_____ 3. "A community has *some* rights, and a law against burning the very symbol of community is not a lot to ask."

_____ 4. "It's been fun, but maybe it's time to recognize that something more complex is going on than yet another First Amendment dispute."

_____ 5. "All such a group has to do is manage to get arrested, and the media moguls will descend on them with millions in free advertising."

_____ 6. "But of course, the newspapers defending the 2 Live Crew lyrics or the Mapplethorpe photographs somehow desist from inflicting them on their readers."

_____ 7. "I need a minister to write a big sermon saying I'm Satan, worse than vermin."

_____ 8. "So, please, oh someone, censor my rhyme, and we both can be on the cover of *Time*."

_____ 9. "Liberals are not only not allowed to deviate from the claims of their most extreme members on any of these matters, they will be denounced or driven out if they do."

_____ 10. "Hospitals will close, children will wail, bridges will collapse, banks will fail."

C   ESSAY QUESTIONS

Choose one of the following topics and write an essay. Try to integrate ideas, vocabulary, and writing techniques that you have studied in this unit. In this essay, try to incorporate the following:

- an introductory paragraph that presents both sides of the argument and clearly states your thesis (whether you support censorship practices or not);

- paragraphs (at least three) that develop your argument with supporting evidence;

- a conclusion that reinforces the position you have taken. It should also end with a new idea (a warning, prediction, value judgment) that has not been mentioned before.

1. According to Peter Plagens, who writes on censorship:

The social cohesion of a society assumes some censorship—this is, it requires individuals to put limits on what they say or do. Sometimes—whether it's

Granny sending kids away from the table for swearing or kiddie pornographers getting thrown in jail—brakes have to be applied.

Do you agree with his statement? If so, where do the brakes need to be applied, in your opinion?

2. React to the following statement in an essay: "Censorship cannot eliminate evil—it can only kill freedom."

Do you agree or disagree? Use specific cases to support your opinion.

TAPESCRIPT

UNIT 1
MEN WHO KNOW WHERE THEIR BULLETS ARE GOING

Introduction

Across much of the nation this week, there are pickups parked on the sides of country roads near the woods, and you can hear the pop of rifles firing in the distance. Hunters are still out. Recently, commentator Donald McCaig came on the air and said a few kind things about hunters, but since then there's been some trouble at his Virginia sheep farm, the kind of incident that farmers dread.

Commentary

I'd like to speak directly to the boys in the lime-green Chevrolet who shot two of our sheep Monday, opening day of deer season . . . shot them from the road and left them to die.

Since you boys had to flee, you'd be interested to know what's happened once you'd gone. The ewes you shot had been just turned out onto pasture so they could graze; their lambs could frolic and play. When we found them, the lambs were banked up against their dead mothers. I rolled a ewe over, and when we saw the bullet hole, my wife, Anne, cried.

You should understand that we're lambing, and not getting much sleep, and Anne's worked so hard, you see, to nurture those ewes that the thought that someone could just kill them, for the pleasure of it, for a moment that unhinged her mind. "How could anyone do this?" she said. "What kind of a person could do this?" And then she threw up.

Hunters—men—don't kill animals with young at their side. Without their mothers, young animals starve to death. Hunters—men—know where their bullets are going. One of your bullets went through the mother and severed her lamb's leg, and the vet had to put the lamb down, she was in such pain. Of course you didn't know that; you had to flee.

You mightn't have noticed our farm is not posted. Over the years, a good many hunters—men—have hunted deer and turkey, grouse, rabbits, and squirrels here. In the years they've been hunting, none of them has so much as left a gate open. Some of these hunters have taken supper with us; we've met their families.

I confess my first thought, when we'd found out what you'd done, was to post the farm: "No hunting. No trespassing." But, you see, that would be penalizing honest men for what you did. So, today we'll burn two young ewes and one lamb, and we'll try to get the lambs you orphaned on a bottle. That's harder to do than you might think. Of course we've called the sheriff, and if you're caught, we'll prosecute. But, I don't expect you'll be caught.

Two thousand years ago, Plato looked around and saw that sometimes evil-doers are not caught. Sometimes villains get away with it. Plato said the evil man has a sick soul, and every cruel, thoughtless act a man commits soils and coarsens his own soul.

You killed without reason. You are less than you were.

UNIT 2
WHEN DOES LIFE BEGIN?

Introduction

In this country, the convergence of medical and legal issues is being spotlighted this summer in the case of the Tennessee couple and their frozen embryos. As with many other things he reads about these days, commentator Andrei Codrescu finds the case complicated by implications.

Commentary

The husband, Junior Lewis Davis, wants the fertilized eggs disposed of. The wife, Mary Sue Davis, is infertile and wants the eggs to hatch. The husband's lawyer calls the eggs "a group of undifferentiated cells," while the wife's attorney has labeled them "preborn children." Between these two definitions lies the entire range of current propositions as to when exactly does a human being become one.

Here in Louisiana, life begins at conception. But, the law's unclear whether what goes on in a petri dish can possibly be called "conception." Other laws envision a human as beginning either from the minute it loses its flippers or from the time it does its first uterine somersault. Other opinions maintain that there are no human beings until they complete a scouting program or even pass an SAT test. I've heard an advocate for the proposition that human beings aren't human beings until they prove it themselves, in a court of law.

Clearly, there are seven lawyers for seven embryos, in every case. The seven frozen embryos in the Tennessee case could be used as tests for the various laws. One embryo could be a group of undifferentiated cells; that one would be thawed. Another could testify to the validity of petri dish conception; that one could stay. Another could be raised into a fine Boy Scout and sent out to fight drugs for the President; that one can prove it's a human being in a White House ceremony.

One shouldn't look at these embryos as merely frozen lumps, contending for definition. They are seeds of the very laws they might spawn. Mr. and Mrs. Davis should not fight for these eggs as if they were a private matter between themselves and their petri dish. They are sitting on the very basis of our future definition of human beings. Their divorce mirrors the divorce of the diverse philosophies at work here. They should work out a custody arrangement for these eggs that requires a constitutional lawyer to babysit.

UNIT 3
TO KNOW MORE ABOUT LESS OR LESS ABOUT MORE

Introduction

Common wisdom has it that an expert is someone who knows more and more about less and less. Substitute the word "specialist" for "expert," and ask whether it's better to believe someone who knows more about less or less about more and you have the subject of writer Rod MacLeish's essay this morning.

Commentary

Archilochus, the Greek poet, left us only bits and pieces of his writings; the most famous is Fragment 103: The fox knows many things, but the hedgehog knows one big thing. No one is certain about Fragment 103's original meaning. But it has become a metaphor for a modern dilemma: the increasing dominance of Western society by specialists, hedgehogs, if you will. This means, inversely, the decline in influence of generalist foxes.

The supremacy of hedgehogs is dangerous because it creates a climate of rarefied ignorance. The man who invents an exotic new form of chemical weaponry has probably forgotten—if he ever knew—the generalist's view of history, with its lessons about the origins of war. The junk bond and insider-information scoundrels, who sullied the reputation of Wall Street, were obsessed with the one big thing they knew. The prudence and moral balance, which comes from a broad general vision of society, were lost on them.

Perhaps the dominant power of the specialist hedgehogs was inevitable, as science and technology became increasingly complex after the mid-nineteenth century. The argument here is not *against* specialists, but rather their inordinate influence over our lives. In the mores of Western society, the generalist fox, who knows (but is not expert in) many things, is dismissed with such derisive clichés as "jack-of-all-trades, master of none."

At the turn of this century, there was an acerbic classicist at Oxford who used to tell newly arriving students, "Nothing you will learn here in the course of your studies will be of any use to you in later life save only this: If you pay attention and work hard, you may eventually come to know when a man is talking rot." In other words, Oxford taught you how to think by teaching you many subjects that enriched and broadened the mind. The hedgehogs know how to think, but only about one big thing. The time may be approaching when the people who dominate our lives won't know when a man is talking rot.

UNIT 4
ECONOMIC MIGHT VS. ECOLOGIC RIGHT

Introduction

Seven weeks from now, a new dam in the Amazon will flood millions of trees and animals out of the rain forest. Environmentalists have criticized the plan because they say many endangered animal species will be destroyed. Physicist Jim Trefil has been thinking about the situation in the Amazon, and he has these observations.

Commentary

Some of my colleagues are starting to publicize their worries about the rate at which plants and animals are disappearing from the earth. Things like the destruction of the tropical rain forest are described in somber tones. The destruction of a habitat, we are told, is equivalent to the destruction of all the species that live in that habitat. We are told that mankind must not contribute to the demise of other living things.

I have to admit that my reaction to this line of reasoning is a bit schizophrenic. On the one hand, I have a strong emotional commitment to the notion that any argument that keeps people from cutting down a tree is a good argument. For years, I've managed a twenty-acre wood lot in Virginia, taking out deadwood to keep my family warm in the winter.

And yet, I've been trained as a scientist. And one of the first elements of that training was to learn to put feelings aside and examine arguments solely on their merits. When I do that with the arguments about the dangers of extinctions and loss of biological diversity, some very disturbing questions arise in my mind. I worry that the people involved may be overselling their case, that the situation may be neither as serious nor as dangerous as they say.

Species, like individuals, do not live forever. Over the past 600 million years, almost every form of life that existed on the earth has become extinct. Paleontologists estimate that, even in normal times, species become extinct at the rate of several hundred per year. Governments can no more pass laws to stop the death of species than they can pass laws to stop the death of individuals. Dying is just another part of life.

So the real question is how the extinction rate today compares to what it's been in the past. I don't know the answer to this question, but I don't think anyone else does either. I do know that until it's answered, I'm going to be very skeptical of headlines about impending doom.

Another problem I have is with this word "species." When we hear that a species is endangered, we usually think of whales or whooping cranes or ivory-billed woodpeckers—something spectacular. In fact, most of the tropical species that are being wiped out today are insects that live in very restricted locations. The beetles in one mountain valley may look just like their neighbors in the next valley. But they're counted as separate species because of very fine technical differences between them.

My experience has been that when people learn that all this fuss is being made over bugs and not large animals, they feel cheated and lose interest in the whole extinction question. People listen to what scientists have to say because they

believe we are capable of making objective judgments, regardless of our own beliefs and feelings. If the public comes to regard us as just another pressure group crying wolf, they may just stop listening. If that happens, we will have lost the most important battle of all.

UNIT 5
"JUST SAY 'NO' TO DRUGS"?

Introduction

This year Congress has been willing to debate almost any proposal in the war against drugs. Commentator Linda Chavez says the legislators "just can't say no."

Commentary

Drugs have become a political obsession this election year. The House recently passed a bill that would impose a federal death penalty for drug-related murder. The House bill also calls for widespread mandatory drug testing and would permit the use of illegally gathered evidence in criminal trials. The Senate is considering ways to bring the House bill to a quick vote, without going through the normally lengthy committee process.

Every politician is eager, it seems, to cast a tough antidrug vote before his constituents cast their votes in November. It's as if politicians feel they have to come up with some new and drastic measure that hasn't been tried before, in the hopes it will make the drug problem disappear. The death penalty for drug pushers or those who commit drug-related murders seems to be the favorite of conservatives this year.

Now, a handful of liberals, led by Baltimore Mayor Kurt Schmoke, have come up with a radical approach at the other extreme: decriminalize drug use in the hopes that it will take the profit out of drug sales. Schmoke built a reputation as a hard-nosed state prosecutor before he was elected mayor of Baltimore. But like most law-enforcement officials, he faced frustration in his own war on drugs in Maryland.

But the alternative that he and others propose would amount to a surrender. And what's worse, drug use would not diminish. It hasn't in countries like the Netherlands or England, which have similar policies. Lives would continue to be lost to the ravages drugs inflict on the bodies and spirits of those who take them.

There aren't any easy answers to the drug problem in America. And election years certainly aren't conducive to discussions of the hard truth of drug use. Drug dealers push their wares because there is a market for them in this country. Legalizing drugs won't affect that market and, arguably, might increase it by removing the penalties.

Nancy Reagan took a lot of flak when she proposed a program to "just say 'no' to drugs." But is there really any other answer? Americans are going to have to face up to some hard questions about ourselves and our values if we're really going to eliminate drugs. Most of us, unfortunately, would rather talk tough or redefine the problem.

UNIT 6
BRIDGING AN UNCOMMON PAST WITH A COMMON FUTURE

Introduction

Mastering the English language once was considered indispensable for immigrants seeking their place in America. Commentator Linda Chavez says this should hold true for the country's newest immigrants as well.

Commentary

America is a nation of immigrants. Every once in a while, we're reminded of that simple fact. We were reminded of it last summer, when we celebrated the one-hundredth anniversary of the Statue of Liberty. And we were reminded of it again in recent days as we watched thousands of illegal immigrants apply to live here legally under a new law that grants them amnesty.

Many of these immigrants are Hispanics. They come from Mexico but also from Central and South America and the Caribbean. And they join millions of other Hispanics, some of whom trace their roots in what is now the United States to a time before the Pilgrims landed at Plymouth Rock. Demographers tell us that by the year 2050, one out of every three persons living in the United States will be of Hispanic origin. The face of America is changing. So too, some warn, will the sound of America change. Already it is common in many parts of the country to encounter neighborhoods where little English is spoken, even in public. In some places, ballots are required by federal law to be printed in Spanish and other languages in addition to English. Many schools teach Spanish-speaking children in their native language, and all schools are required by law to allow such children to speak Spanish among themselves, on the playground or in lunchrooms, for example.

One school district in Texas that recently tried to enlist parents' help in encouraging their children to speak only English while at school dropped the plan when Hispanic organizations objected, even though the proposal had received early support from the parents themselves, who presumably thought it would help their children learn English more quickly.

One of the reasons that the United States has succeeded in becoming a nation with its own identity and culture, despite the disparate nature of its population, is that it has been bound by a common language. Many Americans—in fact, if lumped together, perhaps a majority of Americans—did not have ancestors whose original language was English. Nonetheless, English is our language now.

We are a nation of immigrants with no common past, but with a common future. The bridge between the two has been and should continue to be our common English language. The United States is a richer and more vibrant society because of its immigrant heritage. The increase in the proportion of Hispanic Americans can add to the richness and vibrancy of this nation, but it can do so only if Hispanics, as all other ethnic groups, decide to be woven into the culture of our society by the common thread of the English language.

UNIT 7
HAVE ALL THE HEROES DIED?

Introduction

"Today's the day I consider myself the luckiest man on the face of the earth". . . Lou Gehrig saying good-bye to the fans at Yankee Stadium on July 4th, 1939. A hardworking ballplayer, dedicated to his family, Gehrig was courageous in his battle against a fatal disease. He was a role model, the type of athlete that commentator Frank Deford says you don't hear much about these days.

Commentary

While drugs remain(s), and surely will so, the crux of the issue separating owners and players in all sports—the umbrella of dispute—involves the question of definition: How are players perceived?

Curiously, it's upside-down. The players' unions—and this is a matter that crosses all sports lines—the unions maintain that players are just like everybody else, while the owners argue that players are very special folks. Crazy, isn't it?

The buzzword is *role model*. For some reason, people are embarrassed to even use the word *hero* anymore. So ballplayers are, well maybe they are, role models. Unfortunately, being a role model is like being tall, or bald, or freckled. You don't have any control over it. And like it or not, kids are always going to make ballplayers their heroes, their role models. This is one of the reasons that ballplayers get paid much more than most other folks.

So, I'm getting very tired of players and the players' union people saying "they don't want to be role models; they're just like everybody else." I'm also getting very tired of people dredging up poor Babe Ruth's name and then putting him down. Babe Ruth was a terrific hero in his time. People say, "See! What a sham it all is! Babe Ruth drank too much, he ate too much, and he chased women." Yeah, but who knew? What they knew was he hit home runs. John Kennedy was a terrific hero. OK, OK, he was committing adultery in the White House with a Mafia mistress. But who knew? What they knew was he stood up to Khrushchev.

Unquestionably, though, it's tougher all the time to be a totally successful role model. It's a very prying world. And you can't get away with the same stuff nowadays. Maybe this is good. It's a different world now. Babe Ruth wouldn't have a potbelly if he were a star today. Civilization marches on.

I think ballplayers, in their selfishness and their self-centered escape mode, miss the point. Of course children should choose saints and statesmen and educators and preachers as their role models, but you know very well that they're not going to; that's why they're children, and also why they grow up to be grown-ups.

Do you know who children also choose as their role models? Well, rock singers, disc jockeys, anybody older who drives a red sports car, comedians who say very dirty words out loud. These, by and large, are today's role models for today's children. And, by comparison, ballplayers, I think, make very good role models, indeed. I think the unions ought to recognize that and make the players aware of it, too.

I have no idea where the idea grew up that sports was supposed to be perfect. And just because it isn't, then everyone can go around talking about Babe Ruth's failures of the flesh and abdicate all personal responsibility themselves. Children are going to look up to ballplayers, and so, for that matter, will some adults. And in a very honest way, this shows what a healthy society we really are. Heroes have never been gods. Heroes, OK, "role models," are very human, and what is more human than a young man with a number on his back able to deal with curveballs better than temptation? We're in a sorry state if we can't relax and let ballplayers be heroes, the way they're supposed to.

UNIT 8
THE RIGHT TO DIE VS. THE RIGHT TO LIFE

Introduction

It is often argued that no one on earth is equipped to judge the proper moment to end a life. But, in fact, people make those decisions every day. And commentator Philip Gerard found sometimes they live to regret their choices.

Commentary

Just over a year ago, after fighting Parkinson's disease for almost ten years, my mother suffered a massive heart attack. She survived it only because she was already in the hospital. She stopped breathing for at least eight minutes, possibly as long as half an hour, before she was revived by extraordinary means: defibrillator, adrenaline, the whole crash-cart, Code-Blue scene. My father got a phone call demanding that he make an immediate choice: Put my mother on a respirator or let her die right then. Under pressure and unprepared for the awful circumstances, my father made the instinctive human choice: Try to save her.

At the hospital, the doctors gave us their prognosis. For my mother to come out of her coma would be a miracle and a hideous one. The massive brain damage would leave her in a persistent vegetative state. Then, the family decided, unhook the machine and let her die. Impossible, the doctors said. Under state law, once my mother was hooked up to the machine, she could not be unhooked without a court order. She might live for as long as a decade. My father would have to petition the court to allow his wife of forty years to die.

When I first heard the word "coma," I imagined serene catatonia. But my mother's coma began as constant convulsions. With each breath the respirator shoved into her lungs, her body shuddered. She frothed at the mouth. Her eyeballs rolled back, white, into her head. She was strapped down to the bed or she would have fallen to the floor. This lasted day and night for three days. After that, her nervous system virtually destroyed by the unrelieved trauma, she quieted. My sisters and I took turns sleeping on a cot in my mother's room. We didn't want her to be alone when she died.

After a week of that, I recall lying awake into the small hours of a snowy morning, listening to the hum of the monitors and the "suff'ing" of the respirator. I prayed for the courage to turn off the machine and let her die in peace. It would have been easy—just click off the toggle. No one would have known for hours. I didn't have the courage.

My mother lasted three months. In the end, she was breathing through a tube permanently inserted in her throat. She weighed almost nothing. The doctors were keeping tissue alive, but the woman was long gone. Honoring state law, the doctors weaned her off the respirator a little each day, forcing her to labor for every breath. They said she was in no pain, but her face contorted and her body convulsed. Then she died.

You can argue the fine medical ethics of the thing. All I can add is this: I'd whip any man who treated a dog so cruelly.

UNIT 9
REDUCING INEQUALITY IN EDUCATION

Introduction

This country's racial segregation in public schools was banned by the Supreme Court on this date in 1954. Commentator Askia Muhammed believes the ruling came as a mixed blessing.

Commentary

It's odd that on this thirty-fifth anniversary of one of the most momentous Supreme Court decisions there are no national celebrations. Or, maybe it's not so odd.

I think there's a sense of national weariness at various court-imposed school-integration-by-busing schemes over the years. So who wants to celebrate *that* anniversary? It's ironic because the Washington D.C. plaintiffs, whose case was joined into the *Brown v. Topeka, Kansas Board of Education* suit, were parents who complained that their children had to ride buses past an all-white junior high school in their neighborhood. But the whole concept of integration or desegregation is full of ironies, as far as I'm concerned.

The *Brown v. Board* decision had to be, however. Historically, the doctrine of "separate but equal" from the 1896 *Plessy v. Ferguson* decision had to be repudiated in U.S. law if the country was to refer to itself sincerely as "one nation under God."

My only problem with the notion of integration, though, is having to automatically concede that, unless white children are around, black children cannot possibly be learning anything in school. It breeds unacceptable inferiority thinking among blacks, the descendants of slaves in this country.

We paid a dear price for integration. The well-educated blacks were free to move anywhere they chose when segregation was outlawed. And they chose, increasingly, to leave the masses of suffering people most in need of their presence, their guidance, their stability, their leadership by example. The black communities' role models, once forced to live in predominantly black neighborhoods by segregated housing laws, were at last able to flee to the suburbs. They fled, leaving the ghettos to be vied over by the pushers and the poor.

As a nation, we gained as much as we lost when the Supreme Court overturned "separate but equal." But I, for one, wish we hadn't so quickly lost the sense of self-sufficiency, of pride, of self-help, self-government that African-Americans surrendered. We thought, "let George do it," instead of wanting to do it for ourselves, mostly so we could get along with the majority, the European-Americans, as we integrated into the country's mainstream.

UNIT 10
ANOTHER FIRST AMENDMENT ISSUE?

Introduction

Commentator Jerry Stern thinks there's a buck to be made in all this censorship business.

Commentary

Please, oh please, oh censor me.
Please, someone, outlaw my poetry.
I tried lyricism and profundity,
but I got ignored completely.

I need a senator, I need a judge,
I'll take a governor, I don't need much.
I just need someone to make me famous
by arresting me and calling me names.

I need a minister to write a big sermon
Saying I'm Satan, worse than vermin.
I need politicians to make their speeches
Saying I'll corrupt their Georgia peaches,
to claim I'm a threat to civilization,
a malignant blemish on our fair nation.

Tell the world, oh tell them please
That my kind of art will bring the nation to its
  knees.

Hospitals will close, children will wail,
Bridges will collapse, banks will fail.
Sodom, Gomorrah, and even worse . . .
That's what'll happen if you read my verse.

Oh please, oh media, attack my squalor,
The righteous love outrage, and they like to
  holler,
"He's awful, he's sinful, his mind's in the gutter.
Slice him to pieces, fry him in butter."

Churches will get filled, candidates get votes,
Artists can make statements, critics give quotes,
Records'll sell more, art prices rise,
The courts will be busy, the lawyers thrive.

Censorship's good for all concerned.
It's only a few who really get burned.
So, please, oh someone, censor my rhyme,
And we both can be on the cover of *Time*.

ANSWER KEY

UNIT 1

Men Who Know Where Their Bullets Are Going

II. A. VOCABULARY
Suggested answers:
1. light trucks   2. game birds   3. die of hunger   4. cut off; separate   5. kill to end suffering   6. criminals   7. spiritual principles   8. fear greatly   9. forbid trespassers on   10. female sheep   11. run away from 12. having legal action taken against them 13. shocked them

II. B. SUMMARIZING THE ISSUE
Suggested answers:
1. The issue: Is hunting an acceptable sport? Is deer management an appropriate reason to hunt?
2. Proponents' (of hunting deer) arguments:
   —management is necessary because
     1) overpopulation
     2) destruction of property
     3) Lyme disease
     4) car accidents
3. Opponents' (of hunting deer) arguments:
   —alternatives could be used to manage deer
   —farm animals often get killed
   —suburban accidents

III. A. LISTENING FOR THE MAIN IDEA
3. Donald McCaig feels ambivalent about hunting.

III. B. LISTENING FOR DETAILS
1. b   2. b   3. c   4. b   5. b   6. c   7. b   8. c

IV. A. READING FOR THE MAIN IDEA
1. Although Bass feels guilty about being a hunter, he must hunt.

IV. B. READING FOR EXPLICIT AND IMPLICIT MEANING
Suggested answers:
3. E   4. I   5. E   6. I   7. E   8. E   9. E 10. I
11. E   12. E   13. I   14. E   15. I

IV. C. WORD SEARCH
Nouns: hide; prey; heifer; roaming; elk; gluttony; predator
Verbs: wrestled with; pursue; loll around; groaned
Adjectives: liable; insatiable; heartthrob; shaky

V. C. VOCABULARY REINFORCEMENT
  Movement:
    flee
    loll around
    roam
  A legal action:
    post
    prosecute

A separation of some kind:
  sever
  unhinge
An eventual death:
  put (something) down
  starve
Dealing with something unpleasant:
  dread
  flee
  groan
Those in the hunt:
  predator
  prey
Animals that can be hunted:
  deer
  elk
  grouse

VII. A. EXERCISE
1. should not have fled   2. must not have been brought up   3. might not have realized   4. could have given up   5. must have been   6. could not have been kept   7. must have liked   8. could have posted   9. might have been   10. should not have killed

VII. B. EXERCISE
1. sight, sound, taste, touch
2. a. red, almost purple heartthrob steaks; b. groaned c. black as coal, shiny and greasy . . . winged, black devils
3. desire/guilt
4. a. eyes. . . like a bear's or a wolf's or even an owl's; fall comes like a splash of water; ravens, black as coal. . . like winged black devils   b. ravens calling to ravens c. ravens

UNIT 2

When Does Life Begin?

II. A. VOCABULARY
Suggested answers:
1. meeting of separate things   2. proposals 3. unable to have children   4. small glass concave plate   5. unfrozen   6. female organ where baby develops and grows before birth   7. guarding of children   8. thrown away   9. bring life into being from an egg (*used figuratively here; usually chickens' eggs hatch*) 10. brought forth; generated   11. microscopic units of living matter 12. the meeting of a sperm and an egg   13. difficult tasks; maneuvers (*used figuratively here*)   14. pieces of indefinite size and shape   15. suggestions   16. struggling

II. B. SUMMARIZING THE ISSUE
Suggested answers:
1. The issue: The development of medical technology has presented us with ethical issues that we are only beginning to deal with.
2. The wife's view:
   —does not want eggs disposed of
3. The husband's view:
   —no longer interested in seeing his ex-wife bear his children
4. The judge's view:
   —embryos are people, not property
   —the wife should have the embryos

III. A. LISTENING FOR THE MAIN IDEA
3. Our laws are not prepared to deal with new ethical questions.

III. B. LISTENING FOR DETAILS
1. c 2. a 3. b 4. b 5. c 6. c

IV. A. READING FOR THE MAIN IDEA
2. We should consider the negative consequences of medical technology.

IV. B. READING FOR FACT VS. OPINION
Suggested answers:
3. F 4. F 5. O 6. O 7. F 8. O 9. O 10. F 11. F
12. O 13. F

IV. C. WORD SEARCH
Nouns: blobs; broken home; limbo; surge; forbears; toddler; continuum; nurture
Adjectives: infinitesimal; iffy; arrant; unbridled; prolonged
Verbs: mend; grappled with; endured; infringes upon; unsnarl; purify; bestowed on; inflict; envision; outstrips

V. C. VOCABULARY REINFORCEMENT
1. has spawned   2. had never been envisioned
3. have grappled with   4. be conceived   5. implied
6. will have unbridled   7. dispose of   8. hadn't endured   9. mending   10. having bestowed

VII. A. EXERCISE
2. On no account did Mr. Davis want children now that he was divorced.   3. In few cases has the subject of where life begins been an issue in divorce.
4. Neither did Mrs. Davis.   5. Under no circumstances was Mrs. Davis willing to give up her chance of becoming pregnant with the frozen embryos. 6. Not until she sought the help of invitro fertilization could Mrs. Davis consider having children.   7. Not only did Mrs. Davis's attorney view the embryos as human life, but the judge also saw them as "preborn children."
8. At no other time has technology outstripped our ability to resolve legal issues. 9. Only in developed countries do people fight over frozen embryos.

10. By no means will lawmakers ignore the Davis case when deciding how to define when life begins.

VII. B. EXERCISE
a. Introduction: facts
   Conclusion: own conclusion
b. Introductions: facts and statistics; anecdote; questions
   Conclusions: prediction; quotation/call for action; quotation

UNIT 3

To Know More About Less or Less About More

II. A. VOCABULARY
1. b   2. a   3. b   4. a   5. a   6. b   7. a   8. a   9. b
10. a   11. b   12. a   13. a

II. B. SUMMARIZING THE ISSUE
Suggested answers:
1. The issue: Whether a specialized or generalized approach to learning is most appropriate for today's world
2. a. Advantages to the specialists' approach to education:
   —more technical jobs available (computers, etc.)
   —professional needs require specialization
   —higher salaries
2. b. Disadvantages to the specialists' approach to education:
   —some specialized jobs related to crime
3. a. Advantages to the generalists' approach to education:
   —shared knowledge with a common core
   —enriches the mind
3. b. Disadvantages to the generalists' approach to education:
   —useless
   —not easy to determine what everyone should know

III. A. LISTENING FOR THE MAIN IDEA
1. A generalist approach to education is necessary for today's world.

III. B. LISTENING FOR DETAILS
1. c   2. c   3. c   4. b   5. a   6. a   7. b   8. a

IV. A. READING FOR THE MAIN IDEA
3. Today's generalist approach to education is no longer relevant for today's world.

IV. B. READING FOR FACT VS. OPINION
Suggested answers:
1. O   2. F   3. F   4. F   5. O   6. O   7. O   8. F
9. O   10. O   11. F   12. F   13. O

IV. C. WORD SEARCH

Nouns: flaws, synthesizing, paradigm, scourge, stasis, vocationalism
Adjectives: trendy, salient, suspect, fellow, calcified, lopsided, predicated, backlogged, bankrupt
Verbs: lag, run the gauntlet, edge, clamor, faring, recedes, whisked

V. C. VOCABULARY REINFORCEMENT

Nouns	Verbs	Adjectives	Adverbs
bankruptcy	**to go bankrupt**	bankrupt	X
calcification	**calcify**	calcified	X
clamor	clamor	**clamorous**	X
derision	**deride**	derisive	X
edge	edge	**edged**	X
enrichment	**enrich**	enriched	X
fellow	X	fellow	X
flaw	X	**flawed**	X
X	X	inordinate	**inordinately**
inversion	**invert**	**inverted, inverse**	inversely
lag	lag	**lagging, lagged**	X
metaphor	X	**metaphoric, metaphorical**	**meta- phorically**
recession	recede	**recessive**	**recessively**
suspect	**suspect**	suspect	X
synthesis	synthesize	**synthesized, synthesizing**	X
trend	X	trendy	X

1. trendy 2. inordinately 3. enrichment 4. suspect
5. recession 6. bankruptcy 7. derisive 8. synthesize
9. fellow 10. metaphorically

VII. A. EXERCISE

(Check tapescript.)

VII. B. EXERCISE

1. C 2. C 3. C 4. M 5. M 6. C 7. C 8. C
9. C 10. M 11. C 12. C 13. C 14. M 15. M

UNIT 4

Economic Might vs. Ecologic Right

II. B. SUMMARIZING THE ISSUE

Suggested answers:
1. The issue: To what extent we should try to save species from extinction or allow for man's development

2. Proponents' (of saving endangered species) arguments:
   —extinction is now 10,000 times greater than before man
   —tiny species keep the earth in balance
   —need diversity for food and drugs
3. Opponents' (of saving endangered species) arguments:
   —proponents oversell case by creating fear
   —species have always gone extinct
   —man's need to survive is more important

III. A. LISTENING FOR THE MAIN IDEA

2. The dangers of extinction may not be as serious as they are made out to be.

III. B. LISTENING FOR DETAILS

1. b 2. c 3. b 4. a 5. a 6. c 7. b 8. a

IV. A. READING FOR THE MAIN IDEA

2. The number of species becoming extinct each day is frightening.

IV. B. READING FOR FACT VS. OPINION

Suggested answers:
1. O 2. F 3. O 4. F 5. F 6. O 7. F 8. O
9. F 10. O 11. F 12. O 13. O

IV. C. WORD SEARCH

Nouns: annihilation; might; wreaking havoc; pharmaceuticals; butchering; handwringing; malls; hectare; drop in the bucket; shrubs
Verbs: weeds out; portends; died off; thrive
Adjectives: slashed; razed; countless; vacated; chilling; eradicated; history; harvestable; mind-boggling

V. C. VOCABULARY REINFORCEMENT

2. diverse 3. species 4. endangered 5. harvested
6. mall 7. drop in the bucket 8. schizophrenic
9. thriving 10. overselling

VII. A. EXERCISE

Suggested answers:
   1. My experience has been that when people learn that scientists are making all this fuss over bugs and not large animals, they feel cheated and lose interest in the whole extinction question. (The writer may not want to "point the finger" at those who are making the fuss: the scientists.)
   2. In fact, most of the tropical species that we are wiping out today are insects that live in very restricted locations. (Here, the people who are committing the action, we humans, are less important than those who are receiving it, the tropical species.)
   3. Subdivisions and malls are increasingly replacing

grasslands and wetlands. Acid rain is poisoning trees and lakes. (The effect is more important than the cause.)

4. Occasionally the annihilation was unintentional, as when early explorers introduced predators to remote locales—such as the dodo on the island of Mauritius. (The receiver of the action is more important than the agent.)

5. By the middle of the next century, according to the Nature Conservancy, we may have lost one-half of all the earth's species, largely as a result of man's greed. (The blame on "man" is somewhat removed by using the passive voice.)

6. Scientists (or journalists) describe things like the destruction of the tropical rain forest in somber tones. They tell us that the destruction of a habitat is equivalent to the destruction of all the species that live in that habitat. (The description and the telling are more important than "who" describes or tells.)

7. And yet, professors at the university of _____ trained me as a scientist. (The place where he was trained is not as important as his being trained.)

8. If loggers raze that hectare of hardwood—whether to make cardboard packing boxes for VCRs or disposable chopsticks—they remove the species forever. (The writer does not want to blame anyone in particular for deforestation.)

9. The beetles in one mountain valley may look just like their neighbors in the next valley. But scientists count them as separate species because of very fine technical differences between them. (The focus is more on the insects than on the people who categorize them.)

VII. B. EXERCISE

Suggested answers:
Statistics:
—Tropical forests are slashed and burned at the rate of 100 acres a minute.
—Since 1900, Africa's wildlife population has declined by more than seventy percent as the human population has grown sixfold.
—In the early twentieth century, the earth was losing one species a year; today it's one species a day—400 times the natural rate.
Personal Testimony:
   (none is used in this essay)

Factual Reference:
—When the dinosaurs were killed off 65 million years ago, flowering plants survived.
—Already the Tasmanian wolf, the laughing owls of New Zealand, the Caribbean monk seals, and many more are history.
—The Madagascar periwinkle, for example, is a key

ingredient in curing lymphocytic leukemia.
Appeal to Authority:
—the Nature Conservancy
—the World Wildlife Fund

UNIT 5

"Just Say 'No' to Drugs"?

II. A. VOCABULARY
1. a   2. a   3. b   4. b   5. a   6. b   7. b   8. a   9. a
10. b   11. a   12. a   13. b

II. B. SUMMARIZING THE ISSUE
Suggested answers:
1. The issue: Whether or not the U.S. should consider legalizing drugs as a method of controlling the drug problem in America.
2. Proponents' (of legalization) arguments:
   —current policies are a waste of money
   —need to spend on education and treatment
   —black market prices are an incentive to get into drug business
   —gangsters disappeared with prohibition
   —drugs = health problem, not crime problem
3. Opponents' (of legalization) arguments:
   —legalization = surrender
   —legalization would increase:
   1) drug use
   2) crime
   3) child abuse
   4) AIDS
   —legalization didn't work in China
   —policies for legalization remain unclear

III. A. LISTENING FOR THE MAIN IDEA
2. Linda Chavez opposes the legalization of drugs in the U.S.

III. B. LISTENING FOR DETAILS
1. b   2. a   3. b   4. c   5. a   6. b   7. a   8. c   9. c

IV. A. READING FOR THE MAIN IDEA
1. Drug legalization could begin to control the U.S. drug problem.

IV. B. READING FOR AUTHOR'S INTENDED MEANING
Suggested answers:
1. D   2. A   3. A   4. D   5. A   6. D   7. A   8. D
9. A   10. A   11. A   12. D   13. A

IV. C. WORD SEARCH

Nouns: panacea; prescription; oblivion; substances; affliction; epidemic; free rein; addiction
Adjectives: lucrative; key; petty; alienated
Verbs: conjures up; condone; deprive

VII. A. EXERCISE

1. would be   2. had never entered; would consider/ would have considered   3. will probably buy
4. decriminalizes   5. had been; would never have proposed   6. would be; had continued   7. won't be able
8. restrict   9. spent; wouldn't decrease/spend; won't decrease   10. hadn't called for; wouldn't have paid

VII. B. EXERCISES

a. Suggested answers:
2. A smaller market would exist to support the drug-pushing business.   3. Drug abuse would continue, but more addicts would use clinics rather than pushers.
4. If drug addicts used clinics, there would be fewer babies born into drug addiction.   5. Legalization would provide assistance and safety to addicts.
6. Addiction would be viewed as a health problem rather than a criminal problem.

b. Suggested answers:
2. If drug pushers don't have a lucrative market in which to push their wares, fewer people will use drugs.
3. Other countries have decreased drug use with legalization policies.   4. Decriminalizing drugs would mean addicts could get assistance to help them get off drugs.   5. Drug pushers won't be able to make as much money with decriminalization, so they will leave the business. 6. The "just say 'no' to drugs" approach is a simplistic policy that hasn't worked.

UNIT 6

Bridging an Uncommon Past with a Common Future

II. A. VOCABULARY

9, 6, 3, 2, 5, 11, 1, 4, 8, 10, 7

II. B. SUMMARIZING THE ISSUE

Suggested answers:
1. The issue: Whether or not English should be made the official language of the U.S.
2. Proponents' (of official English) arguments:
  —English binds people together
  —ancestors learned English successfully when it was expected of them
  —countries with more than one language are emotionally and politically divided

  —need a common language to participate in a democracy
3. Opponents' (of official English) arguments:
  —violation of free speech
  —xenophobia could be the result
  —need to preserve ethnic pluralism

III. A. LISTENING FOR THE MAIN IDEA

1. All immigrants to America should be required to learn English.

III. B. LISTENING FOR DETAILS

1. c   2. a   3. c   4. b   5. c   6. b   7. c

IV. A. READING FOR THE MAIN IDEA

3. The official-English movement is taking the wrong approach to language policy in the U.S.

IV. B. READING FOR AUTHOR'S INTENDED MEANING

Suggested answers:
1. D   2. A   3. A   4. A   5. D   6. A   7. D   8. A
9. A   10. D   11. A   12. A   13. D

IV. C. WORD SEARCH

Nouns: mantel; bedrock; shop steward; naysayer; incursion; gerbils; spokesman; musket; bugaboos
Verbs: hinder; prosper; sponsor; take them lightly; proliferated
Adjectives: sanctioned; conversant; mellifluous

V. C. VOCABULARY REINFORCEMENT NOUNS

1. bedrock   2. spokesman   3. naysayer
4. demographer   5. amnesty   6. incursion   7. ballot
8. ancestor   9. common thread   10. musket

VII. A. EXERCISE

1. Alistair Cooke, who is a spokesman for U.S. English, speaks English English.
2. Immigrant children whose first language is not English may study in bilingual education programs before being mainstreamed into the English-speaking school system.
3. In the 1930s, there were entire neighborhoods in which only Italian, Polish, or Greek was spoken.
4. There are many children in the U.S. today whose families have been in the country for more than 100 years and still don't speak English well.
5. The constitutional amendment that is being proposed by the group for U.S. English would have an impact on schools and ballots.
6. Hispanic parents who originally thought their children could learn English more quickly if they

spoke it at school objected to a proposal to make English the school's only language.

7. Some people remember a time when all immigrants were expected to learn English in the United States.

8. Many immigrants to the U.S. are Hispanics, most of whom come from Mexico, Central and South America, and the Caribbean.

9. Some Americans fear that the multilingual nature of their country will result in another Quebec, which is a province with its own distinct language and culture.

10. Some people say that there is no proof that a constitutional amendment that makes English the official language of the U.S. would bind Americans together.

VII. B. EXERCISE

1a. had their downside   1b. nostalgia
2a. handsome, silver hair and tongue   2b. shopping
3a. humor/irony   4a. irony (a language other than English is used)   4b. anger/irony   5a. nostalgia/irony
6a. sadness/irony   7a. resignation   8a. bugaboos
8b. irony/humor   9a. fight in the kitchen
9b. irony/humor

UNIT 7

Have All The Heroes Died?

II. A. VOCABULARY

1. with small spots   2. curious inquiring   3. bring to light by searching deeply   4. give up   5. something that covers a broad range of items   6. false; a hoax
7. criticized   8. big stomach (usually from eating and drinking too much)   9. respect   10. key word or phrase   11. defended themselves with courage against   12. causing death or disaster   13. central point   14. pursue successfully a course of action that might usually be expected to result in blame or misfortune

II. B. SUMMARIZING THE ISSUE

Suggested answers:
1. The issue: Is it possible to have and do we need heroes (or role models) in today's world?
2. Examples of past heroes:
   —George Washington
   —John Kennedy
   —Martin Luther King
   —Lou Gehrig
   —Babe Ruth
3. Examples of present-day role models:
   —sports heroes
   —Lee Iacocca
4. Problems with heroes/role models today:
   —they use drugs and alcohol
   —they are greedy
   —they may be too self-possessed

III. A. LISTENING FOR THE MAIN IDEA

2. Ballplayers should be considered heroes, in spite of their flaws.

III. B. LISTENING FOR DETAILS

1. c   2. c   3. c   4. b   5. a   6. a   7. b   8. a   9. a
10. b

IV. A. READING FOR THE MAIN IDEA

3. Today's role models have many failings.

IV. B. READING FOR AUTHOR'S INTENDED MEANING

1. A   2. D   3. A   4. A   5. A   6. D   7. D   8. A
9. D   10. A   11. D

IV. C. WORD SEARCH

Nouns: pickle, threshold, trouser cuffs, rot
Adjectives: hasty, lush, rampant, tenured, bush-league, onerous, blessed, harsh
Verbs (idiomatic expressions): put him to pasture, has the world handed over on a plate of solid silver, has gone down the tubes

V. C. VOCABULARY REINFORCEMENT

People's physical appearance:
   bald
   freckled
   potbellied
Antisocial behavior:
   adulterous
   prying
   selfish
A difficult and weighty task:
   burdensome
   onerous
Something very positive:
   blessed
   lush
Something changed from its normal condition:
   rotten
   upside-down

VII. A. EXERCISE

2. Although it is an unfortunate fact that children make ballplayers their heroes, children will always look up to them.

3. Even though people are embarrassed to use the word, a ballplayer should be considered a "hero."

4. In spite of the fact that they tried to show the world the shame underlying old heroes, reporter heroes had feet of clay, too.

5. While it is said that John Kennedy had affairs, he was a heroic president.

6. Children choose ballplayers and rock singers as their heroes, even if they should choose saints and educators.

7. The public chooses who it wants as role models, even though some role models do not want this role.

8. Though players have failures or shortcomings, they make very good role models.

9. Despite the fact that they have the world handed over on a plate of solid silver, Harvard Law students want to have role models.

UNIT 8

The Right to Die vs. the Right to Life

II. B. SUMMARIZING THE ISSUE

Suggested answers:
1. The issue: Whether or not we have the right to end our lives when medical technology can keep us alive
2. Proponents' (of euthanasia) arguments:
   —the family lives in trauma
   —keeping someone alive with artificial means prolongs death (not life)
3. Opponents' (of euthanasia) arguments:
   —we can't be sure of a comatose person's desires
   —euthanasia could be used to "eliminate" people

III. A. LISTENING FOR THE MAIN IDEA

3. Keeping people alive on life-support systems can be cruel.

III. B. LISTENING FOR DETAILS

1. b   2. c   3. b   4. c   5. a   6. b   7. c   8. c   9. c

IV. A. READING FOR THE MAIN IDEA

3. We must work toward respecting life, as we don't know the consequences of euthanasia.

IV. B. READING FOR THE AUTHOR'S OPINION

Suggested answers:
1. O   2. O   3. O   4. O   5. O   6. B   7. B   8. B   9. B   10. B   11. B   12. O

IV. C. WORD SEARCH

Nouns: torture, preoccupation, longevity, forethought, stratagem, living wills
Adjectives: extant, chronic, mortal, viable, empirical, provocative, insensate, creeping, arrested
Verbs: torments, subsidizing, collude, mandates

V. C. VOCABULARY REINFORCEMENT

Nouns	Verbs	Adjectives	Adverbs
X	X	chronic	**chronically**
coma	X	**comatose**	X
ethics	X	**ethical**	**ethically**
miracle	X	**miraculous**	**miraculously**
preoccupation	**preoccupy**	**preoccupied**	X
provocation	provoke	provocative	**provocatively**
revival	**revive**	revived	X
serenity	X	serene	**serenely**
torture	**torture**	**torturous**	**torturously**
trauma	**traumatize**	**traumatic**	**traumatically**
vegetable	**vegetate**	vegetative	X
viability	X	viable	X

1. ethical   2. revive   3. vegetables   4. serenity
5. viable   6. traumatic   7. provokes   8. chronically
9. miraculous   10. torturous   11. preoccupation
12. comatose

VII. A. EXERCISE

1. Having fought   2. Being   3. demanding
4. (Having been) confused. . . shocked   5. Having been given   6. Respecting   7. Hearing   8. (having been) destroyed   9. Lying   10. Hoping   11. having been weaned

VII. B. EXERCISE

Suggested answers:
1. first person; yes
2. Beginning: his mother's suffering from Parkinson's disease, her heart attack, and her survival; Middle: the family's experience with their mother on a respirator; End: his mother's death
3. What: his mother was put on a respirator; To whom: his mother and the family; Where: the hospital; when: nine months ago; How: she suffers with her prolonged life and then dies
4. "defibrillator, adrenaline, the whole crash-cart, Code-Blue scene"; "With each breath the respirator

shoved into her lungs, her body shuddered. She
frothed at the mouth. Her eyeballs rolled back, white,
into her head";   "the hum of the monitors and the
'suff'ing' of the respirator"; "but her face contorted
and her body convulsed."

5. Euthanasia may be less cruel than keeping a
person alive at all costs.

6. "Just over a year ago . . . ;" "Then . . . ;" "After that
. . . ;" "After a week of that . . . ;" "In the end. . . ."

UNIT 9

Reducing Inequality in Education

II. A. VOCABULARY

a. 3   b. 9   c. 8   d. 12   e. 6   f. 5   g. 7   h. 4   i. 11
j. 2   k. 10   l. 14   m. 15   n. 13   o. 16   p. 1

II. B. SUMMARIZING THE ISSUE

Suggested answers:
1. The issue: How best to achieve racial integration in
America through the public school system
2. a. Busing
   Pros:
   —racial balance
   Cons:
   —too much time traveling
   —"white flight" has led to more ghettos
   —flight of African-Americans has left inner-city
     school children with fewer role models
   b. Magnet schools
   Pros:
   —voluntary desegregation
   —quality education incentive
   Cons:
   —African-American parents insulted by focus on
     white students
   c. Voucher programs
   Pros:
   —everyone has equal choice
   Cons:
   —not everyone is able to make an informed choice
     (unequal)

III. A. LISTENING FOR THE MAIN IDEA

1. The African-American community is losing its identity through integration efforts.

III. B. LISTENING FOR DETAILS

1. c   2. a   3. c   4. b   5. c   6. c   7. b   8. a

IV. A. READING FOR THE MAIN IDEA

3. We must continue to use integrated schooling as a
means for ending discrimination.

IV. B. READING FOR AUTHOR'S INTENDED MEANING

Suggested answers:
1. A   2. D   3. A   4. D   5. D   6. A   7. D   8. A
9. D   10. A   11. A   12. D   13. D   14. A

IV. C. WORD SEARCH

Nouns/phrases: in this vein, polity, vantage point, arenas, preeminence, impulses, the public good
Verbs: tackle, sparked, press for, nurture, relinquish,
ensure, level, capped, remedy, preempted
Adjective: hospitable, crucial, counterproductive,
telling, feasible

VII. A. EXERCISE

1. Many white parents enrolled their children in private and suburban schools as a result of busing.

2. The Supreme Court's 1954 ruling came with not
only many advantages but also many disadvantages for
African-Americans.

3. Busing attempted to end segregated schooling,
eliminate racism, and create the common school in
America.

4. Some people view the _Brown v. Board of
Education_ case as a mixed blessing, while others view
it as a momentous decision.

5. The doctrine of "separate but equal" was support-
ed in the _Plessy v. Ferguson_ case, overturned in the
Brown v. Board of Education case, and debated in the
Kansas City case.

6. Because of "white flight," many African-
Americans have been left to live in ghettos that are
dangerous, drug-infested, and poor.

7. Because of their inability to draw suburban children back into the inner cities and their loss of money
because of empty spaces, some magnet schools may
have to close.

8. American public schools have instituted three
major policies involving schools and race: segregated
schooling, mandatory busing, and school choice.

9. Some parents don't want to bus their children
outside their communities, but they do want "excellence" programs for their children.

10. The American common school was designed to
provide resources for individual development, to teach
an appreciation of the common good, and (to) provide
a setting in which children from different backgrounds
could learn together.

VII. B.a. EXERCISES
Suggested answer:

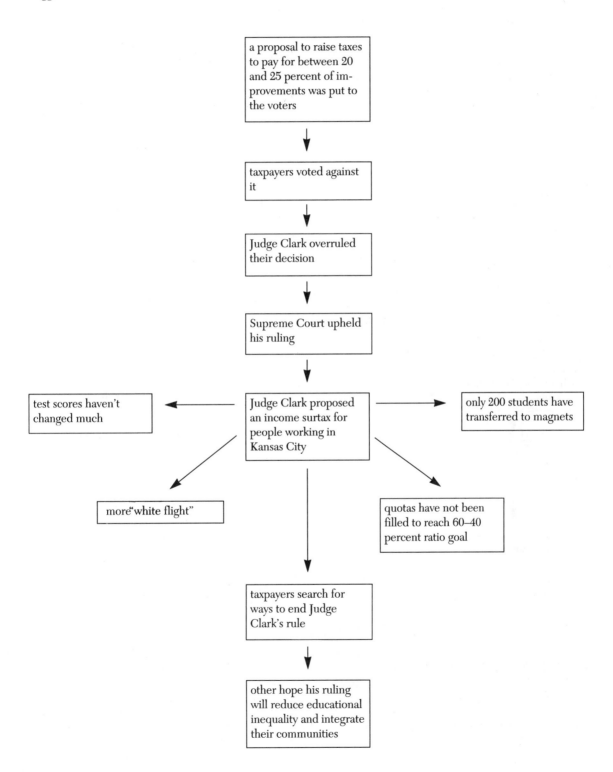

a proposal to raise taxes to pay for between 20 and 25 percent of improvements was put to the voters

↓

taxpayers voted against it

↓

Judge Clark overruled their decision

↓

Supreme Court upheld his ruling

↓

Judge Clark proposed an income surtax for people working in Kansas City

test scores haven't changed much

only 200 students have transferred to magnets

more "white flight"

quotas have not been filled to reach 60–40 percent ratio goal

taxpayers search for ways to end Judge Clark's rule

↓

other hope his ruling will reduce educational inequality and integrate their communities

VII. B.b. EXERCISES
Suggested answer:

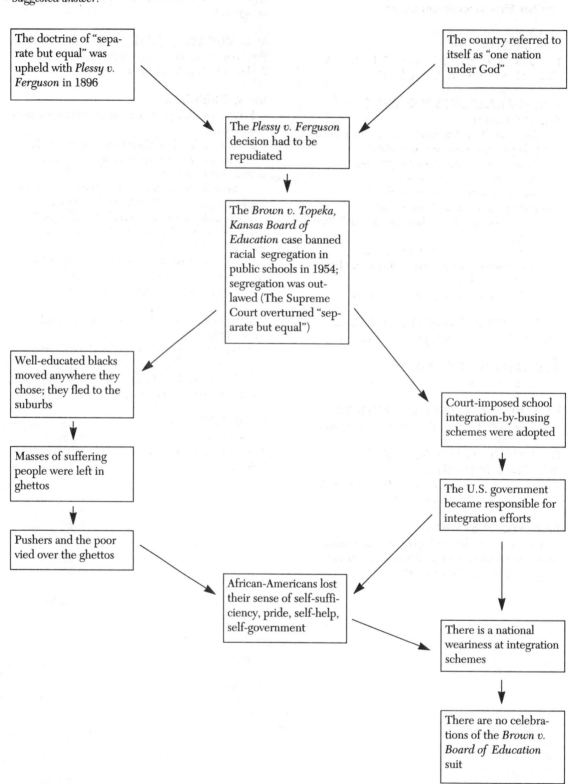

The doctrine of "separate but equal" was upheld with *Plessy v. Ferguson* in 1896

The country referred to itself as "one nation under God"

The *Plessy v. Ferguson* decision had to be repudiated

The *Brown v. Topeka, Kansas Board of Education* case banned racial segregation in public schools in 1954; segregation was outlawed (The Supreme Court overturned "separate but equal")

Well-educated blacks moved anywhere they chose; they fled to the suburbs

Masses of suffering people were left in ghettos

Pushers and the poor vied over the ghettos

Court-imposed school integration-by-busing schemes were adopted

The U.S. government became responsible for integration efforts

African-Americans lost their sense of self-sufficiency, pride, self-help, self-government

There is a national weariness at integration schemes

There are no celebrations of the *Brown v. Board of Education* suit

UNIT 10

Another First Amendment Issue?

II. A. VOCABULARY
1. a   2. b   3. a   4. a   5. b   6. b   7. b   8. a   9. b
10. b   11. b   12. a   13. a   14. b   15. a

II. B. SUMMARIZING THE ISSUE
Suggested answers:
1.   The issue: Have Americans reached the point at which they should limit free expression?
2.   Proponents' (of censorship) arguments:
   —certain books promote racism
   —obscenity in music and art is offensive
   —pornography is offensive to women
   —some material offends the religious sensibilities of people
3. Opponents' (of censorship) arguments:
   —censorship erodes the free exchange of ideas
   —creativity suffers
   —society's concept of morality always changes

III. A. LISTENING FOR THE MAIN IDEA
3. Censorship helps people to become famous.

III. B. LISTENING FOR DETAILS
1. c   2. b   3. a   4. a   5. b   6. b   7. c

IV. A. READING FOR THE MAIN IDEA
2. Our communities have the right to set standards.

IV. B. READING FOR AUTHOR'S INTENDED MEANING
1. A   2. A   3. A   4. A   5. D   6. D   7. D   8. D
9. A   10. A   11. D   12. D   13. A

IV. C. WORD SEARCH
Nouns: elites, seamless web, political arena, zealots, yahoos, flaps, slippery slope, intelligentsia, scams, shades of gray, moguls, mind-set

Verbs: obliterate, desist, be denounced
Adjectives: iconoclastic, preposterous, crude, corrosive, antagonistic

V. C. VOCABULARY REINFORCEMENT
2. yahoos   3. verse   4. righteous   5. obliterate
6. obscene   7. political arena

VII. A. EXERCISE
   1. What the U.S. political arena resembles is a traveling circus.
   2. What made 2 Live Crew famous is the media.
   3. What the media moguls provide for artists is millions in free advertising.
   4. The author questions whether the prohibition of flag burning is really a First Amendment issue.
   5. The author asks how it ever happened that it is now a settled "right" to spend public money to promote Robert Mapplethorpe's photographs.
   6. The author wonders why it is an indisputable crime to spend public money on school prayer.
   7. What the broader public wants is some sense of community.
   8. Basil Patterson explains where everything has gotten so crude.
   9. The author observes when the elite culture presses its position.
   10. The author believes that a law against burning the very symbol of community is not a lot to ask.

VII. B. EXERCISE
Suggested answers:
1. b   2. e   3. d   4. a   5. b   6. b/e   7. a/c/d   8. b/c
9. b   10. c/d